PRAISE FOR *A NEW U*

"Technology has provided us with limitless opportunity to innovate and customize every aspect of our lives, but our education system regretfully remains stuck in the past. Ryan Craig makes a compelling argument for positively disrupting the concept of higher education in America so that we can continue to drive the competitive global economy."

—*Jeb Bush, 43rd Governor of Florida and founder and chairman of the Foundation for Excellence in Education*

"Every parent, counselor, mentor, and educator should read this book. We owe it to our students and kids to understand what's happening in higher education in America to prepare ourselves to provide the best possible advice on college."

—*Allen Blue, co-founder of LinkedIn*

"Ryan Craig succinctly outlines how higher education will be reshaped by forces already seeded and in play. College and university leaders must listen to these signals from the future to effectively chart the path forward."

—*Van Ton-Quinlivan, executive vice chancellor of California Community Colleges*

"Ryan Craig is one of the great thinkers and disruptors in postsecondary education today. He provides important insights into the challenges students face in navigating our current system, and offers provocative ideas on how to think differently about multiple pathways and new delivery models that can empower all individuals with the education and training they need to achieve the rewarding careers and fulfilling lives they deserve."

—*William D. Hansen, president and CEO of Strada Education Network and former US Deputy Secretary of Education*

"*A New U* documents the clear misalignment of higher education's promise and delivery for students of today and the future. Craig makes a compelling case for transformative innovation in higher education and provides numerous examples of emerging opportunities. The question: Will the higher ed community respond or become obsolete?! This is a must read for anyone who is committed to finding innovative, responsive pathways forward."

—*Hanna Skandera, former New Mexico Secretary of Education*

"Ryan Craig demonstrates that in a time when talent is at a premium, producing that talent in new and different ways must be a priority. *A New U* is really about a New Us, a world where faster, cheaper—and arguably better—learning will produce the talent we need in the 21st century."

—*Jamie Merisotis, president and CEO of Lumina Foundation*

"Fasten your seat belt! Ryan Craig takes us on an eye-opening journey through the world of higher education, and the many rapidly-emerging alternatives, in this must-read book. I couldn't put it down, and as soon as I finished I wanted to re-read it. It's brimming with the most compelling anecdotes, examples, and statistics, and will forever change your view about the role of postsecondary education in launching young adults into careers, and leveling society's playing field."

—*Ted Dintersmith, executive producer and author of* Most Likely to Succeed *and* What School Could Be

"*A New U* is the book I wish I had written—minus Ryan Craig's hilarious stories from his own college experience. This book paints a plausible portrait of how the disruption of traditional colleges will occur and should be required reading for all who care about the future of higher education."

—*Michael B. Horn, cofounder of the Clayton Christensen Institute for Disruptive Innovation*

"Don't be fooled by Ryan Craig's new book. It's not another anti-college diatribe. Instead, Craig proposes a more rational approach to making decisions about postsecondary education, laying out a method to help families make sense of a confusing panoply of alternatives. Unfortunately, these alternatives are not yet widely known. Whether you are a parent, a student in high school, a policy maker, or an employer, you should read this book to better understand these broader alternatives."

—*Marie Cini, president of the Council for Adult and Experiential Learning (CAEL)*

"*A New U* details the new landscape of alternative education providers outside the walls of traditional colleges and how new providers are putting pressures on existing colleges to focus on employment outcomes while lowering their prices. This witty and sharp book is an important read for those of us in traditional higher education as well as for policymakers and people considering college."

—*Robert Kelchen, assistant professor of higher education at Seton Hall University*

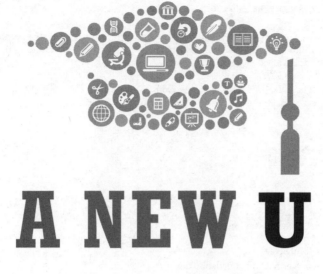

A NEW U

FASTER + CHEAPER
ALTERNATIVES TO COLLEGE

• • •

RYAN CRAIG

BenBella

BenBella Books, Inc.
Dallas, TX

"Bank" icon on page 184 by Lance Hancock from Noun Project
"Interview" icon on page 184 by Gan Khoon Lay from Noun Project

BenBella Books, Inc.
10440 N. Central Expressway, Suite 800
Dallas, TX 75231
www.benbellabooks.com
Send feedback to feedback@benbellabooks.com

Printed in the United States of America
10 9 8 7 6 5 4 3 2 1

Library of Congress Cataloging-in-Publication Data:
Names: Craig, Ryan, 1972- author.
Title: A new U : faster + cheaper alternatives to college / by Ryan Craig.
Description: Dallas, TX : BenBella Books, Inc., 2018. | Includes
    bibliographical references and index.
Identifiers: LCCN 2018012771 (print) | LCCN 2018013525 (ebook) | ISBN
    9781946885579 (electronic) | ISBN 9781946885470 (trade cloth : alk. paper)
Subjects: LCSH: Education, Higher—Aims and objectives—United States. |
    Educational change—United States.
Classification: LCC LA227.4 (ebook) | LCC LA227.4 .C735 2018 (print) | DDC
    378/.01—dc23
LC record available at https://lccn.loc.gov/2018012771

Editing by Vy Tran
Copyediting by J. P. Connolly
Proofreading by Lisa Story and Cape Cod Compositors, Inc.
Indexing by WordCo Indexing Services, Inc.
Text design by Publishers' Design and Production Services, Inc.
Text composition by PerfecType, Nashville, TN
Cover design by Oceana Garceau
Jacket design by Sarah Avinger
Printed by Lake Book Manufacturing

Distributed by Two Rivers Distribution, an Ingram brand
www.tworiversdistribution.com

Special discounts for bulk sales (minimum of 25 copies) are available. Please contact Aida Herrera at aida@benbellabooks.com.

This book is dedicated to the promise of socioeconomic mobility that was once met by America's colleges and universities, and that will be again.

CONTENTS

FOREWORD

I've spent a lot of time thinking about robots. And about their brains. And specifically about what those robots, whether they work in factories or live entirely inside the Internet, will mean for our economy and our culture.

When you watch a robot assist a surgeon as she performs a delicate operation, you can really feel the potential of the technology. When you see robots and humans working side-by-side on an assembly line, or choose from possible job candidates filtered by a robot, or talk to accountants who can now work on tougher problems because robots are doing a lot of their basic calculations, you can really understand how they will change our work.

The fact that none of these capabilities existed even five years ago makes me want to kick our education and training system into a much higher gear. Education must prepare us with more than new work skills. More than ever, we live in a culture mediated by powerful technology. Machine learning and artificial intelligence determine in no small way what news we read, what shows we watch, who we talk to and how. If we are going to be good citizens, good neighbors, and good caretakers of our society, we must be educated about how to live in the world alongside this new technology.

At LinkedIn we've seen an explosion of new ways to learn among our customers and members—and are even part of the mix ourselves. I've spent much of the last five years thinking about what we would need to learn and how we would need to learn it. I've met traditional educators and innovative ones. I've talked to software developers making education freely accessible through the Internet and to organizations leaping the digital divide by providing learning on phones. Each organization, whether a big employer or startup, a state university or nonprofit, bridges a gap. Some train missing skills in new ways, some forge links between educators and employers, some help kids become curious through innovative programs, some guided young people as they explore careers.

Today this work is more crucial than ever. The deepening crisis of college affordability makes it even more urgent that we come up with answers to bridge skill gaps. In this book, Ryan Craig documents a number of promising answers. Ryan explains how this urgency has inspired new schools, new pathways and business models, new approaches to public policy and placed tremendous pressure on existing education to change.

Higher education needs disruption. It must keep up with the changes in our economy and our society if America is to continue to make good on its commitments to its citizens and the world. This important book tells the stories of the innovators who are already blazing the trail toward a more responsive and responsible education. I hope you find it as useful as I have.

—Allen Blue
Co-Founder, LinkedIn
Los Angeles, California

INTRODUCTION

I have a test today . . . I must take it. I want to go to a good
college, so I can have a fruitful life.

—*Ferris Bueller's Day Off (1986)*

I loved college and was exceptionally fortunate to attend a good one. But none of my memories of Yale involve classes or faculty. They involve my roommates and their antics in the ample interstitial time—oh, and also my wife, whom I met there. Better not forget that.

One joke we played at college has lasted nearly a quarter century. Senior year, we decided to turn an issue of *Rumpus,* the tabloid newspaper we founded, into a parody of *People* magazine's "50 Most Beautiful People." The issue featured photos of students posing like fashion models accompanied by fawning profiles: "She's got legs and she knows how to use them. In cross-country, that is."

According to the editorial for the first issue of "Yale's 50 Most Beautiful People":

> In the world, there are those that have and those that have not. Most at Yale fall into the former category, and yet we are not all equal . . . Everyone at Yale has secretly admired and desired someone on this list. Let us end this secrecy! Shower the Beautiful People with garlands of praise. They have been chosen.

It was clear to most that this was a joke. To find fifty willing subjects, we had to cajole; the letter that the "BPs" received didn't even use the word "beautiful" but rather euphemisms such as "pulchritude" and "campus presence." As many rejected or ignored their selection, the editorial defended our authority: "By our logic, one of the defining characteristics of being one of the 50 Most Beautiful People at Yale is having the courage to stand up and proclaim one's beauty. Thus, anyone who lacked this courage is not beautiful. By this tautology, our list is perfect and complete."

"50 Most" made a splash and has been doing so annually ever since. But perhaps the most surprising lesson to come from the BPs was how quickly something that started as a joke became a status symbol. Within two years of the inaugural issue, being selected as a BP had become a badge of honor. It became commonplace to lobby editors for inclusion. And we learned that at least one of the original BPs had listed her selection on her résumé, the one whose profile started with, "The Yale attack-wing streaks down the lacrosse field with the ferocity of a velociraptor. But we've never seen a velociraptor look quite the way Jane does."

Today, the "50 Most" of higher education aren't leggy cross-country runners or fierce attack-wings but rather faster + cheaper alternatives to college that started as an afterthought or joke but are quickly finding their way onto résumés.

Almost everything is getting faster + cheaper. Watching a movie used to require going to the theater or video store. Now thousands of films are available without leaving the couch. Rides appear at the touch of an icon for less than the cost of a taxi. Dates are arranged by swiping right. With "1-Click" Amazon will deliver any of 500 million products to your door.

For Millennials and Generation Z (those born starting in the late 1990s and now reaching college age), convenience, speed, and value are fundamental to modern American life. So it's surprising that school, where young people spend the bulk of their waking hours, has hardly changed at all. Sure, students use technology at home and in class, but it remains supplemental to and not much more effective than traditional chalk-and-talk teaching. When teens finish high school and begin making independent decisions, one would think they'd seek a faster, cheaper pathway to real life rather than spending four years attempting to earn 120 credits and a bachelor's degree. They haven't yet, because there haven't been great alternatives—until now.

●　●　●

Clayton Christensen's seminal 1997 work *The Innovator's Dilemma* introduced the concept of disruptive technologies: "cheaper, simpler, smaller, and, frequently, more convenient to use." And while they may "underperform established products in mainstream markets . . . they have other features that a few fringe (and generally new) customers value."[1] Defining technology broadly as the process by which organizations make products and services, Christensen noted that the "most profitable customers generally don't want, and indeed initially can't use, products based on disruptive technologies."[2] But disruptive technologies emerge because, "in their efforts to provide better products than their competitors and earn higher prices and margins, suppliers often 'overshoot' their market: They give customers more than they need or ultimately are willing to pay for."[3]

Replace "customers" with "students," "products" with "degrees," and "suppliers" with "colleges" and you get what's happening in higher education: disruptors are emerging because the college and university product is more than some students need or are willing or able to pay for. Except for the fact that it's not only a "few fringe" customers. Millions of young Americans are dislocated, disgruntled, and burdened by a mountain of student loan debt. A high percentage of Millennials are unhappy with their college and postcollege employment experiences. One recent survey found that only 27 percent of Millennial college graduates agreed with the statement that "higher education leaders put students first," while 66 percent disagreed, saying they put the interests of their schools first.[4]

Meanwhile, millions more students have experienced career Armageddon by trying and failing to get over the bar of four years and 120 credits. Degreeless twenty-somethings who have wasted money and valuable time without attaining any credential of value are what kept former Secretary of Education Arne Duncan up at night: "If you have inordinate debt and no degree, you're in a worse situation than where you started," he said.[5] Unfortunately, this describes nearly half of all students who undertake degree programs. America has by far the lowest rate of college completion as a percentage of students who matriculate.[6] And adding dropouts to graduates working in jobs that don't require a college degree yields a majority, which is proving dangerous to the social fabric of our country.

Educators are waking up to this new reality. Barnaby Lenon, former headmaster at one of the UK's most elite private schools, recently launched a stinging critique of education leaders who signal to students that progressing to university is the only acceptable path because other options are seen as a "failure" or even a "disgrace." He said, "I am sick of not particularly academic students saying they are going off to [study] English or Psychology—just because they have been told to."[7] And Anthony Carnevale, director of the Georgetown Center on Education and the Workforce, has commented: "Higher education has become a $500 billion computer without an operating system."[8] Simply put, college has gotten far too expensive and employment outcomes for new graduates have deteriorated significantly.

Mark Zuckerberg famously dropped out of college; so did Bill Gates. But they recognize that their success is highly exceptional, which is why both these American icons strongly urge young Americans to start what they were unable to finish. For more than fifty years, families have heard from Gates, governments, and every group imaginable that the key to socioeconomic success in America is attending and completing college. College is not only the best way to ensure a good job and career, it's really the only way. So for most families with children approaching college age, anything less than college is seen the same way we saw "Yale's 50 Most Beautiful People"—as a joke. Why would anyone forgo the "college premium," the income jump everyone sees upon completing a bachelor's degree?[9]

But as we learned from the Beautiful People, jokes have a funny way of becoming the status quo, and many policy makers also view the status quo as something of a joke. As former Secretary of Labor Robert Reich has said, "It's an absurd conceit of contemporary America that the only route to a middle-class life must be through a four-year university degree."[10]

In this book, I document the early days of a faster + cheaper revolution that will upend the traditional college route as America falls out of love with bachelor's degrees, particularly from nonselective schools. Alternative pathways are sprouting up everywhere. As these "disruptive technologies" proliferate, employers are undergoing simultaneous changes in their approaches to sourcing talent and hiring. These trends will snowball as more and more talented and motivated Millennials and Gen Z-ers opt out of a system that is unnecessarily lengthy and costly, at least to get a good first job. To get a sense of what I'm talking about, let me introduce you to Samantha, Simon, and Tommy.

The Graduate: "I'd Do It Differently"

Samantha Wolverton attended George Mason University, majoring in global affairs with a minor in software engineering. She supported herself by working in a restaurant and, after graduating, moved back home to save money and set out to find her first "real" job. The problem was that although Samantha applied to ten to fifteen jobs a day, no one responded. This went on for a year before Samantha found Revature, which provides advanced coding training to recent college grads.

For Samantha, Revature gave her "an overview of technologies that are actually used in entry-level development jobs—and the technology was much more up to date." While computer science assignments at GMU might involve modifying Java code to rotate a figure, at Revature she was tasked with designing an entire project. She learned to use "struts": existing code that developers call upon for common functions. It was fast-paced and challenging and exciting. She spent her weekends working on projects and preparing for mock interviews, knowing that real interviews for jobs with Revature clients were just around the corner.

Near the end of her training, Samantha interviewed with managers at Capital One. In November 2016, Revature hired Samantha for a minimum period of two years and staffed her out to Capital One. Samantha loves her job.

"They're focused on learning and growth of new developers," said Samantha. "Most of the skills and technologies I use in this job I learned in the Revature program. The software engineering minor in college taught me the basics of only one programming language. In this job, I get way more experience and in-depth understanding of the programs we use."

After her time with Revature is done, Capital One has the option to hire Samantha directly. "Capital One tends to hire Revature developers," she said, "and we're just starting those discussions now." A position at Capital One would pay $80–90,000 a year.

Samantha doesn't regret her time at George Mason. She made great friends, enjoyed studying global affairs, and grew up a lot. Yet if she could go back in time and do it differently, she would.

"Keep an open mind," Samantha advises. "There are other options."

The Dropout: "Going to College Is Like Gambling"

If Simon Kim could press reset, like in a video game, he "definitely wouldn't go to university." He started at West Hills Community College and then transferred to the University of California, Merced, the newest of the UC campuses (and closest to his home), to pursue a degree in business management. He took morning or afternoon classes, completed his coursework as quickly as possible, then went home to play video games and online poker. In his final semester, he met with a counselor to check that he had all the credits he needed to graduate. That was when he learned for the first time that UC Merced wouldn't accept some of his transferred credits from West Hills.

Rather than retake the courses, Simon decided to drop out and play poker full time. After all, he was already making $25,000 a year from online poker and he knew lots of people making more. But after a year and a half of playing poker, the site he played on most made some changes that didn't work to his advantage. Now at a crossroads, Simon remembered a fellow poker player who had left the game and started a career in sales. Simon thought maybe he could do that too and started searching for sales jobs. Up popped AlwaysHired, a training program that prepares students to work in sales for technology companies. AlwaysHired doesn't have a requirement that candidates finish college, so Simon applied, was accepted, and started the program a week later.

At AlwaysHired Simon wrote scripts, pitches, and email campaigns, practiced cold calling prospects, and was trained on how to use Salesforce, the most common customer relationship management (CRM) platform. One particularly memorable assignment was to go out, meet strangers, engage them in conversation, and keep drilling them.

"It helps you to get out of your comfort zone," Simon recalls. "It was awkward, but it was good preparation for working as a sales rep, because you have to ask people a lot of questions, and questions that you're not always going to want to ask."

AlwaysHired also guided Simon on how to identify hiring managers—making sure he was talking to the right people—and prepared him for interviews. In the third week of the program, AlwaysHired set up an interview with TMC Software, a San Francisco recruiting firm for IT consulting and staffing services. Simon met various account executives and the CEO. His lack of a degree came up in the interviews, but the CEO was clear that it wasn't a problem given Simon's skill set. TMC made him an offer, which he was happy with. Simon started work one week after AlwaysHired ended.

Simon's goal now is to gain experience in sales and move up into an account executive position. His current sales development (lead generation) position pays around $65,000 if he meets his quotas. Most account executive positions pay $90–100,000. Simon isn't considering going back to university to finish his degree.

"College was super useless for my current job," he said. "It's almost like college is not necessary. Nothing I learned in those business classes taught me how to sell. I definitely wouldn't go back."

The Builder: "There Are New Ways to Have a Career"

Tommy Gaessler always liked to build things: first with train sets and Lego blocks, then with computers. During Tommy's freshman year at Regis Jesuit High School in Aurora, Colorado, his dad, an entrepreneur, started a company at Galvanize, a technology community in Denver. The idea for Tommy to take Galvanize's immersive web development program instead of going to college came from his dad. It was a hard decision. His high school boasts a 99 percent college placement rate, and his classmates got into prestigious schools like Harvard, Yale, and Princeton. Also his mom wasn't for it; she believed Tommy needed a degree for people to take him seriously.

Tommy avoided meeting with his guidance counselor to talk about college until the end of senior year, when he got called into her office. He told her about Galvanize and instead of getting upset, she got excited. She said she might want to go there as well and began recommending it to a few other students.

"My friends thought it was cool that I was doing something different," Tommy said, "and Dad and I eventually won Mom over."

After graduating, Tommy began Galvanize's six-month full-stack immersive development program. "At Galvanize, the curriculum for each quarter is different but the schedule is the same," he said. "Each lesson builds on the last one. First you learn a static website, then a database, then a server so you can change things or post things. It was really encouraging to understand that the entire internet only involves four things: get, put (update), post (publish), and delete. That simplifies a lot."

In the afternoons, Tommy and his classmates would code along with the instructor or take notes, build their own projects with that code as homework, then review it with the instructor the next day.

Galvanize also helped Tommy with career development skills such as writing a résumé and cover letter, networking, and preparing for interviews. "We practiced doing coding challenges by hand on a whiteboard so we could demonstrate those skills in an interview setting and stand out," said Tommy.

He thinks one of the most important skills Galvanize furthered was problem solving: "We had to learn different ways of thinking to complete the coding challenges. And if I needed help finding a solution to a problem, I had to figure out how to ask the right questions."

Straight out of his six months at Galvanize, Tommy was recruited by a start-up, Airstream Health. In his current job as a software developer for Airstream, Tommy works on front-end development using Angular, Google's newest language, which he'd learned at Galvanize. "One cool thing about Galvanize is it teaches new technology," Tommy said. "College teaches Seed, which is forty years old. Everything I learned at Galvanize I use today."

● ● ●

The experiences of Samantha, Simon, and Tommy show why many Millennials have begun to question the conventional wisdom that college is the only pathway to a good first job. As Gen Z begins graduating from high school, questions are flying fast and furious. Many wonder whether it's worth taking on tens of thousands of dollars in student loans. Others ask what they'll study that will help them get (and keep) a good job. Even those that are privileged enough to not worry too much about the cost or economic outcome of committing to a degree program are starting to question whether there might be better paths for development and personal growth than four years on a college campus.

If you're wondering the same thing, here's a simple framework for making this critically important choice. Green means go to college. Red means don't. And yellow means it depends (and read on).

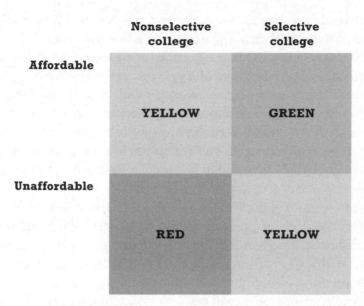

Although I'll add complexity by defining terms later on, the simple reality is this: if you're admitted to a selective college that provides scholarships or grants to make tuition, fees, and room and board affordable, you should put down this book, hurry up, and enroll. Conversely, if you're admitted to a nonselective school without the requisite college grants or scholarships to make it affordable, keep reading before you make a big mistake. And if you're in a yellow quadrant, you'll want to be very careful about how you think about selectivity and how you define affordable. Prior to the emergence of viable alternatives, the question of whether college was affordable was moot for most families. If you couldn't afford college, you borrowed. Well, guess what? It's not moot anymore. And you'll want to recognize that your definition of affordable might be very different for a selective college than a nonselective one. We'll pick up this framework in chapter 9, after completing a whirlwind tour of new, faster + cheaper alternatives.

• • •

At the start of each chapter, I tell what I hope is a funny college story. This is because it's somewhat relevant. But it's also to provide a sense of what might be lost as we shift to faster + cheaper alternatives. At the same time,

I'm constantly pausing mid-elegy to remind myself that if we don't shift, we'll lose a lot more than funny stories; we'll lose generations.

All students must have a good chance at achieving positive outcomes from postsecondary education. Make no mistake: every shred of evidence tells us that some form of postsecondary education is more important than ever. Failure to do so will mean relegation to a lifetime of menial work and will also limit one's ability to take full advantage of the blessings of American citizenship. And as a nation in today's global knowledge economy, any reduction in postsecondary education would be tantamount to economic suicide.

But the central point of this book is that it doesn't have to be "traditional" postsecondary education; it doesn't have to be college. You'll be able to tell from my stories that I truly loved college; I met my future wife, Yahlin, the first day of freshman year, in English 129. So I have no desire to take anything away from those who succeeded and will succeed at a traditional four-year journey of discovery, and I'll mourn the loss of that experience. At the same time, I'm honored to be able to provide the first roadmap to this next generation of programs, illustrated with inspiring stories of student pioneers, along with the first directory of faster + cheaper alternatives to college.

Fostering the development of a diverse set of faster, less expensive, and respected pathways to high-value employment is the calling of our time. Let's hope we get the job and do it well. America's future depends on it.

PART I

A Generation at Risk

CHAPTER 1

The Ol'
College Try

LELAINA: Quick, Vickie. What's your social security?

VICKIE: Uh, 851-25-9357.

TROY: Very impressive.

VICKIE: That's the only thing I really learned in college.

—*Reality Bites (1994)*

Most students learn a lot more in college than Vickie from *Reality Bites*. One of the most important lessons I learned in college is that labels matter a lot. During sophomore and junior years I dated a girl whose last name was Hong and who had the unfortunate habit of writing "HONG" with a black Sharpie in big block capital letters on literally everything she owned. Every book, clothing label, even her wastebasket was inescapably, inevitably HONG. Sometimes, sitting in her room looking at a plethora of HONG, it was all I could think about.

Back in the day, we listened to music on CD. Over the course of my relationship with Hong, our CD collections became intermingled and remained so even after we broke up. In my senior year I began dating Yahlin. One day when Yahlin was in our common room, she came across a copy of Cat Stevens's *Greatest Hits* with the telltale HONG obscuring poor Stevens's face. Yahlin knew exactly what the label meant and, in front of my roommate

Dave Friedman, spent the better part of the next hour alternatively asking questions and griping. After a while, Dave had had enough and took matters into his own hands. Taking a black Sharpie from his room, he grabbed the CD from Yahlin and vigorously covered HONG until all we could see was Sharpie. Then, immediately below, he wrote in equally large block capital letters: FRIEDMAN.

Dave might have saved my future that day, since Yahlin and I remained together and got married. The point is, labels matter (thanks for the lesson, FRIEDMAN). And while the label of "college graduate" has apparently become a prerequisite for a successful career, it's important to begin any discussion of college with its underlying substantive value. College's educational goals are ambitious and important for both the wealth and health of our country.

When I entered college in 1990, I fell in love with the promise of truly learning to read, write, and think. The physical manifestation of this promise was a thick blue book titled *Yale College Programs of Study.* It wasn't just the multitude of fascinating courses—each unpacking a suitcase of previously hidden knowledge while also signaling a potential future journey of study and work—that cast a spell. It was also the well-written introduction to the undergraduate curriculum. A college education, the book began, should "cultivate a broadly informed, highly disciplined intellect . . . [and provide] a phase of exploration, a place for the exercise of curiosity, and an opportunity for the discovery of new interests and abilities."[1]

The Blue Book went on to say that "to ensure that study is neither too narrowly focused nor too diffuse," students are required to take at least two courses in each of the following areas:

1. Humanities and arts: Exploring "the broad range of human thought, expression, and endeavor—cultivates an educated recognition of the greatest accomplishments of the past and enriches the capacity to participate fully in the life of our time."
2. Science: Developing "critical faculties that educated citizens need. These include an ability to evaluate the opinions of experts, to distinguish special pleading and demagoguery from responsible science, and to realize which things are known and which unknown—which are knowable and which unknowable—to science."

3. Social sciences: Understand the "connections between the familiar and the exotic, the traditional and the contemporary, the individual and the group, the predicted result and the anomalous outcome."
4. Foreign languages: To enhance "understanding of how languages work, often resulting in heightened sophistication in the use of one's own language."
5. Quantitative reasoning: "An educated person must be able to use quantitative information to make, understand, and evaluate arguments."
6. Writing: "The ability to write well is one of the hallmarks of a liberal education."[2]

But, as Yale notes, "the distributional requirements constitute a minimal education, not a complete one."[3] Students are also expected to concentrate their studies in the form of a major. According to the Blue Book:

> to study a subject in depth can be one of the most rewarding and energizing of human experiences and can form the basis of the interests and occupations of a lifetime. Knowledge advances by specialization, and one can gain some of the excitement of discovery by pressing toward the outer limits of what is known in a particular field. Intense study of a seemingly narrow area of investigation may disclose ramifications and connections that alter perspectives on other subjects. Such study also sharpens judgment and acquaints a person with processes by which new truths can be found.[4]

Beyond breadth and depth—and what the Blue Book doesn't call out—is that the third leg of the college edifice is perspective transformation: changing frames of reference to reflect on assumptions in order to develop valuable critical thinking skills. Every argument or idea is built on a scaffold of assumptions that may be sturdy enough to last ages or flimsy enough to crumble when poked and prodded. Perspective transformation involves looking at the same argument or idea through different frameworks, typically showing it in very different lights. More than anything else, the ability to do this well is the mark of what we consider an "educated" person (as opposed to intelligent, because this ability comes naturally to few and requires significant training and practice). Perspective transformation is easier to do in liberal arts courses than in science, technology, engineering, and math (STEM) courses. But it's essential: the best way to equip students with the skills they'll need to constructively make, advance, and counter ideas and arguments over the course of their lives.

Naturally, all three legs are strengthened by rigor. College is not supposed to be easy. Challenging readings, discussions, problem sets, projects, exams, and lots and lots of writing do improve thinking, not to mention work habits. Students who make it through the four-year gauntlet will have developed skills that will be useful for life.

Sounds good, right? Done right, it is a very good thing—not only in terms of personal development but economically as well. As one college president wrote recently, "an effective traditional college experience pushes students to learn beyond their own bubbles, exceed their perceived limits and discover new strengths and interests they have not thought about—skills that are crucial to career success."[5] College degrees have become the ticket to upward mobility and a symbol of the American Dream: an investment in college is an investment in yourself and your future.

● ● ●

College has become so engrained in the modern mind as the path to a good life that it's hard to fathom that there wasn't always a higher education monoculture of bachelor's degrees.[6] But back in the colonial era very few students actually completed degrees or earned any credential. Students attended college for a year or two and then departed. And why not? After all, college degrees weren't required for professions like law or medicine.[7] Some historians believe the growth in demand for degrees was initially a by-product of the popularity of commencement ceremonies.[8]

Ultimately, as our oldest institutions began to develop elite reputations, degrees became an alumni quality assurance mechanism: if this student says he was educated at our institution, we'd best ensure he's been educated to our standards. Still, throughout the eighteenth and nineteenth centuries, colleges and degrees served the sons of the merchant elite. College attendance and the bachelor's degree signified the social status of the father as much as the education of the son.

It was only after World War II—with the GI bill and massive new investments at the state (public university systems) and federal (Pell Grants and student loans) levels—that college degrees became commonplace, rising from 5 percent of adults to more than 30 percent. So it's really within the past two generations that college has expanded from an elite audience to the mass market pursuant to the belief that bachelor's degrees should and could serve all students. As degree prevalence doubled between 1970 and 1990, employers across virtually every industry began to utilize them as a crude general ability screening mechanism for most entry-level jobs.

So when young adults entered the labor market, the prevailing view was that if you wanted to get a good job, you needed a college degree. And there's no question that this remains the prevailing view, substantiated by the fact that employment outcomes remain far better for those with a degree than those without: Unemployment rates are much lower for college graduates as a group,[9] and over the course of their lives, college graduates earn nearly $1 million more than high school graduates.[10]

Of course, if all talented and motivated students feel compelled by the social norm to go to college and earn degrees—leaving behind less talented and motivated students—it would be awfully strange if college graduates didn't earn more. This self-selection bias gives rise to what I call the "dystopian counterfactual": what if the many documented advantages of earning a college degree stem primarily from the talent and motivation required to complete a college degree—not to mention the family background, wealth, and support that provided the path to college—rather than from value added by a college education?

There's no easy solution to the dystopian counterfactual. So we will try to triangulate our way to a point of view on whether the institution of college is working and, if so, for whom.

The first and most important point is that only about half of all students who enroll in four-year colleges in the United States complete a degree within six years.[11] While it's possible some may take longer, the overall completion rate is not higher than 55 percent, meaning 45 percent of students who attempt college fail to get over the bar. That means no credential of value and therefore wasted time and money.

And yet each year hope springs eternal as millions of new students enroll in thousands of colleges and universities. Eighty-one percent of students who start at community college for the first time think they'll eventually earn a bachelor's degree, but only 12 percent do.[12] In this respect September on campus is reminiscent of New Year's Day at the gym: everyone signs up with the best of intentions, but life tends to get in the way. Although there are signs hope may be dissipating. The 2017 College Confidence Index from

Allianz Tuition Insurance indicates 55 percent of entering college students are "not very confident" that they will successfully earn a degree.[13]

The fact that college degrees have become the primary screening mechanism for good jobs, and that nearly half of all Americans who attempt the credential fail to complete it, creates a feeling that our system is rigged. For those without degrees, there's a strong sense that no matter what they do, they're unable to get ahead and, in fact, are falling behind.

● ● ●

Students who are talented and motivated enough to complete degree programs are not without their own challenges. First and foremost, there's substantial evidence that many students are not benefiting from teaching and/or learning. By filing public records requests at one hundred public colleges and universities, the *Wall Street Journal* obtained test results from sixty-eight institutions for the Collegiate Learning Assessment (CLA) Plus, a cognitive test administered to freshmen and seniors by about two hundred colleges and universities. The *Journal* found that one-third of seniors are unable to make a coherent argument, interpret data in a table, or assess the quality of evidence in a document. While the majority of students demonstrated some measurable progress in critical thinking, some flagship universities like the University of Texas at Austin and the University of Kentucky showed little improvement. And at universities like the University of Louisiana at Lafayette, three-quarters of seniors demonstrated critical thinking skills that fell in the "basic" or "below basic" categories.[14] Nationwide, CLA reports that 40 percent of seniors fall into these two lowest categories.[15] Further, a recent survey of employers by the Association of American Colleges and Universities revealed only 26 percent thought new college graduates had "excellent" critical thinking skills.[16]

The National Survey of Student Engagement (NSSE) surveys hundreds of thousands of American college students on their attitudes toward higher education. According to NSSE, only 10 percent of students are fully engaged. Somewhere between 20 to 40 percent of students are fully disengaged. And the remainder are in the middle.

These numbers are consistent with the findings of Richard Arum of New York University and Josipa Roksa of the University of Virginia, who in their 2011 book *Academically Adrift* reported that more than one-third of students failed to materially improve critical thinking and writing capabilities over the course of their college experience. They also found that college is much less rigorous than generally thought. Few courses demand that students read more than forty pages per week or write twenty-page papers. Average study time is only twelve hours per week. A third of students surveyed study less than five hours per week.[17] In fact, the Heritage Foundation has calculated that the average college student spends 2.76 hours per day on education-related activities but 4.4 hours per day on leisure activities "not including shopping, grooming, personal care, housework, cooking, or eating."[18]

In *The Five-Year Party*, Craig Brandon, a former journalism instructor at Keene State College in New Hampshire, describes a typical day in his class: "None of my twenty-two students would be taking notes and only a few would be paying attention. Two would be asleep with their heads down on the desks, three would be listening to their iPods or texting messages on their cell phones, four would be engaged in a lively conversation among themselves about the awesome party they went to last night . . . Only two or three students would have read the assignment for the day . . . No one would ask a question and 90 percent of them were simply filling a seat."[19] He reports conversations with "more than a hundred professors" who have dumbed down courses and lowered the grading curve.[20]

Brandon lays the blame squarely at the feet of administrators focused on enrollment, retention, and the bottom line rather than ensuring students actually learn something. He has choice words for the current system, alternating between "massive scam" and "widespread fraud."[21] "The inconvenient truth," claims Brandon, "is that only the best colleges in America still consider 'education' to be their primary mission."[22]

One UK commentator, writing in the *Times of London* in 2017, claimed the problem was the "all must have prizes" approach, which eroded the meaning of educational achievement. When everyone was supposed to be able to get university degrees, she said, universities were forced to lower their standards. According to her, "standards did indeed fall" in the UK. "It wasn't just questionable courses being introduced in adventure tourism, personal training or the like. It was a devaluation across the board."[23]

Adding the 45 percent of students who don't complete to the percentage of graduates who don't appear to be learning anything of note—which I conservatively estimate at about one-third—only 37 percent of students are experiencing positive outcomes from college; 63 percent are not.

• • •

Another inconvenient truth is that only $0.21 out of every tuition dollar is actually spent on instruction.[24] What colleges and universities are spending on is administration, for one. At small colleges, spending on administrative staff (deans and associate deans) amounts to $0.64 out of every $1.00; instruction is the remaining $0.36. And this only includes support of core academic operations, not student activities, financial aid, or any other of the many functions provided by colleges and universities.[25] Over the past twenty-five years, the number of administrators grew twice as fast as the number of students.[26]

For the average American, the most visible spending is on college athletics. Only 10 percent (23/228) of NCAA Division I universities generate enough revenue from their athletic programs to cover expenses, and this number is misleading since sixteen of those twenty-three programs only broke even as a result of alumni contributions directed to athletic programs (some of which, presumably, would have found their way to the alma maters independent of sports). So only 3 percent (7/228) truly break even on an operating basis.[27] The rest are funded in part or virtually in whole by state subsidies or, more commonly, student tuition and fees. According to Robert Kelchen, Assistant Professor at Seton Hall, since 1999 mandatory student fees have risen 30 percent more than tuition at public four-year schools. Last year, the average mandatory fee was $1,700.[28]

Schools are also spending money on facilities. Hundreds of millions of dollars have been spent on aquatic features ranging from lazy rivers to paw-print-shaped hot tubs to grottos modeled after the one at the Playboy mansion.[29] It's even more helpful if these features are visible on the campus walk, which is where many families decide whether to enroll. According to Mitchel Livingston, VP for Student Affairs at the University of Cincinnati, families not only make their decisions on the walk but during the first fifteen minutes of the walk. "They want to be wowed," he said. "If we don't wow them they go somewhere else that has more wow."[30]

And speaking of wow, there's the example of North Carolina's High Point University, which operates a first-run movie theater and steak house for students and which actually hired a Director of "WOW" to please students by keeping track of their favorite movies, sodas, and candy. High Point has become infamous for operating like a resort, complete with valet parking, concierges, and lobster lunches.[31] It's an outlier for sure, but most schools are spending money on facilities and services that point in this general direction.

Finally, colleges and universities continue to prioritize research over teaching, which while often serving the advancement of knowledge—particularly in the hard sciences—also serves the dual purpose of allowing faculty to do what they want and providing a much easier metric than teaching or learning for determining faculty quality (i.e., number of publications). And as for the conventional wisdom that top researchers are better teachers, that may be a useful fiction. According to a Brookings study that utilized unique "matched student-faculty data" from Northwestern University between 2001 and 2008, "there is no relationship between the teaching quality and research quality of tenured Northwestern faculty." The authors went on to say that their estimates are "precise zeroes, indicating that it's unlikely that mismeasurement of teaching or research quality explains the lack of a relationship between the two."[32] A new book by Georgetown University professor Jacques Berlinerblau, *Campus Confidential: How College Works, or Doesn't, for Professors, Parents and Students,* is quoted in the *New York Times* as reinforcing the important point that "while teaching undergraduates is normally a very large part of a professor's job, success in our field is correlated with a professor's ability *to avoid teaching undergraduates*."[33]

● ● ●

All this might be fine if college didn't cost so much. In the 2017 film *The House*, Will Ferrell and Amy Poehler's daughter Alex, who is attending Bucknell University, has lost her scholarship. As a result, mom and dad are forced to come to terms with the list price: "It's $50 million!" Ferrell's character mistakenly exclaims when he sees the tuition bill. Desperate to raise the cash to keep their daughter in school, they open an illegal casino in a residential neighborhood.

When there's a Hollywood comedy about the outlandish cost of college, it's a sign that affordability has gone from being a consideration or constraint to the first thing everyone except the wealthiest families thinks about when they think about college.

Schools have hiked tuition at roughly double the rate of inflation (and recently room, board, and student fees at double the level of tuition).[34] Over a thirty-year period, that's the difference between affordable and ridiculous. Ridiculous as in the basis for a Hollywood comedy. Ridiculous as in the *New York Times* interviewing the President of the University of Notre Dame, noting that it would take students more than four thousand hours (or 100 weeks of full-time work) at prevailing campus wages to pay for half of the annual tuition, and asking him if he thinks God wants families to spend $300,000 for college.[35] Ridiculous as in Duke University sophomore Miriam Weeks attributing her involvement in the adult film industry to the cost of college. Speaking at the University of North Carolina at Chapel Hill's Student Union, Weeks, also known as Belle Knox, reportedly said, "I felt that being screwed on camera was the best way to avoid being screwed by the higher education system."[36] And as she then wrote in *Time*:

> Officials at my school responded that $60,000 is a bargain—they actually spend $90,000 a year on each student. Let's break that $90,000 down. Building and maintaining physical infrastructure on campus gets $8,000. Another $14,000 goes to pay a share of administrative and academic support salaries, which in Duke's case includes more than $1 million in total compensation to the university president, Richard Brodhead, and more than $500,000 to the provost, Peter Lange, according to 2011 tax filings. Also, $14,000 goes to dorms, food, and health services; $7,000 goes to staff salaries for deans and faculty; and miscellaneous costs take up another $5,000.[37]

And ridiculous as in President Trump, in his first official remarks on higher education, belittling the sector with the term *crippling debt*, bringing to mind one of my favorite headlines from *The Onion*: "Online University Allows Students to Amass Crippling Debt at Own Pace."[38]

Contrary to popular belief, unacceptably high tuition isn't only a problem at private colleges. Tuition has increased faster at the public colleges and universities attended by the majority of students. According to the College Board, public university tuition, fees, and room and board averaged about $20,000 in 2017—more than double the cost of a generation ago (adjusting for inflation).[39] Faced with declining state support following the Great Recession, many public schools saw no alternative but double-digit tuition hikes.

Of course the problem is not only tuition. It's the total cost of going to school—including housing, food, transportation, and health care—and colleges and universities often radically underestimate these other expenses. A

2017 paper by the University of Wisconsin–Madison's HOPE Lab and Seton Hall's Robert Kelchen compared actual living costs with estimates used by colleges and universities in their financial aid calculations. The study found that more than 40 percent of four-year colleges are utilizing a cost of living estimate that is at least 20 percent off from actual costs (almost always under). Tufts University utilizes a cost of living estimate that is almost $11,000 below the actual cost of living in Boston.[40]

The upshot is that new college graduates who avail themselves of federal financial aid owe an average of $37,000 in student loan debt.[41] Total student loan debt is over $1.4 trillion, the second-highest form of debt (behind mortgages but more than car loans or credit card debt). Average student loan debt per household has grown an unfathomable 828 percent since 1999 and now constitutes 10.6 percent of total household debt—more than double the level of 2008.[42]

Student loan debt is growing by about $50 billion every year, primarily because graduates aren't paying it down. The 12 million student loan borrowers in their thirties still owe an average of $34,000, which translates into about $400 every month.[43] More than a million borrowers now default on their loans each year.[44]

Overall, only 57 percent of the 22 million Americans with federal student loans are current on their payments; 43 percent (nearly 5 million) are in default, delinquent, or in forbearance.[45] Fifty-seven percent may be a high estimate given a recent Department of Education coding error indicating that actual repayment rates could be as much as 20 percent lower.[46] There are almost 1,500 colleges and universities where the majority of students who borrowed federal loans are making interest-only payments on their loans or no payments at all.[47] Debt is also feeding back into low completion rates. Between 2013 and 2016, more than 30 percent of students failed to settle their balances, triggering institutional holds, forced withdrawals, and collection agencies.[48] One recent headline I stumbled upon: "Stop Calling Millennials the Facebook Generation. They're the Student Loan Generation."[49]

So it's not surprising that alumni are unhappy. In a recent poll of 30,000 college graduates, only half strongly agreed their college investment was a good one.[50] For younger alumni, it was only 38 percent, which makes a lot of sense given that a shocking one-third of all borrowers who graduated between 2006 and 2011 have already defaulted on their student loans.[51] In another survey, 71 percent of graduates with loan balances say they "would have made different education choices if they could have forecast the burden of repaying student loans," perhaps because the imperative to repay nondischargeable student loans is causing them to make different job choices: 40 percent of graduates with debt take jobs unrelated to their major or training vs. 20 percent of graduates without debt.[52] Even those who find good jobs say they find the debt "distracting" at work.[53] So it's no wonder that 17 percent say they would have forgone college altogether if they knew they'd owe so much money from loans.[54] And 30 percent say they would sell an organ to be rid of their loans.[55]

Parents of alumni have become equally disenchanted; in a Kaplan/ MONEY survey of more than five hundred parents of prospective college students, only 21 percent say the cost of college is justified.[56] This may have something to do with the fact that Millennials have been unable to move out of their parents' homes.[57] From 2007 to 2016, homeownership by thirty year olds dropped from 32 percent to 21 percent. In 2004, 33.5 percent of twenty-three- to twenty-five-year-olds lived with parents. In 2015, it was 45 percent, posing real costs for young people as well as their parents. In a recent poll by the Canadian Imperial Bank of Commerce, 76 percent of parents with adult children living at home said they'd willingly contribute an average of $24,000 to get them out of the house.[58] And how about this dismal statistic? In 2005, the majority of young adults in thirty-five states lived independently; in 2015, this was true in only six states.[59] That's a shocking turnabout in a single decade.

Dependence on parents is not good for economic activity. When young adults live with their parents, 25 percent are idle (i.e., neither working nor going to school).[60] It's also hurting new business creation. The Kauffman Startup Activity Index, which explores national trends in new business creation, shows that the share of young adults engaged in entrepreneurial activities declined from more than 34 percent in 1996 to 24.7 percent in 2014.[61] In 1995, 15 percent of working adults under forty were self-employed and 21 percent had student loan debt. In 2010, 12 percent were self-employed and 37 percent had student loan debt.[62] Young adults with student loan debt are less likely to apply for business loans (17 percent of young households with debt vs. 27 percent of households without debt).[63] And when young adults with loans go into business, they're not doing as well (an average of two employees vs. nine for those who graduated without debt).[64]

So while everyone acknowledges college affordability is a problem, for Millennials (and soon for Gen Z), it's a crisis. Which explains a recent survey that found 70 percent of Millennials believe student loan debt is a "bigger problem" than North Korea for the United States.[65]

• • •

In response to these unprecedented questions about the value of college, aside from building climbing walls and lazy rivers, most schools have resorted to two primary strategies: discounting and marketing.

Prior to the Great Recession, families were willing to believe that price was a signal for quality, which enabled colleges to continue raising list prices. But no longer. Average tuition discounts provided by private colleges have increased 10 percent since the Great Recession to nearly 50 percent for first-time freshmen.[66] Most colleges call these discounts "scholarships," and many prey on students' desire to play a college sport by calling them "athletic scholarships." They stock teams in popular sports with more players than needed or launch new teams in esoteric sports or even e-sports (i.e., video games).

Overall, though, more than 85 percent of discounts are not real scholarships. Real scholarships require real funds provided by real private donors, foundations, or employers, which is different from slashing prices to convince students to enroll. (Most wealthy donors are more interested in putting their names on buildings, funding research, or supporting athletic programs than funding scholarships.[67]) And as average discount rates for upperclassmen are significantly lower than for freshmen, the whole pricing enterprise has a bit of a "bait-and-switch" smell to it.[68] Pine Manor College in Massachusetts was recently called out for significantly reducing aid to sophomores. According to one observer, "It felt like it was a marketing tool. They needed to fill their freshman class."[69] Matriculating students are fearful of exactly this, which explains why a recent University of California, Los Angeles (UCLA) survey found that two-thirds of all incoming freshmen—the majority of whom received financial aid packages—expressed some or major concern about their ability to afford college for all four years.[70]

In terms of marketing, colleges and universities are constantly revamping print collateral and digital assets and increasingly hiring agencies to manage "campaigns." Some, unfortunately, have gone further—and not only the "predatory" for-profit universities that the *New York Times* and other media outlets love reporting on. East-West University is a private nonprofit institution on the South Side of Chicago that recruits low-income students to programs with a 9 percent graduation rate and where former students make less than high school dropouts. Until recently, the university offered students iPads if they could convince their friends to enroll. According to a former admissions officer quoted in a *Wall Street Journal* article, "Some of these kids couldn't write at all, you would just look at their essays and you knew they weren't going to make it."[71]

In addition, recent stories of admissions officers intentionally and materially misreporting test scores, GPAs, and class rank of enrolled students in order to inflate rankings have tainted schools like George Washington University, Emory University, Bucknell University, Tulane University, Claremont McKenna College, and Flagler College, where the VP of Enrollment Management memorably explained to the *St. Augustine Record*: "I really love this college so much, and there had been a decline a little bit in the profile of the incoming class . . ."[72]

● ● ●

Of course, most of this misery relates to alumni; that is, the 55 percent who actually complete their degrees. So what about the 45 percent who don't complete degrees? Most of them are Millennials: America has 12.5 million twenty-somethings who attempted but failed to earn degrees.[73] As Arne Duncan, President Obama's Secretary of Education, said, having debt but no degree can be "the end of the world" and "catastrophic" for students.[74] And while the level of debt held by noncompleters is lower—thereby permitting higher education officials, such as the former President of the American Council on Education, to brazenly calculate that "average" student loan debt is only $13,000 (i.e., not a major problem, nothing to see here, move along)—defaults are concentrated amongst noncompleters.[75]

The one-two punch of low completion rates and student loan debt has thrown America's engine of socioeconomic mobility into reverse for young adults. Today, while 50 percent of twenty-four-year-olds with family incomes of $90,000+ have earned bachelor's degrees, the number for families with incomes under $35,000 is less than 6 percent.[76] Families with incomes of $116,000+ represent more than half the degrees awarded to traditional-age students (eighteen to twenty-four).[77]

American higher education has become segregated by wealth. At the top two hundred colleges, 75 percent of students come from the top income quartile and only 5 percent from the bottom quartile. Shockingly, at thirty-eight of our most selective institutions (sadly including Yale), there are more students from the top 1 percent than the bottom 60 percent.[78] Public colleges and universities are also heading in the wrong direction. A clear majority of top public institutions are admitting more wealthy students and fewer low-income students than they were back in 1999.[79] We're also seeing a dismaying level of racial segregation: 80 percent of whites attend the top five hundred colleges while 75 percent of minorities attend institutions outside the top five hundred.[80]

Increasingly, lower-income students are staying away. The percentage of low-income students who enroll in college immediately after high school has declined by 10 percent since the Great Recession.[81] Some of this decline is a result of fewer low-income students applying—a new poll from the Jack Kent Cooke Foundation reveals that more than a third of high-achieving low-income students are refraining from applying to any college due to concerns about college cost[82]—but much of it is "melt" between application and start of school; up to 40 percent of low-income students who accept admission never attend the first day of class.[83] Last summer, *New York Times* columnist David Brooks wrote a great column titled "How We Are Ruining America," about how "members of the college-educated class have become amazingly good at making sure their children retain their privileged status . . . [and] making sure the children of other classes have limited chances to join their ranks."[84] It's the sort of thing that makes you think a revolution might be just around the corner.

● ● ●

College is a lot like marriage. Both college and marriage have many social and psychological benefits and are the mark of successful people. They also exist, at least in part, for the benefit of others. Marriage is a better arrangement for raising children, which is one reason it's important to grant marital status to all couples who desire it. And college produces an educated citizenry, which benefits society as a whole, and in particular, employers.

Both are also terrific unless you fail to stick with it. All other things being equal, divorced people are worse off across the board—less healthy, less happy—than people who never married to begin with. They're certainly worse off financially. Likewise, those who get "divorced" from college—by starting and failing to complete—are worse off than those who never enrolled.

Both marriage and college are social constructs: marriage since the dawn of recorded history, college much more recently. Age aside, college is different from marriage in one crucial way: While marriage saves money through splitting housing and other costs and remains a great financial investment for those who stick with it, the social, psychological, and societal benefits of college now cost so much that the return on investment is increasingly uncertain for those who stick with it.

This is because the income premium correlated with college is in decline. Census data shows that the average annual earnings differential between high school and four-year college graduates rose sharply, from $19,776 in 1975 to $32,900 in 2000 (expressed in 2015 dollars)—only to fall to $29,867 by 2015. In the late twentieth century, rising higher-education costs were offset by the increasing financial benefits associated with a bachelor's degree. Since 2000 these benefits have declined while costs have continued to rise.[85] According to a 2015 Goldman Sachs research note, the return on college is falling: "In 2010, students could expect to break even within eight years of finishing school. Since then, that has increased to nine years. And if the trend line continues, students who start college in 2030 without scholarships or grants . . . may not see a return on investment until age 37."[86] Clearly, there will come a point at which the price is too high for a social construct that, as it pertains to success, may be more of a signifier than signified, and a diminishing one at that.

It's possible we've already passed this point, at least for some institutions. During the summer of 2017, the Department of Education's National Center for Education Statistics released a report showing the fourth consecutive year of reductions in the number of colleges and universities eligible for federal financial aid programs. After declines of 0.3 percent, 1.2 percent, and 2 percent the previous years, the decline from 2015–16 to 2016–17 was a whopping 5.6 percent. Since 2013, the number of colleges has fallen from 7,416 to 6,760, or by 9 percent.[87] Over the past six years, total federal student loan borrowing for college is down 20 percent.[88]

Last summer, Mitch Daniels, the former Governor of Indiana and current President of Purdue University, appeared at a forum on higher education in Washington, DC, and shared his conclusion that colleges and universities need to take responsibility for outcomes. "I think schools like ours should be at risk," said Daniels. "If we're going to take on students who have borrowed money, there's so little accountability in the system right now."[89]

Daniels is still a voice in the higher education wilderness; no other college or university president has espoused a similar view. But it's consistent with his approach since taking the reins at Purdue in 2013. His first initiatives: freezing tuition, then hiring loan counselors to warn students about borrowing too much. Coming from outside the system, Daniels realized college's day of reckoning was nigh. "Higher education has to get past the 'take our word for it' era," he said. "Increasingly, people aren't."[90]

CHAPTER 1 • KEY POINTS

- The college income premium is largely a product of self-selection.
- Overall student outcomes haven't been great for the past decade; more than 60 percent of students who enroll have experienced negative outcomes.
- Colleges aren't spending as much on teaching and learning as on arguably extrinsic pursuits.
- Affordability and debt have been game changers in public perception of college.

CHAPTER 2

The Employment Imperative

Would you mind telling me then—what were those four years of college for? What was the point of all that hard work?

—*The Graduate (1967)*

I learned in college that when you take someone's word for something, you're likely to get fooled. Sophomore year, my best friends lived across the hall from a suite of unhappy seniors. Why so glum? First, they picked the lowest card of all the seniors in the college room draw and were relegated to a room more appropriate for sophomores. Second, as a consequence, they had to share a bathroom with my friends. So on day one the seniors made clear that the bathroom was theirs exclusively; my friends were expected to walk through the adjoining suite to the bathroom on the other side. That was the first shot in the Bathroom War.

My friends fired back not only by using the bathroom anyway but also becoming energy efficiency zealots, particularly when it came to turning off the bathroom lights when one of the seniors was in the shower. The seniors complained to the dean, and then the master, who called my friends into his office for a dressing-down. A cold war ensued for a few months but returned to hot one afternoon when my friend Chris Douvos came bounding up the stairwell with a delicious New Haven pizza, only to lose his balance as he reached the top of the stairs. As if in slow motion, we all watched the pie tumble out of its box and land toppings-down on the very dirty floor (to this day, my friends refer to this event as "the worst thing that ever happened"). Grieving, my friends left the pizza on the ground, shunted to the side of the stairway, right in front of the bathroom.

A week later, one of the seniors, Mimi, complained bitterly about the pizza. Sensing a potential silver lining in "the worst thing that ever happened," Chris told Mimi that his roommate Dave was battling a nasty cough, but his father had no health insurance and Dave couldn't afford penicillin. As a result, their other roommate Alex, a molecular biology and biochemistry major, was attempting to grow mold on the pizza to make penicillin for Dave. Mimi backed away, apologetic, until the next day when the seniors realized the story was too ridiculous to be true and promptly bagged and tossed our toiletries from the bathroom. But my friends wouldn't be cowed. That night we all went out for chicken wings and returned with a bucket of bones, which—in a gutsy move that turned the tide in the Bathroom War—Chris arranged on the floor of the shower to spell "Hi Mimi."

●   ●   ●

Today's students are not as easily fooled as Mimi and her friends. Not even close. The single biggest change in higher education in the past decade is the percentage of students who say they're enrolling for job, career, or income reasons. Today, in survey after survey, more than 90 percent of students provide this as the critical reason for going to college[1]—what I call the "employment imperative." More and more students don't want to be wowed by lazy rivers or concierges. They want to be wowed by a good first job. To paraphrase James Carville from President Clinton's successful 1992 election: "It's the job, stupid."

Why an employment imperative? The primary reason is poor employment outcomes experienced by college graduates during the Great Recession. Most students have older siblings or friends who were unemployed or underemployed, often significantly, for many years. In *Academically Adrift*, Arrum and Roksa found that of students who graduated in 2009, eighteen months later 35 percent were living with their parents or other family members and only 17 percent were making more than $40,000 per year.[2] Likewise, a longitudinal study by the National Center for Education Statistics of students who were high school sophomores in 2002 (and therefore would have graduated from college in 2008) found that 41 percent were unemployed at least once between 2009 and 2012, and 35 percent were persistently underemployed.[3]

Few college graduates are actually unemployed for extended periods of time, in large part because they need to pay off student loans and so are likely to pick up work where they can find it. The $25,000 question (or whatever amount they were paying annually for tuition) is whether it's the kind of work that requires a college degree.

Underemployment is a lot harder to define than unemployment. The Rockefeller Foundation found that 49 percent of recent college graduates reported they didn't need to go to college to do their current jobs.[4] Accenture found 51 percent of 2014 and 2015 graduates considered themselves to be underemployed.[5] Avenica (formerly GradStaff), a provider of career pathways for new college grads, found that 86 percent of brand-new college graduates reported having no job offers.[6] In *The Five-Year Party*, Brandon said the "vast majority" of his students "were employed after graduation as clerks and waiters." He continued:

> Whenever I encountered them in these jobs where they were making absolutely no use of the skills I taught them, I would ask them what had happened. Most of them were vague and unwilling to discuss how they were paying off their student loans. The ones who did open up said they were still waiting for their big break, for the fickle finger of success to bestow its wealth upon them.[7]

More authoritatively, the National Bureau of Economic Research has found that the unemployment rate of recent college graduates spiked at 7 percent postrecession and remains north of 5 percent, while underemployment remains near an all-time high of around 45 percent.[8]

In his 2016 book *There Is Life After College*, Jeff Selingo found that only about a third of all new graduates were successfully launching careers. Two-thirds were suffering through what the media has taken to calling Millennials' "failure to launch,"[9] which has led to headlines in *The Onion* like "Company Immediately Calls Job Applicant Upon Seeing 'B.A. In Communications' on Résumé." There is a cottage industry for journalists writing articles like this one in *Cosmopolitan*: "10 Reasons Why You Shouldn't Freak Out if You're Graduating Without a Job (You are *so* not alone)." Among the silver linings: you don't have to deal with coworkers you don't like, moving back home is the best living situation you'll have for a long time, and you can sleep all you like.[10]

More frustrating is that wages haven't improved for college graduates since the Great Recession. In fact, they've continued to fall, even for students who majored in STEM subjects. In 2015, new graduates who majored in biology had average salaries of $31,000, down from $35,000 in 2010. Even computer science and engineering grads saw a decline.[11] As a generation, Millennials are earning 20 percent less than Baby Boomers did at the same stage in their lives.[12] Which explains why only 41 percent of recent graduates have been able to pay down any principal on their student loan balances in the first three years after leaving school.[13] And why the Federal Reserve Bank of New York found that the bottom 25 percent of new college graduates are incurring debt but earning no more than high school graduates.[14]

We also know that lower wages for new graduates tends to result in "wage scarring"—lower wages that persist for decades.[15] A new study from the Social Security Administration and a number of researchers, including Fatih Guvenen, an economist at the University of Minnesota, attributes the increase in lifetime inequality over the past fifty years to "a result of lower incomes at younger ages." According to Guvenen, "It all starts at age twenty-five," or with suboptimal first jobs.[16]

Beyond demonstrably poor employment outcomes, a second reason for the employment imperative is that students tend to have less exposure to paid work. When Baby Boomers and Gen X-ers were in high school, even if they weren't working during the school year, it's likely they worked over the summer. Maybe they scooped ice cream, delivered papers, mowed lawns, or worked as lifeguards. But in the summer of 2017, only 43 percent of sixteen- to nineteen-year-olds were working or looking for a job—down from nearly 70 percent a generation ago.[17] While McDonald's is now advertising itself as America's "Best First Job," fewer teens are working there. The Bureau of Labor Statistics predicts teen workforce participation will drop below 27 percent by 2024.

Why is this occurring? *Bloomberg* cites crowding out by older workers and immigrants.[18] Other explanations are stricter teen driving laws and compressed summer calendars. But the most plausible explanation is that jobs like dishwasher or busboy have been devalued by society in general, and parents in particular, as useful steps on the road to a successful career.

Instead, students are being encouraged to study and participate in as many extracurricular activities as possible in order to burnish their college applications. Jeff Selingo noted as much in the *Washington Post*, quoting one expert as saying: "Upper-middle class families and above have made the determination that college admissions officers devalue paid work and that if you're not pursuing a hectic schedule of activities you'll be less appealing to colleges."[19]

I agree that sacrificing paid work at the altar of college admissions and the almighty bachelor's degree has not only been short-sighted but harmful. As Selingo shared:

> I worked in a hospital kitchen filling orders for patients. It was probably the worst job I ever held, but it was the first time I wasn't surrounded by my peers, so it taught me how to interact with people of all backgrounds and ages. I also learned the importance of showing up on time, keeping to a schedule, completing tasks, and paying attention to details (after all, I didn't want to mess up a tray for a patient on a specific diet).[20]

This disconnection to paid work has been exacerbated by the rise of unpaid internships during and after college. The National Association of Colleges and Employers (NACE) reports the percentage of college graduates participating in at least one internship is now more than 80 percent (up from less than 10 percent a generation ago).[21] Technically, unpaid internships are illegal unless the employer is a nonprofit organization or unless interns receive college credits. Sadly, by broadly awarding credits for unpaid internships, many colleges and universities are enabling this system of internship-peonage, thereby furthering young people's distance from paid work.

The result is that for most Millennials—and now Gen Z-ers—there's no sense of easing into paid work, no gradual evolution. It's now binary: at the end of college, switch off childhood and switch on employment and adulthood. The anticipation of this sudden shift is producing a great deal of anxiety around the issue of employment and the first paid job in particular. (This is an anxiety older generations never felt because most of us had a sense we were employable—maybe not in the jobs we wanted, but we believed we'd be able to get by.) Of course, having tens of thousands of dollars in student loan debt hanging over your head makes this anxiety all the more acute.

So many of today's college students are dreading graduation, paralyzingly anxious at the question of what they'll do for paid work. This is why today's students no longer buy the time-honored college line: "We prepare you for your fifth job, not your first job." Today's students know that if they don't get a good first job, their fifth job is likely to be lousy as well.

• • •

Colleges and universities have not been responsive to students' views on the importance of a good first job, preferably in a growing sector of the economy (and preferably for a winning employer rather than an also-ran).[22] If they had paid attention to the employment imperative, they'd be busy aligning degree programs, courses, and curricula to actual entry-level positions and also significantly increasing investment in career services. Unfortunately, they're doing neither.

First, it's important to acknowledge that existing degree programs are not well aligned to first jobs. Only 16 percent of students believe college is preparing them for first jobs.[23] One human resources executive at a major North American company shared with me that he had mapped all degree programs to jobs and found only 30 percent were 1:1 (really few:few) relationships. The rest were either many:many or many:few—both "risky education paths."

But even the degree programs that are ostensibly aligned may not be properly preparing students for good first jobs. Roger Schank, former chair of the Computer Science Department at Yale, recalled a "mini-revolution" when students began complaining that Google wasn't hiring Yale CS graduates. According to Schank, "The reason was clear enough. The faculty, many of whom were still there from my day, are, in essence, theoreticians. They may know how to program but they don't really do it anymore and they want to teach about their new ideas and their latest theories." Schank went on to report that the chair of the Economics Department at Columbia told him that the only reason calculus is a requirement for the economics major is that the department didn't want to deal with the volume of students who want to work in finance, and so calculus is utilized as a filter.[24]

The challenge of aligning degree programs, courses, and curricula to employer requirements—specifically what employers are looking for in entry-level jobs—is exacerbated by faculty control over academic matters. This doctrine evolved over the course of the twentieth century and is now embedded in accreditation standards.[25] Faculty control means curriculum decisions occur within academic departments, which are structured according to an encyclopedic organization of knowledge. However, that means yesterday's knowledge, which yields academic silos and big gaps.

Take business or data analytics. Hundreds of thousands of new entry-level jobs have been created in this area over the past several years. But where do they fit into existing departmental structures? Some business schools have added relevant curriculum; at other universities, it's the statistics department. Under faculty control, most universities haven't yet come up with an adequate answer. We're seeing the same thing in cybersecurity. The skills required for cybersecurity require some computer science curriculum but are a distant relative from learning C++. At Texas A&M University, cybersecurity courses have been offered by engineering as well as agriculture and life sciences departments.

Many faculty members resist the idea that teaching should be aligned to employment opportunities. Last year, after I proposed as much in a series of articles, I found myself under attack on what's referred to as "Academic Twitter." Several academics found "outrageous" the notion that aligning curriculum with employer needs was a goal that faculty members shared. One prominent professor with an army of over 21,000 followers tweeted, "Sorry, that isn't a shared goal. It is a questionable goal, in fact." She then went on to dismiss the idea that students are focused on employment, saying, "The research shows today's students consider community and family [not employment]." Another professor who was more accepting of the notion that students might care about getting a good first job said, "That's a labor-market problem that is not going to be solved by the educational system."

An article last year in American higher education's paper of record, the *Chronicle of Higher Education*, summed up the view of traditional colleges and universities on this question. In an article on Texas A&M's effort to launch courses in cybersecurity, the *Chronicle* reached the following conclusion: "Work-force demand can lead some institutions to teach students the skills needed for today's entry-level jobs. But those tools may well be obsolete five or ten years from now."[26] The implication—one that is absolutely in the mainstream of faculty thinking—is that updating curriculum to reflect current labor market needs may not be a worthwhile pursuit because such needs will change in five to ten years.

Can you imagine similar thinking in any other sector of the economy? Does Apple let a year go by without a new iPhone release, let alone five or ten? Do health care professionals skip continuing medical education for

years at a time because the new information will be outdated? If they did
so, it would cost lives. Likewise, it should be unacceptable to sacrifice one
class of college graduates, let alone five or ten.

Even colleges that explicitly aim to align academic programs to labor
market needs fall far short. Last year, Kimberly Cassidy, the President of
Bryn Mawr College, and Gina Siesing, the college's chief information officer, wrote an op ed in *Inside Higher Education* on their institution's new
initiative to infuse "digital skills . . . throughout the entire curriculum" to
"provide long-term employability" for graduates. Here's how they described
Bryn Mawr's approach:

> Our colleagues at Bryn Mawr College have developed just such
> an approach to maximize our students' digital competencies. We
> obtained extensive information from faculty members, staff mem-
> bers, parents, and graduates from a diverse set of fields and pro-
> fessions to create a matrix of the kinds of technical understanding
> and critical use of data and digital tools that students need to thrive
> in their course work, research, internships, and future professional
> pathways.[27]

See if you can guess what's missing from this list (hint: it starts with
"EMP" and ends with "LOYERS"). Colleges are either ill-suited to or inca-
pable of this kind of engagement with the labor market.

● ● ●

Another area where colleges and universities fail to meet the employment
imperative is career services. Career services is the Las Vegas of the university; with the various brand-name firms that recruit on campus, it looks
glitzy, but the façade conceals cheap construction. Outside of the most elite
schools, the commitment of these firms is tenuous at best. Are they actually
coming to campus? In the unlikely event they are, how many students did
they hire last year?

Students who rely on career services are like Vegas gamblers. They may
win, but the odds are against them, as demonstrated by poor employment
outcomes. According to a recent Gallup poll, only 8 percent of graduating
students found career services "very helpful."

Andy Chan, Wake Forest University's vice president for personal and career development, got some attention a few years ago for declaring "Career Services Must Die." His primary critiques:

1. The very concept of "career services" conveys to students that they aren't expected to think about employment until senior year, and also that it's merely one office of dozens that performs a specific service (when it's the most important question students have when they enroll).[28]
2. The classic career services model is six to twelve overbooked counselors sitting in an office, advising seniors who show up to get help. About half don't bother.[29]

To Chan's two points, I would add four more:

3. With more recruiting and hiring occurring online, fewer employers feel a need to recruit on campus.
4. Most career services counselors are career services lifers rather than professionals with relevant experience and networks in the sectors students are seeking to enter.
5. Many career services offices are located in out-of-the-way locations, often on the periphery of campus, and rarely open in the evenings and on weekends.
6. The challenge of defining underemployment allows career services to hide their heads in the sand via silly employment numbers like "more than four-fifths (82 percent) of the class of 2015 bachelor's degree graduates were employed or in graduate school within six months of graduation."[30] (Sure they were employed, but doing what?)

These challenges are echoed in student responses to a survey of new graduates' experiences with career services by Avenica:

- "I used career services a lot because I was an English major and I didn't know what exactly to do. But they basically just led me to different websites online."
- "Career services didn't bring any employers to my attention. It was more along the lines of 'where best fits you' and then you were on your own from there."

- "I sought out a lot of professors for advice because they shared my same major, and I asked them what they did. And they all said grad school."
- "I did a practice interview with career services, and the lady who was interviewing me didn't want to be there at all."

If colleges and universities understood the employment imperative, they'd pursue a less glitzy, more substantive, and more challenging approach to career services. Imagine integrating career services into the student lifecycle from freshman year. Students could be thinking about career options every year—not only for part-time or summer work but also for course and major selection. Unfortunately, many career services offices have a bureaucratic reflex, resisting efforts to infuse career services across the university. Because if everyone is responsible for career counseling and employer connections, there would be no need for a central function (and no employers paying on-campus recruitment fees to fund career services budgets).

There also needs to be a shift in attitude. Colleges and universities have always taken the labor market as a given. Over the past few years, in response to articles on the skills gap, I've received comments from faculty members and administrators to the effect of "that's a labor market problem, not our problem." What colleges and universities may not realize is that decision makers in the labor market are as fallible as any of us. Most hiring and HR managers aren't particularly adept at understanding what skills are required for a particular job and then reducing that understanding into a job description. Few enterprises are able to envision the hit products and services of tomorrow, and even fewer are able to determine what new skillsets and positions will be required to execute on these opportunities. Hiring decisions are susceptible to change. If you're charging tens of thousands of dollars a year for a postsecondary program, you have an obligation to work hard to help your graduates get jobs.

Unfortunately, colleges and universities have obstinately moved in the opposite direction: they are failing to innovate career services while cutting spending at the same time. Since the Great Recession, colleges and universities have cut spending on career services by 11.4 percent.[31] According to Brandon Busteed of Gallup, students with the most student loan debt—those who need career services most to recoup their investment—are the ones who say career services are least helpful. "Poor career counseling services at a time of high student loan debt . . . [means] you're going to have graduates in a really bad place," said Busteed. All schools "should be investing more in career services," he said. "And apparently the opposite is true."[32]

One area of career services where there has been movement is internships. Virtually all colleges and universities now welcome employers offering internships and encourage students to participate. Most students participate in internships, and while many graduates do land jobs from internships, they're a flawed pathway. First, most internships are unpaid (about a million each year in the United States), which means employers and students are less likely to take them seriously. (If they're paid, many employers don't resort to calling them "internships," they're real jobs!) Second, unpaid internships add to the total cost of the degree; students need support until they land a paid job. Finally, even if unpaid internships lead to employment, it's likely to be lower-paid employment; one estimate has unpaid interns starting work at $37,000 vs. $51,000 for paid interns.[33] Hillary Clinton has argued against unpaid internships and a number of employers have been sued for the practice.

At a speaking engagement a few years ago, I was taken to task for calling career services a "backwater." Upon reflection, I take it back. Career services can't be a backwater because backwaters actually have water. Like Sin City in the Nevada desert, glitzy career services offices with abysmal placement rates neither have nor carry any water.

●   ●   ●

Student frustrations around failure to launch and employment outcomes are now manifesting themselves in three distinct ways.

The first and most prominent is the "free college" movement. Birthed by Senator Bernie Sanders as part of his 2016 presidential bid, and incorporated in part by Hillary Clinton into the Democratic Party platform, free college has quickly become Democratic Party orthodoxy (to the point that leading candidates for the 2020 nomination apparently feel compelled to announce free college programs).[34]

Free college reminds me of a restaurant I frequented as a child. Fran's was the tavern where my dad would take my brother and me to get a banquet burger (my choice, served with Toronto's finest relish tray—delicious in memory, mediocre in reality) and a pancake with a banana smiley face (my brother's selection—always mediocre; he has no excuse). Fran's low prices were outdone only by its indifferent service. Two years ago, Fran's celebrated its seventy-fifth anniversary by offering 1940 prices for one afternoon. My banquet burger would cost a quarter, my brother's smiley pancake twenty cents. What happened? Lines were four hours long. So while lunch might have been (close to) technically free, due to the hassle and inconvenience, it wasn't exactly worthwhile.

With both Fran's and free college, the salient trade-off isn't between debt and free, but between free and good. Free college that requires navigating oversubscribed classes and transfer credits without clearly leading to a good first job may not be worthwhile, particularly since tuition is only a part of the total cost of attendance. According to the College Board, annual living expenses for full-time students are over $8,000—more in high-cost metro-politan areas.[35] Given capacity and transfer issues, few "free college" students will finish in four years, which could translate to $50,000-plus in debt.

As with Fran's, the line between free and good isn't a fine line but a big honking bright line; and that's not the only line I'm worried about. Just as Fran's $0.25 burgers drew a long line, free college will draw a line of tens of thousands who otherwise wouldn't have attempted a degree. Some will complete college and get better jobs, without massive improvements in completion and employability at newly "free" colleges—an announcement that's not nearly as advantageous in Democratic political jockeying—but a much greater number will incur debt without achieving positive outcomes.

The second expression of student frustration is the rise of what I call the "anticredential." Silicon Valley venture capitalist Peter Thiel's fellowship program, launched in 2012, provides $100,000 grants to college students who drop out of college in order to pursue an entrepreneurial project. Thiel Fellows, who, the program director states are "a league of extraordinary, courageous, brilliant individuals who should be a shining light for the rest of society," were profiled in a recent article that recounted how, at the annual retreat, all Fellows received "Everlane backpacks and sweatshirts with DROPOUT written in black letters."[36]

In an era when college dropouts (Zuckerberg, Gates) are our biggest (and wealthiest) heroes, it's not a surprise that students are taking pride in dropping out. But flaunting it is leading to rude behavior, like that of Billy Wilson, a Kansas State University student with a 4.0 GPA, who made his dropout announcement on Facebook accompanied by a photo in which he literally gives the finger to Kansas State.[37]

Most important, but overlooked by many people (with the notable exception of the provosts and college CFOs responsible for balancing budgets), is the fact that higher education enrollment is already declining rapidly. In the 2016–17 academic year, 18 million students were enrolled in American colleges and universities. That's 2.4 million fewer than in the fall of 2011, a 12 percent decline; 58 percent of schools have seen an enrollment decline since 2013.[38] According to a survey by Gallup and *Inside Higher Education* released in September 2017, only 34 percent of American colleges and universities met 2017–18 enrollment targets.[39]

Much of this is a product of fewer high school graduates and a nearly full-employment economy, but at least some is due to students simply steering clear—no wonder, when only 16 percent of students believe a college degree prepares students "very well" for employment.[40] In a survey by the National Association of College and University Business Officers, 68 percent of colleges reported that "price sensitivity was eating away at enrollment."[41] The same survey by Gallup and *Inside Higher Education* found that 71 percent of public institutions and 89 percent of private colleges and universities "believe they are losing applicants due to concerns over debt."[42]

The *New York Times* recently profiled 2017 high school graduates who planned to skip college, reporting 30 percent of high school graduates were now in this category (a recent high).[43] Among the comments to the *Times:*

- "College has gotten so expensive. They leave with so much debt, and walk away with an $11-an-hour job."
- "College isn't something to play around with. You don't go just to go."
- "I didn't want to take the same path everyone was taking."
- "I'm ready to jump out there and start doing my career."

None of this should be surprising. Millennials value transparency above all else. But colleges and universities have not done a good job of being transparent with students. Discounting is not transparent from financial aid packages including "scholarships." Lack of alignment with entry-level jobs is not transparent from today's authoritative programs of study "Blue Books." Student outcomes like debt and employment are not transparent from the first fifteen minutes of the campus walk. All of which leads influential commentators like Matt Taibbi of *Rolling Stone* to level some serious charges:

The education industry as a whole is a con. In fact, since the mortgage business blew up in 2008, education and student debt is probably our reigning unexposed nation-wide scam. It's a multiparty
affair, what shakedown artists call a "big store scheme," like in the
movie *The Sting*: a complex deception requiring a big cast to string
the mark along every step of the way. In higher education, every
party you meet, from the moment you first set foot on campus, is
in on the game.[44]

In a very real sense, over the past decade American colleges and universities could not have done more to turn off their current and future
customers. New surveys demonstrate this in spades. A poll by NBC News
and the *Wall Street Journal* released in September 2017 showed that 47
percent of Americans no longer believe that earning a college degree will
lead to a good job and higher lifetime earnings. Among Millennials, only
39 percent continue to believe in college; 57 percent of Millennials do not.[45]
Skepticism of the college enterprise seems to be increasing monthly; in
December 2017, *Time* magazine reported on a survey by the research firm
Culture Co-op that found "78 percent of Gen Z-ers say getting a four-year
degree no longer makes economic sense."[46]

CHAPTER 2 • KEY POINTS

- The employment imperative—students' overwhelming focus on
  employment and a good first job—is the single-most important
  change in higher education in the past decade.
- Colleges have not been responsive to this change.
- The free college movement, the rise of the "anticredential," and
  enrollment declines have resulted.

CHAPTER 3

Hiring and Jobs

Mom: Why don't you get a job at Burger-Rama?

Lelaina: I was valedictorian of my university.

Mom: Well, you don't have to put that down on your application.

—*Reality Bites (1994)*

Freshman year marked my first experience with the issue of privacy in higher education. It wasn't the typical "roommate hangs sign on door to warn he's in there with a girl." That didn't happen until sophomore year. It involved something much simpler. (On my floor, the simplest things were often most perilous. Like sleeping. One roommate enjoyed hiding under beds for hours, waiting for someone to go to sleep. Then, just as you'd be nodding off, he'd reach up and grab your leg, causing panic and injury.)

In this case, the simple act was attempting to take a shower. I turned on the water, took off my glasses, and hopped in the shower. Without my glasses, I'm fairly blind. So as I was washing my hair, I failed to notice that my roommate Chris had decided to hop in the shower with me. He claimed he was in the stall with me for well over a minute before he decided to get my attention with, "Hey, can you pass the soap?" It was likely that everyone in Welch Hall that evening heard my reaction: "AAAARGH. GET OUT! WHAT ARE YOU DOING?! GET OUT!"

One thing hiring has in common with college is very little privacy. When you apply for a job, you don't know how many people will look at your résumé. It could be five, ten, or more, or it could be zero.

Why zero? Because today more than 85 percent of all job openings (and nearly all positions college graduates might want) are posted online. As a result, the typical job posting generates hundreds of applications; in some cases, more than a thousand—way too many résumés for any hiring manager to wade through.[1] In July 2017, Alan Ripp, owner of a public relations firm, wrote in the *New York Times* about how difficult hiring had become. In the "vast online jobs marketplace . . . restless applicants shoot off their résumés like one of those T-shirt cannons at a football stadium, firing without aiming."[2] For an account director position, Ripp received applications from an auto collections manager, a home health aide, a visual merchandiser, a fiscal benefits analyst, an emergency medical technician, and a brand ambassador. Naturally, "it didn't take long for the résumés to blur."[3]

This is why experts estimate that more than 80 percent of employers have resorted to applicant tracking systems (ATS) to manage their hiring processes.[4] Arising more than a decade ago as a system of compliance or record keeping for employers to demonstrate that no discrimination is occurring in hiring—a fundamental principle of employment law—an ATS keeps track of who is applying to their jobs and manages contacts with candidates as well as interview scheduling. Early systems had rudimentary capabilities around matching keywords in the job description to keywords in the résumé. File types and formats really mattered. For example, a PDF was not a good document to submit because some applicant tracking systems didn't know how to open them up and run keyword searches. Also, some text formats were easier to search than others.

Today, every applicant tracking system can open PDF and other file formats. So that's not an issue. The big issue today is matching keywords in the résumé to keywords in the job description. Because the average employer will only actually look at a small fraction of résumés that seem to be the best fit according to the keyword filter, savvy candidates increase their odds of making it through the filter to a human hiring manager by engaging in "keyword packing" (keywords from the job description) or even "résumé spam" (literally copying the job description into the résumé in white font).

The rest of us are subject to the vagaries of keyword matching, which is notoriously imperfect. Josh Bersin, a leading human resources consultant, once tested a leading ATS by creating a fake résumé for a candidate who met all specified qualifications. The ATS ranked the candidate as a 43 out of 100, primarily due to the way the candidate's graduate degrees were formatted on the résumé.[5]

With online job postings and applicant tracking systems, most candidates never receive a response to a job application other than perhaps an automated "Thank you for submitting your application." A satire by *The Onion*—headlined "'I Would Be Absolutely Perfect for This,' Report 1,400 People Looking at Same Job Posting"—gets to the heart of the matter: convenience actually means horror show for the vast majority of job seekers.[6] This state of affairs is highly relevant for higher education: whereas a college degree used to be more meaningful in the job search process, the vast number of applicants for each open position has significantly reduced the signal-to-noise ratio of the college degree.

● ● ●

Beyond the long odds, the keywords that the rest of us need to match are increasingly technical. Over the past decade, Burning Glass, a research and data firm at the intersection of the labor market and higher education, has determined that technical skills have come to outnumber cognitive and noncognitive skills combined in job descriptions across nearly all industries.[7]

Career Area	Technical Skills Specified	Cognitive and Soft Skills Specified
Information Technology	75%	25%
Health Care	74%	26%
Engineering	71%	29%
Life/Physical Science and Math	68%	32%
Manufacturing and Production	68%	32%
Design, Media, and Writing	66%	34%
Research, Planning, and Analysis	65%	35%
Personal Care and Services	63%	37%

Career Area	Technical Skills Specified	Cognitive and Soft Skills Specified
Finance	62%	38%
Marketing and Public Relations	62%	38%
Management and Operations	61%	39%
Education and Human Services	60%	40%
Hospitality, Food, and Tourism	59%	41%
Sales	59%	41%
Human Resources	57%	43%
Clerical and Administrative	57%	43%
Customer and Client Support	49%	51%

This is undoubtedly a result of two factors unrelated to actual job requirements. First, for any given job, it's easier to come up with ten different technical skill requirements than ten different ways of saying "problem solving," "critical thinking," or "strong communications skills." Second, job descriptions used to be basic. One of the most famous, purportedly posted by explorer Ernest Shackleton for his ill-fated trans-Antarctic expedition, is believed to have read: "MEN WANTED for hazardous journey, small wages, bitter cold, long months of complete darkness, constant danger, safe return doubtful, honor and recognition in case of success."[8] In other words, job descriptions used to describe the job itself rather than desired characteristics of candidates. But in the ensuing century, and particularly in the last decade, the professionalization of the human resources function has resulted in the "best practice" of developing and enhancing position descriptions based on a review of similar positions at competitors. The result is an arms race of job requirements. Faced with a continued deluge of applicants, HR managers are always looking to add necessary skills. Deleting job requirements simply doesn't make sense when what seems to be needed is a finer net.

None of this is of any consequence to the inexorable keyword matching logic of applicant tracking systems, which filter out candidates without a sufficient level of keyword match. This means that candidates with few technical skills are often invisible to human hiring managers.

Of course, the prevalence of technical skills in job descriptions also reflects an underlying reality that nearly all businesses have digitized. Even companies and organizations that have nothing to do with the internet or even e-commerce have replaced paper processes with software and increasingly software-as-a-service (SaaS) products. So there should be no question that employers are experiencing a massive and unprecedented technical skills gap. In a recent survey of US hiring managers, 90 percent reported it difficult to find and hire the right tech talent and 83 percent said the shortage of tech talent is slowing company revenue growth.[9] A survey of 42,000 global employers by Manpower, a staffing firm, revealed 40 percent reported talent shortages.[10]

It's incorrect to generalize about a tech skills gap. For example, we don't have a shortage of C++ or Fortran coders. The tech skills gap actually consists of thousands of microlevel or tactical technical skills gaps. These gaps are particularly obvious for entry-level positions outside the tech sector. I'm talking about jobs across all industries that use SaaS platforms to manage functions like supply chain, sales, marketing, customer service, finance, IT, and HR. So candidates who don't have keywords like Pardot (marketing), Marketo (digital marketing), Google Adwords (digital marketing), ZenDesk Plus (customer service), NetSuite (finance), Financial Force (finance), Workday (HR), and Salesforce on their résumés are unlikely to be considered. According to Burning Glass, jobs demanding Salesforce experience have quadrupled in the past five years; in 2017, more than 300,000 open positions called for Salesforce skills.[11] In addition to these cross-sector SaaS platforms, every industry has its own SaaS platforms for specific functions. For example, insurance companies and third-party claims administrators have a range of SaaS options for claims processing. All these platforms are increasingly likely to be included in job descriptions (as HR managers scramble to beef up job descriptions in the face of the résumé deluge), so candidates who don't name these platforms on their résumés are less visible to hiring managers.

● ● ●

Beyond simply knowing how to use software—which could be a "middle skills" job (78 percent of which require digital skills), what's increasingly in demand are coding skills.[12] In a recent paper, Robert Cohen, a senior fellow at the Economic Strategy Institute, found that job postings requiring less than two years' experience (i.e., entry-level jobs) require a "noticeably high level of proficiency with software programming and development skills."[13] According to Burning Glass, a stunning 49 percent of open jobs with a starting salary over $70,000 require coding skills.[14] In 2017, there were 33,000 *sales* jobs posted that demanded coding skills.[15]

Matt Sigelman, founder and CEO of Burning Glass, points to job descriptions for desktop publishers to demonstrate the additional earning power of coding. Desktop publishing positions that don't specify HTML5 skills have an average salary of $54,000. Desktop publishing positions with HTML5 average $75,000.[16] *USA Today* recently ran a feature on "America's best jobs" and wrote: "The nation's best jobs boast salaries that average $100,000 and up, offer generous company benefits, and promise to have recruiting suitors fighting for your hand. But they are highly technical roles carrying job descriptions like DevOps engineer and analytics manager that demand an alphabet soup of computer skills."[17] Four of *USA Today*'s top five jobs were "highly technical." The only exception was "Tax Manager," a profession few young people aspire to.

LinkedIn has found that "while the ability to lead, collaborate and communicate are still critical to landing a job, it's having experience in the latest technical skills that will get hiring managers at the top companies clamoring for your attention."[18] In a 2016 report, HR leaders from top companies in technology, finance, management consulting, and media told LinkedIn they "all want the same thing: people with experience in machine learning, cybersecurity, data analytics and cloud technology. And the most in-demand roles: engineers and data scientists with these skills."[19] According to LinkedIn, eight of the fifteen highest-paid entry-level jobs are in technology:[20]

1. Data scientist ($93,000)
2. Hardware engineer ($90,000)
3. Software engineer ($80,000)
4. Technology analyst ($76,000)
5. Operations engineer ($75,000)
6. Security engineer ($74,000)
7. Process development engineer ($73,000)
8. UX design ($72,000)

Meanwhile, CompTIA, an IT industry association, reports[21] that the largest technology skill gaps are in:

1. Emerging technologies like the internet of things, artificial intelligence, and automation
2. Integration of apps, data, and platforms
3. Cloud infrastructure and apps
4. Digital business transformation
5. Cybersecurity
6. Software or app development
7. Data management and data analytics

I could go on, but you get the idea. If you have digital skills, you have a reasonable chance in the entry-level hiring game. Otherwise you'll have better odds in Vegas.

• • •

As I noted in the last chapter, colleges haven't been good at adapting to these changes in the job market. For reasons of academic organization, faculty control, and the rigid nature of credentials and credit hours themselves, I don't believe there are any accredited higher education institutions that have relevant programs in *all* of the aforementioned areas. At the vast majority of colleges and universities, across the vast majority of departments, lower-level course curriculum is rigid and rarely changing. Most departments offer the same lower-level courses they offered twenty or thirty years ago. Meanwhile most upper-level courses are dictated by faculty research priorities, which operate independently of labor market needs.

Even for programs that appear highly relevant—BSc in computer science, for example—the curriculum is much less applied than employers want. Very few schools incorporate real-world projects or hackathons into their programs. While all schools teach Java, few computer science programs actually expose students to how coding projects work in practice (e.g., using struts: existing code that developers call upon for common functions). According to the Center for American Progress:

Undergraduate computer science core curricula . . . remain firmly entrenched in technical and mathematical fundamentals. For example, most of the courses needed for a bachelor's degree in computer science at Carnegie Mellon . . . fall under computer science fundamentals; mathematics and probability; and engineering and life sciences. The program offers electives in applications . . . and software systems . . . yet there is no requirement that students take those particular courses.[22]

South Korea, the country with the highest level of postsecondary education attainment among Millennials, represents the logical extreme of this lack of alignment. In 2017, the *Wall Street Journal* reported that about 500,000 South Koreans between the ages of fifteen and twenty-nine were unwillingly unemployed, the highest rate of youth unemployment in decades. In order to avoid a "national disaster" of youth unemployment, the government is seeking to create 810,000 new public sector jobs over the next five years, at a cost of $18 billion. So as a result of public spending to produce university graduates with skills that are inconsistent with employer needs, South Korea is contemplating significant additional public spending to create public sector jobs for these graduates.[23]

Many students have an intuitive sense of this inherent disconnect and are trying to hedge their bets by double majoring. According to the US Department of Education, the percentage of students who double majored jumped 96 percent between 2000 and 2008. A 2012 Vanderbilt University study on double majors found that double majoring was up significantly at almost all colleges and universities, with some schools reporting that as many as 40 percent of students are pursuing more than one major.[24] To be clear, students have done this on their own, without pushing or prodding from faculty members, advisors, or career services counselors.

● ● ●

Most experts agree that a combination of technical skills and soft skills is the sweet spot in the labor market. Burning Glass shows fastest growth for these "hybrid" jobs, and a recent poll by the Pew Research Center showed that 85 percent of employers said this combination was "critical to succeed in the workforce."[25]

Employers have become increasingly vocal about the soft skills of new college graduates. By soft, or noncognitive, skills, I'm referring to fundamental capabilities such as teamwork, communication, organization, creativity, adaptability, and punctuality. In a LinkedIn study of hiring managers, 59 percent said soft skills were difficult to find and this skill gap was limiting their productivity.[26] A 2015 *Wall Street Journal* survey of nine hundred executives found that 89 percent have a very or somewhat difficult time finding people with the requisite soft skills.[27] According to LinkedIn economist Guy Berger, "There are more employers that claim that soft skills are hard to find than hard skills. It's a pretty pervasive problem."[28]

But I don't believe Millennials are significantly delayed in their development of soft skills relative to prior generations. What I think is happening is that employers' own hiring practices are causing them to look for soft skills in the wrong places.

One of my favorite metaphors is the guy who stumbles out of the bar late at night and can't find his car keys. Although the keys are probably somewhere back in the bar, he doesn't look back there. Nor does he look around his car—too dark in both those places. Instead, he looks under the street light. Now it's probably a good thing this guy never finds his keys; he shouldn't be driving. But the main point is that he's looking where it's easy to look, not where he should be looking.

The Millennials who are visible to hiring managers are the ones with technical skills, and it is they who consistently get past the applicant tracking system filters. And guess what? For many of these technically prepared Millennials, soft skills aren't their strong suit.

Does this mean there's a soft skills shortage or that Millennials are all late, disorganized, and poor communicators? Quite the contrary; the punctual, organized, and well-spoken Millennials whom employers should want have played by the rules and completed college degrees. But because nearly all colleges and universities continue to float high above the mundane concerns of the labor market, and because they continue to believe that the job of higher education is to prepare students for their fifth job, not their first job, Millennials with strong soft skills are missing key (or at least keyword) technical skills. As a result, it may be that the soft skills crisis is overblown. By triaging the skills gap and addressing the primary issue of technical skills, employers will be happier in the soft skills department.

● ● ●

You probably get the sense, though, that employers aren't happy. The truth may be that they're even unhappier than students. They're not seeing new college grads with the skills they need, and they're flailing about, reacting in different ways. According to research from the Rockefeller Foundation, nearly half of all employers say it's hard to source entry-level candidates.[29] A more recent survey by the Society for Human Resource Management shows only one-fifth of HR professionals are fully confident in their organization's ability to effectively assess the skills of entry-level job applicants.[30]

The first reaction is to refrain from hiring. There are 6 million unfilled jobs in the United States today (many of which require high skills and have high salaries), and perhaps as many articles featuring employers complaining about the skills gap. In the first quarter of 2017, 45 percent of small businesses said they couldn't find qualified applicants to fill job openings.[31] As Peter Capelli of Wharton notes, American employers have developed a global reputation for wanting the perfectly qualified candidate delivered on a silver spoon—or they simply won't hire. According to Capelli, "Employers are demanding more of job candidates than ever before. They want prospective workers to be able to fill a role right away, without any training or ramp-up time. To get a job, you have to have that job already."[32] Capelli calls this the "Home Depot view of the hiring process," where filling a job vacancy is "akin to replacing a part in a washing machine." The store either has the part, or it doesn't. And if it doesn't, the employer waits.

A second reaction is degree inflation. If we're not getting what we want from candidates with bachelor's degrees, let's ask for master's degrees. CareerBuilder recently found rampant degree inflation across the economy. Nearly 40 percent of employers report raising degree requirements in job descriptions; 33 percent of employers report hiring more candidates with master's degrees for positions held primarily by those with college degrees; 41 percent of employers report the same phenomenon at the intersection of high school and college: hiring more candidates with degrees for positions held primarily by those with high school diplomas.[33]

Burning Glass calculates what it calls the "credential gap"—the gap between the degree requirements of postings and the levels of educational attainment of people currently employed in those positions—for a range of occupations. The gap is a whopping 57 percent for production supervisors; 52 percent for transportation, storage, and distribution managers; 28 percent for retail supervisors; 25 percent for executive assistants and insurance claims clerks; 13 percent for sales reps; and so on.[34] As Burning Glass facetiously asked in a report on credential inflation, "Half of Supervisors

Now Need a College Degree: Are You Getting Better Service?"[35] A wide range of professions that used not to have degree requirements now ask for college: dental hygienists, police, cargo agents, claims adjusters, health information technicians, IT help desk technicians, fashion designers, and desktop publishers.

Is there some basis for this? Perhaps jobs have become more demanding? Burning Glass investigated and found virtually no difference in skill requirements between some of the above jobs that asked for a college degree, and the jobs that did not specify a degree. This suggests that employers are up-credentialing in a somewhat helter-skelter manner.[36] Richard Vedder, Director of the Center for College Affordability and Productivity at Ohio University, poses a scary question: "In the mid-1970s, far less than 1 percent of taxi drivers were college graduates; by 2010 more than 15 percent were. Is it possible that by 2030 a master's degree in janitorial science could be a prerequisite for a job sweeping floors?"[37]

A third reaction is experience inflation. Instead of asking for more credentials, employers are asking for more experience. In a working paper titled "Unpacking Human Capital: Exploring the Role of Experience and Education in Shaping Access to Jobs,"[38] University of Pennsylvania economics professor Matthew Bidwell evaluated a Burning Glass dataset of 3 million jobs to characterize the "demand" side of the talent marketplace (for which colleges and universities are a major "supplier") and segmented it into a 2 × 2 matrix like the following:

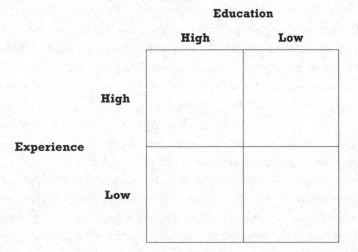

One of Bidwell's key findings was that nearly all jobs with high education requirements (i.e., college and above) also had significant experience requirements (i.e., two or more years of relevant work experience). On average, he found jobs requiring bachelor's degrees asked for four to five years of experience, with some asking for as much as eleven years. In another example of the arms race of job requirements resulting from the professionalization of the human resources function, job requirements that used to be "degree or experience" have become "degree and experience." As a result, one quadrant of this matrix—the high-education-low-experience quadrant nearly all new college graduates fall into—is virtually empty.[39]

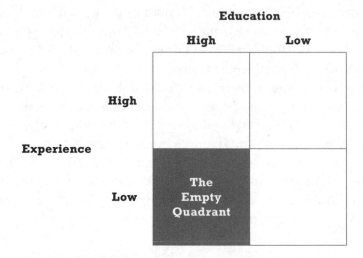

The empty quadrant explains many of the difficulties presented in the last chapter. Whereas a decade ago, many employers were perfectly happy to hire new college graduates into entry-level sales positions, sales today means knowledge of the Salesforce platform. Because few, if any, new college graduates have Salesforce experience (particularly because they're not engaged with paid work before graduating), employers have taken to asking for a year or more of experience with Salesforce.

The fourth and final reaction is to go in the other direction: jettison degree requirements altogether. In the past few years, several employers have either removed degree requirements from entry-level positions or begun proactively masking from hiring managers whether or not candidates have degrees because the companies have ascertained that degree-based hiring tends to result in false positives and false negatives—hiring the wrong candidate or not hiring the right candidate.

In 2015, Ernst & Young (EY) in the UK, which ranks among the largest university recruiters across the pond, removed degree classification from its hiring criteria citing a lack of evidence that university success correlated with job performance. Instead, EY applicants are now offered a battery of assessments to ascertain whether candidates are a good match, regardless of whether they have degrees.[40] In 2017, the *Times of London* reported that EY increased the diversity of its new hires by 10 percent.[41] Penguin Random House is doing the same.[42] Nestlé has done so as well and found that more than 20 percent of new hires would have been immediately screened out under their prior hiring model.

Google is the company most invested in disrupting the degree qualification. In 2008, Google examined what factors best predicted employee performance. Surprisingly, it wasn't attending an elite school or even attending college at all. A significant number of successful executives did not have degrees. So Google began using algorithms to suggest interview questions based on candidate competencies. Google's former Head of People Operations Laszlo Bock went on record saying that grades in degree programs are "worthless as a criteria [sic] for hiring."[43] He added that "many schools . . . generate a ton of debt in return for not learning what's most useful" and "people who don't go to school and make their way in the world . . . are exceptional human beings. And we should do everything we can to find those people."[44] Today, up to 14 percent of employees on some Google teams never attended college.[45]

IBM is also moving in this direction. Sam Ladah, IBM's Head of Talent Organization, is looking "toward different applicant pools to find new talent." IBM wants to hire based on skills, without taking "into account their education background. This includes applicants who didn't get a four-year degree but have proven their technical knowledge in other ways." Already, 15 percent of IBM's new hires don't have college degrees.[46] In a handful of IBM locations, nearly a third of new hires don't have degrees.[47]

What's perhaps most remarkable is that Google and IBM are among America's most prominent and attractive employers. If they can't attract the talent they need via the current degree-based system, what hope do less prominent S&P 500 companies like Air Products or Hormel have, let alone the small and midsized enterprises that employ the other 85 percent of American workers? When our highest-profile employers begin sounding off, it's a fair bet that unhappiness among unsung employers is even higher.

Employers are most certainly not happy. Very few go as far as Craig Brandon, author of *The Five-Year Party,* who claims colleges "have flooded the job market with tens of thousands of semi-literate, unemployable graduates," thereby diminishing the value of the credential.[48] But it is true that only 11 percent of employers believe new college graduates have the skills their businesses need.[49]

This explains why a wide range of employers are following in Google and IBM's wake, using microcredentials from providers like Credly, or e-portfolios from Portfolium, to assess candidates' competencies in a more fine-grained manner. In a survey of four hundred employers by Hart Research Associates, 80 percent said it would be very or fairly useful to see an electronic portfolio of candidates' work product demonstrating cognitive, noncognitive, and technical skills.[50]

The employers of America are beginning to realize that, more than anything else, a college degree means that at the age of eighteen, the candidate was organized enough to apply to college and had the time and resources (i.e., family support) to dedicate four or more years to the task. It's certainly more due to those issues than an accurate indicator for whether the candidate can do a given job (let alone whether he or she will stay in that job).

Employers' unhappiness with the current pedigree- and degree-based hiring also explains this remarkable result from a 2013 survey: when asked whether they would consider hiring a candidate without a degree over someone with a degree, 71 percent of employers said they would.[51] Perhaps some employers have begun asking themselves what it says about candidates' judgment that they would attend this kind of college and pile up this level of debt. And that was five years ago. Since then, skepticism among employers has increased to a significant degree.

CHAPTER 3 • KEY POINTS

- Deteriorating employment outcomes for college graduates are primarily a result of changes in the hiring process.
- Employers have been adding technical skills to job descriptions—skills college graduates don't typically have.

- Employers are not seeing the talent they (think they) need, so they are resorting to degree inflation, experience inflation, and leaving positions unfilled.
- A number of leading employers are demonstrating a surprising level of open-mindedness as to whether entry-level candidates actually need degrees.

PART II

Faster +
Cheaper

The Last Mile

College is a four-year delusion so you don't have to deal with reality.

—*St. Elmo's Fire (1985)*

I n college, my roommates and I inherited a GE fridge that was thirty years old and built like a Sherman tank. It seemed like it weighed as much as one—so says my muscle memory from room-to-storage-to-room moves each year. It was so cumbersome that when it came time to finally dispose of it, my roommate Alex, who drew the short straw, hauled the fridge to the middle of Old Campus and then left it there in a fit of pique. It took Physical Plant a week to remove it.

But the fridge was most famous as an all-season font of winter fun. Junior year we occupied a suite on the top floor of Vanderbilt Hall with a skylight that opened onto Chapel Street. My roommate Chris, a formidable pitcher on his high school baseball team, would open the skylight and dream of launching projectiles onto unsuspecting passersby. His dream became reality when he realized our tank of a fridge produced sufficient frost for him to pack snowballs. Now Chris had incredible aim. He never hit anyone, but his snowballs exploded with force a safe distance away. The shocked and puzzled looks on the faces of New Haven citizenry meeting snowballs on hellish summer days provided hours of amusement. We sang our own version of "Peace Frog" by The Doors: "Snow on the streets in the town of New Haven . . ."

Except there was never enough frost. The fridge only produced one snowball per hour and we all wanted more. So Chris called the number on the back of the fridge—still a working number thirty years on—and asked a question that GE refrigerator technical support had never heard before: How do I get more frost in my freezer? The surprised representative nevertheless gave Chris the answer and snowball production increased threefold—a testament to the importance of technical training. (Though I'd be remiss in failing to note that while this increase in frost was good for his pitching arm, it was bad for both Chapel Street pedestrians and yours truly. Frost quickly overtook the entire freezer, causing Chris to remove a box of ice cream to the nearest flat surface—which happened to be my stereo speaker. The next morning, the ice cream had melted down the front of the speaker. Adding insult to injury, Alex, then immersed in Introductory Japanese, happened to be sitting next to the scene of the crime that morning and, rather than cleaning the mess, absentmindedly carved kanji characters into the dried ice cream.)

Two summers after astonishing Chapel Street pedestrians with our snowball extravaganza, I got a job as a management consultant—a new college grad in an ill-fitting suit naively but energetically attempting to convince experienced and jaded managers to do their jobs differently. One question that kept coming up for clients was who was likely to win the war to bring broadband access to homes: telephone companies or cable companies. While we know the answer now (cable), I spent a lot of time studying the technical specifications of cable and telephony "last-mile" connectivity.

The concept of the last mile—the final leg of the connection to each home—originated in telecom but is now a primary focus for supply chain management and e-commerce in particular. The general principle applicable to many contexts is that the last mile is the most difficult and expensive to build but equally the most valuable: dominating the last mile can provide a nearly unassailable competitive position. In telecom and other utilities, the cost of building the last mile is what results in natural monopolies, thereby requiring regulation.

The last mile in higher education is technical training and placement. At a minimum, the technical training must ensure candidates are no longer filtered out by applicant tracking systems; ideally, the technical training will prepare candidates on the exact software/SaaS platforms used by employers so candidates are floor-ready on day one (i.e., meeting the Home Depot test). In terms of placement, the last mile involves building reputations and relationships with employers so that providers are able to promise candidates, implicitly or explicitly, a good first job.

Employers aren't filling this last-mile education gap themselves and neither are colleges and universities. But over the past five years, we've seen the emergence of a powerful new set of intermediaries: last-mile programs. The focus of last-mile programs is on exactly the technical skills employers need (as listed in job descriptions) but that colleges and universities don't teach. Equally important, they're also developing cognitive and noncognitive skills like problem solving and teamwork. Coding bootcamps are the most obvious example, but last-mile programs are emerging in almost every sector.

• • •

One problem our industry has is there's really no school for it. Not only is there no degree in DevOps, if someone did have a degree from four years ago and hasn't been doing it all, their knowledge would be out of touch.

—*Leslie Carr, Infrastructure Engineering Manager at Clover Health*[1]

Last-mile programs offer value propositions that are quite different from traditional colleges. Viewing higher education through a 2 × 2 matrix, where the X-axis shows cost to the student (paid or free) and the Y-axis shows outcomes (no guarantee or some guaranteed outcome), traditional colleges and universities fit in the bottom-left quadrant. Higher education's model has always been, "You pays your money and you takes your chances."

This creates a major opportunity for last-mile providers that offer a more attractive risk–reward profile to students.

Last-mile programs are easy to categorize. There are bootcamp models where students pay tuition upfront and receive an explicit or implicit guarantee of employment. Most student-pay bootcamps show placement rates north of 80 percent into relevant, well-paid jobs. Then there are income share programs where students don't pay anything upfront but where the last-mile program is so confident of a positive employment outcome that it takes payment as a percentage of graduates' income for several years— typically only once students have exceeded a stated income floor. There are

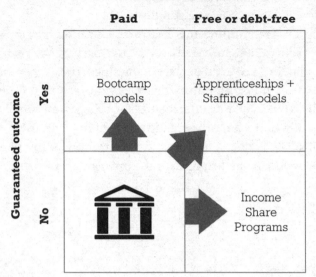

also apprenticeships as well as staffing and placement models, where last-mile providers can guarantee employment outcomes because students are already employees (i.e., apprentices) or because the last-mile programs hire graduates themselves (then staff them out to clients). Both apprenticeship and staffing models typically allow providers to offer the last mile for free, further enhancing the value proposition for students.

• • •

While it's hard to generalize across all last-mile programs, it's fair to say they share the following six characteristics.

1. Technical Skills +

While last-mile programs are laser-focused on the technical skills employers don't typically see in new college graduates, employers also desperately want proven problem solvers who have demonstrated success working in teams. Neil Blumenthal, cofounder of Warby Parker, the leading online provider of designer eyewear, says that "the most important thing is that somebody can come into Warby Parker and get work done. And we find that the biggest predictor of that [is] people that are proactive that have solved problems and worked in teams in the past."[2] Just as traditional colleges aren't focused on technical skills, they're also not nearly as focused as last-mile programs on problem solving and teamwork in a worklike setting.

General Assembly (GA), the largest coding bootcamp, believes its programs develop more than coding capabilities. According to GA:

> Our students learn to solve problems, manage time effectively, and set clear priorities through projects that mimic real-life job scenarios and tasks. They are asked to present and articulate their strategies—both key communication tools for professional success. Our courses foster the motivation and skill that people need for growth in their careers.[3]

So in providing technical skill training, last-mile programs claim to educate more broadly.

2. Intensity

There's a reason many last-mile programs are happy to be called "bootcamps." Like their military progenitors, last-mile programs are intense. Most are taught by practitioners in simulated (or actual) work environments. Students are assigned projects with real deadlines and often work 12-hour days or more. Every bootcamp student I've talked to says the experience was much more intense than college or high school—even more than cramming for final exams. And because students often work in teams, the intensity typically establishes a camaraderie that is rare in traditional college coursework.

David Anderton, who attended a one-week MIT bootcamp called Entrepreneurship 101, says he learned a lot about himself: "With the combination of stress, deadlines, personality conflicts, and lack of sleep, you learn about your limits and weaknesses. Working in teams takes communication, respect, problem solving, and the ability to deal with the unexpected. If you're actually trying to start up a business, these are relevant coping skills."

3. Demonstrate Competencies

The output at most last-mile programs isn't a grade or transcript that employers can't understand. Instead, students complete last-mile programs with a portfolio of work product so employers can actually see their skills. For example, coding bootcamps often have students log their code in GitHub, the primary code repository of the tech sector. Relative to time and effort, last-mile programs do a better job of providing students with something to show the ultimate arbiters of success: employers.

4. Strong Connections to Employers

Last-mile programs engage more with employers than do traditional colleges and universities. They consult employers in the development and continuous revision of curriculum. Most draw upon employers for projects that students work on. Some are physically located with employers—usually in coworking spaces—which enhances engagement in numerous ways. All last-mile providers actively prepare every student for job interviews.

Most critically, all have a refreshingly strong incentive to make sure every graduate gets a good first job: bootcamps cite placement rates and average starting salaries to attract students. Last-mile programs with income share agreements and staffing models are financially invested in the success of graduates. Every last-mile program's business depends on having its fingers on the pulse of the skills employers need right now and then meeting that demand. And some, such as apprenticeships and staffing companies, are employers themselves.

5. Clear Pathways

Many of the college grads who fall into the "education-to-employment" gap are so-called organization kids: they've succeeded at following every defined path and checking every box presented to them through high school—both curricular and extracurricular. They've joined organizations and their college applications present the breadth and depth that top colleges are seeking. Then they graduate into a chaotic labor market and experience poor employment outcomes.

What organization kids need are clear pathways to good first jobs in high-value, high-growth sectors of the economy. These are exactly the pathways opened by last-mile providers. To be sure, these pathways aren't the first or only available pathways to good first jobs. When I graduated in 1994, I followed the pathway offered by management consulting firm McKinsey & Co. McKinsey consultants visited campus and spun stories of how a two-year gig as a business analyst was like being paid to go to business school and of the unlimited career options that would follow. Similar stories ensnare tens of thousands of our most talented grads in consulting and investment banking. And don't get me started on law school, which, if you're lucky, can lead to careers that are either remunerative or enjoyable but rarely both.

But Millennials and Gen Z know that consulting, finance, and law are not the growth sectors they once were. Where are the pathways to good first jobs in growing sectors like technology, biotech, fin tech, and health care? Last-mile programs are charting clear pathways to jobs in the industries of tomorrow.

6. The Credential Is the Job

Unlike colleges and universities, last-mile programs aren't hung up on credentials. Ask most founders of last-mile programs what credential graduates receive, and they're blunt: "The credential is the job. That's the credential students want."

While credentials continue to matter, most students care about a good first job more than a credential. Last-mile programs are betting that once students get a good first job, their second, third, and fourth employers are going to care a lot more about that first job (and demonstrated work product and references from that job) than a credential. They are betting that we have passed "Peak Credential."

•   •   •

We are on the cusp of a faster + cheaper revolution in higher education, and it will be a sea change. The norm has been for the most motivated and talented students to earn bachelor's degrees before launching their careers. In contrast, shorter paths through higher education (i.e., sub-baccalaureate credentials) have always been associated with less talented and motivated students.

The change has already happened in other fields. Take basketball, for example. In the 2017 NBA draft, nine of the top ten picks were freshmen who decided they were done with college after one year ("one-and-done"). Despite the social importance and status of college and despite their free ride, college fell by the wayside as a result of the significant financial pressure of expected future earnings from professional basketball.

While the financial pressure faced by good students staring down tens of thousands of dollars in additional student loan debt is far less welcome than the (positive) pressure encountered by basketball stars, it is of the same behavior-changing genus.

We're on the cusp of disruption, but you wouldn't know it from reading the *New York Times* or listening to the chattering class. To the extent thought leaders focus on postsecondary education, the topic seems to be how to provide free college. It's a sign of how isomorphic and degree-centric our thinking has become that we're talking about "free college" as opposed to "free credentials" or better, "free pathways to good jobs." Of course, the people doing the thinking and talking aren't neutral observers; most attended elite colleges and believe becoming "educated" requires a comparable experience.

Still, there's a burgeoning sense that there should be faster + cheaper options. For the elite, that still translates to career and technical education options leading to blue-collar, middle-skill jobs where there are clear shortages of workers: electricians, welders, and a parade of jobs in the industrial and building trades lead the list. Some examples are quite sensational, as evidenced by last summer's headline in *Bloomberg*: "Want a $1 Million Paycheck? Skip College and Go Work in a Lumberyard."[4] Unfortunately, few upper-middle-income parents want blue-collar jobs for their children. Aren't those the professions their parents and their parents' parents worked so hard to escape from? Moreover, the pathways to these jobs are an associate's degree and certificate programs at community colleges, which are equally uninspiring to most families expecting their children to pursue higher education.

But even if the media and political classes are unaware of it, universities understand the importance of new collar jobs. They know many good digital-centric entry-level jobs in growing sectors are going unfilled, or, via experience inflation, have been recast as jobs requiring a few years of work experience. They know that the 18 million students enrolled in colleges and universities is a figure that's gone down by 2.4 million between 2012 and 2018, and they know that last-mile providers will increasingly compete for their students. This explains why, in a recent survey by the National

Association of College and University Business Officers, 57 percent of colleges and universities are already blaming "the likes of software coding bootcamps" for their enrollment declines.[5]

CHAPTER 4 • KEY POINTS

- The growing gap between college and employer needs is being filled by last-mile programs.

- The risk-return profiles of last-mile programs compare favorably to those of traditional colleges

- Last-mile programs aren't hung up on credentials; the credential is the job!

- Faster + cheaper alternatives aren't pathways to vocational or blue-collar jobs, but rather to digital new collar careers.

CHAPTER 5

Welcome to Bootcamp

You dropped a hundred and fifty grand on an education you coulda' picked up for a dollar fifty in late charges at the public library.

—Good Will Hunting (1997)

P robably the least secret "secret society" at Yale is the Pundits. Founded in 1884, the Pundits are Yale's senior pranksters. When students run naked through the library, dollars-to-donuts it's the Pundits. My brother Aaron was tapped as a Pundit and I'm grateful I'd already graduated and lived eighty miles away when I began hearing stories of his nude cavorting.

On occasion the Pundits put more thought into their pranks. Like the time they called students shopping Jonathan Spence's perpetually oversubscribed course on the history of modern China to say they could improve their chances of getting into the class if they brought woks or kung fu movies to the first discussion section. Or the time they sent notes to ten students named Sarah that read: "Dear Sarah, I am a secret admirer. Meet me at the Atticus Bookstore children's section this Thursday at 7 PM. Love, Dan." Then they sent the same note (in reverse) to ten students named Dan. Ten

Dans and Sarahs showed up that Thursday. It didn't take long for the Dans and Sarahs to figure out they'd been pranked.

One stunt that took longer than you'd think for the victims to figure out occurred two years after my brother had graduated. Aaron and I were back at Yale for law school and the target of an urgent Pundits request: Did we know any law students who were older and who could do a passable German accent? As a matter of fact, we did. Chuck Lane, then a writer at the *New Republic* (now a columnist at the *Washington Post*), was attending law school as a Knight Fellow, a scholarship for working journalists seeking training in the law. He was a few years older, had been Berlin bureau chief at *Newsweek*, had a German wife, and was cantankerous enough to invest significant time in an elaborate joke on undergraduates.

The thrust of the prank was to waste the time of those whom the Pundits viewed as deserving of having their time wasted: students interested in investment banking. The Pundits littered the campus with posters inviting students to come to an informational session for "Banque Hautinger," a private Franco-German investment bank with an exclusive clientele. About sixty students arrived and found a German banker (Chuck) prancing around the auditorium stage:

> CHUCK: Training at Banque Hautinger is very rigorous. It's like—what is word—shoe camp?
>
> AUDIENCE: A bootcamp?
>
> CHUCK: *Ja*, bootcamp.

He then proceeded to construct an elaborate analogy comparing investment banking to war. Sometimes your colleague dies. But you need to keep attacking. It went downhill from there. Chuck began to point to students asking if they had brought résumés as the posters had requested. To a student whose résumé said he spoke Japanese and majored in economics, Chuck barked, "Say something smart in Japanese about economics."

The amazing thing was that no one left. Everyone wanted to believe the simplest explanation: that this was a real (if eccentric) investment bank with real jobs. At the end, Chuck invited students to have a drink with him and other Banque Hautinger professionals at Mory's, the Yale club. The fooled students who showed up found the Pundits in a private room, completely naked. With the Pundits, somehow it always ended with disrobing.

• • •

While bootcamps have their roots in the military—preparing brave young people to fight real wars, not fake investment banking wars—the term has become synonymous with intensive training of any kind. That group of new moms in the park? They're doing a fitness bootcamp. And the last-mile programs that most people have heard of are coding bootcamps.

Coding bootcamps can be as short as four weeks, while a handful last two years. In the tech sector it's generally recognized that coding programs shorter than twelve weeks or three months aren't likely to provide the level of last-mile training that employers want, so I'll focus on programs of this length or longer. The average program lasts fourteen weeks.

Coding bootcamps began life as top-up programs for students who'd already graduated from college. This is particularly true for bootcamps where students pay tuition upfront: most similar to the traditional college model and most accessible to well-off students (the vast majority of whom currently attend college). Galvanize opened its first program in Denver in a coworking space that was attracting tech companies and local college graduates who were "unemployed, which is the worst; underemployed, which is the most likely; or the third category, unhappily employed," as founder Jim Deters was fond of saying.[1] General Assembly's Jake Schwartz says he got the idea because he and his friends from Yale needed an on-ramp to entrepreneurial and tech careers.[2]

How prevalent are coding bootcamps? According to *Course Report*, although the first ones only appeared in 2012, there are now ninety-five coding schools offering programs at three hundred sites in seventy-four cities across forty states. New York has the most programs, followed by San Francisco and Seattle. But Washington, DC, and Atlanta have eight coding bootcamps each. In 2017, coding bootcamps graduated approximately 23,000 students. This is just under one-third of the total of students studying computer science at American colleges and universities.[3] General Assembly itself boasts twenty campuses and more than 35,000 alumni.[4]

Most coding bootcamps are achieving strong placement outcomes for students. For 2016, Galvanize reports 84 percent placement within six months with an average starting salary of $70,000.[5] In the fall of 2016, General Assembly issued an outcomes report audited by accounting firm KPMG. The report showed a 92 percent graduation rate and that 88 percent of graduates were placed in a full-time job within six months. Across the sector, *Course Report* calculates a placement rate of 73 percent with median starting salary of $65,000.[6] The Council on Integrity Results Reporting (CIRR), a new coding bootcamp industry group, found roughly the same result: a 92 percent graduation rate, 80 percent placement rate, and starting salary of $70,000.[7] All programs report graduates are seeing a huge salary jump from prior jobs. Fullstack Academy claims a 65 percent increase.[8]

Employer enthusiasm supports these statistics. A survey by the job board Indeed said 80 percent of American tech hiring managers have hired a coding bootcamp graduate and 99.8 percent say they plan to hire more. Seventy-two percent of respondents believe bootcamp graduates are just as prepared as graduates of computer science programs and 12 percent think they're more prepared.[9] Many of these employers are not Silicon Valley brand names but employers that are digitizing with increasing speed and having trouble finding the requisite level of technical skills. Paycor, a Cincinnati maker of human resources software, has hired many coding bootcamp graduates. According to Jon Toelke, Paycor's senior manager of talent acquisition, "some of the [coding bootcamp] folks I hired two or three years ago are now the managers who are hiring individuals. We've had tremendous success."[10]

Employers also believe bootcamps are a good way to diversify the tech workforce. Seventeen percent of hiring managers say, all other things being equal, they'd hire a coding bootcamp graduate over a university graduate. Sixty percent say coding bootcamp graduates were likely to stay longer; 48 percent say they're easier to hire; and 32 percent say they'll accept a lower salary, probably because they're less likely to have tens of thousands of dollars in student loan debt.[11]

● ● ●

Learning to code is like learning a language. Coding bootcamps train students in various languages. Fullstack JavaScript is the most common, followed by Ruby on Rails, .NET, Python, and PHP. But there's significant fluctuation as new coding demands from employers are quickly reflected in bootcamp curricula. Upcoming languages include Pega, Salesforce, and Spark.

Those names might seem fun to some and daunting to others, but what's the student experience really like? The first challenge might be finding a coding bootcamp. Walk into any of Galvanize's eight campuses across the

United States and one question comes to mind: where's the school? You first see a reception area and a café. When you begin to walk around, it looks like a tech company: open work spaces, team rooms, and "phone booths" (small rooms for making calls). But then you see different company logos on team room windows and you realize it's not just one tech company: it's many. Galvanize is first and foremost a coworking space housing hundreds of tech businesses, from start-ups to teams from large employers like IBM, Google, and Pivotal Labs.

Keep walking and you'll see the classrooms: large open spaces with desks on wheels and screens at the front for anyone to project their work. Only don't call it a bootcamp. Galvanize prefers the term *immersive*. There's the popular web development immersive: a six-month program that aims to take students who've never coded before and produce full-stack developers. There's also the twelve-week data science immersive, which takes students with some background in Python, SQL, statistics, and Bayesian logic, and graduates data scientists. The combination of access to employers—many of which provide projects and contribute to curriculum (not to mention hire graduates)—and immersive teaching programs makes Galvanize a vibrant learning community for technology. Galvanize is somewhat uncommon in only offering two programs. Other last-mile providers like General Assembly offer a wide array including mobile development (iOS or Android), UI/UX design, product management, and cybersecurity.

Not surprisingly, Galvanize generates enough interest from prospective students that it can afford to be selective. Only about 20 percent of applicants are admitted to Galvanize programs. Nevertheless, Galvanize students have included Best Buy clerks, frozen yogurt stand workers, and a homeless candidate.

Students are expected to be at Galvanize full time, just like a job. They'll arrive before 9 AM and typically won't leave before 7 or 8 PM. They're taught in relatively small classes, for the most part with fifteen or fewer students, by instructors who are successful developers but have decided they prefer teaching to coding, although many do both. But the formal instruction occupies only a fraction of that time. Most of the program involves working in teams on projects.

Ryan Burke, a staffer at the National Economic Council, recently decided to go back to school at a coding bootcamp and wrote about her experience in a series of essays on her blog. In "From the White House to Coding Bootcamp," Burke explained why she opted for last-mile training.[12]

In "If You Want to Go Quickly, Go Alone. If You Want to Go Far, Go Together," she described what it was like to work with other students in a bootcamp environment. According to Burke:

> There are a couple of labs (that's how we refer to our assignments) that are notoriously hard. Yesterday morning, I started one of those labs and with some hesitation paired with my classmate Holt . . . I started as the driver with Holt guiding me through the steps he wanted to take to fix the errors . . . The whole time I've been in boot-camp, I had been under the impression that I was slowly mastering an approach called Test Driven Development (TDD). As it turns out, I have been using about 10 percent of the power of TDD. I know from seeing Holt operate. He would spend literally ten seconds looking at lines of code that I had previously ignored and knew exactly what we needed to do next . . . Had I not worked with Holt, there's a decent possibility I would have gone through all twelve weeks of this program without truly realizing the power of TDD. Not only that, but it was a lot more motivating to work together. We spent six hours coding with moments of joy, frustration, and tears (not really, but I came close). When the fifty-third test lit up green, we jumped out of our seats cheering with euphoria (the way that Alabama football fans do when they win a big game).
>
> The other thing they tell you when you start bootcamp is that you will learn just as much or more by teaching others . . . On Monday, my classmate (a former professional poker player turned investor who next year is planning to only eat things he spearfishes) asked me about a lab that I recently completed. As I looked over his code, I realized that I had really not internalized what was actu-ally happening in the problem (that tends to happen when you are learning so fast that you only have minutes to spend on huge con-cepts). So I went back through it trying to explain piece by piece and going back to the lesson together as we needed. No kidding, those ten minutes with him were way more beneficial than when I did the lab the first time.[13]

What projects do Galvanize students work on? In the first month of the web development immersive students learn the basics of JavaScript, then start off building web pages with HTML and styling them with CSS. Then they make them interactive with DOM manipulation and AJAX. The first month concludes with students building an entire client-side app using an agile workflow. In the second month, students learn how to program the server-side: building dynamic server-side apps using Node.js and Express and managing databases using SQL, before completing an entire server-side application. The third month returns to the client side with instruction on frameworks like AngularJS and React before bringing the front-end and server-side together with a team project to build a complete single-page application. The fourth month provides advanced instruction on a range of client-side and server-side topics such as sorting and searching algorithms, as well as training on how to demonstrate live on a whiteboard—an essential skill for technical interviews. The final two months are a capstone project, where students work in a team, supported by the instructor, to complete a project similar in complexity to what employers would expect of entry-level coders.

Students at last-mile programs like Galvanize come from all walks of life. What they have in common is a sense that college did not or would not get them where they want to go: a good first job from which they could begin to build a career.

• • •

On a college track, this story isn't possible. I have sixty credits. It would have taken me two more years to get a bachelor's degree, with no guarantee that it would lead to a higher paying job. The promise of bachelor's degrees leading to lots of money is no longer true. Why would I pay $96,000 for something that might not help me get a good job? I have friends with doctorates who are Lyft drivers.

—*Tosin Awofeso, Galvanize*

Tosin Awofeso had been playing piano for eleven years by the time he finished high school and knew he wanted a career in music. His plan was to get into Texas State University and then apply for its renowned Sound Recording program. He even bought his own equipment. A year into the program, as Tosin was completing prerequisites, musicians started paying Tosin to record. He said, "I started making enough money doing that, so I dropped out of college to work."

Tosin then enrolled in an audio engineering certificate program at San Jacinto College in Pasadena, Texas. "In two semesters," he said, "I got more working and experiential knowledge than my friends who graduated from the four-year program at Texas State." He got an audio engineering job right away. "If I had stayed at Texas State, I would have had another two years to go, and here I was already working as an audio engineer at a TV station."

Tosin worked at the TV station for two years. But he was young, not used to getting up at 4 AM, and had been warned about showing up on time. One morning his car broke down on the way to work and he knew he was done. Later that day he walked into the station and cleaned out his desk. Suddenly he didn't have a job and didn't know how he would pay rent when a friend invited him to Austin.

"So I packed up my stuff and moved to Austin," Tosin said. There he worked at Pei Wei and Subway, then for a few start-ups, and then decided to play piano full time. "I quit working and said yes to everything that's musical." He joined a salsa hip-hop band and between playing music and doing videography and photography projects on the side, made $1,000–$1,500 a month—enough to get by while living with roommates.

Ultimately, Tosin realized that music wasn't going to pay the bills, so he began looking into coding. "I started teaching myself," he said, "but I decided it would take too long to get the skills I needed to be hirable. I needed the connections and help of a being taught in a classroom." He explored bootcamps but couldn't afford the deposits. Then a friend offered to pay Tosin's deposit for Galvanize. He stopped all other work and started the six-month immersive in August 2016.

It was a hard six months. Tosin's partner was pregnant and they had no place to live. "The building we lived in was shut down," he said, "so we stayed in friends' living rooms; we stayed at a hotel owned by the parent of someone I taught music to; a friend let us stay for free in a room she usually rented out on Airbnb."

But when he was at Galvanize, which was most of the time, Tosin was focused. He learned quickly and fell in love with coding. The program focused on the skills he wanted to learn. The applied, project-based learning model worked for his learning style.

"I could lecture you for an hour on functions and scoping, but you won't remember unless you use it," he said. "At Galvanize, we constantly used all the things we learned. In the third quarter, the teachers said, 'We've been teaching you to code in this language. Now try to figure out something you've never seen before.' They made us learn it on our own. In the fourth quarter, they taught some theory behind coding. Instead of saying, 'Copy and paste this and you'll get random colors,' they explained how it works, how you randomize it, and how to make it faster. Galvanize taught me how to ask the big questions, break them into smaller questions, and figure out how to solve the problems."

In the final month of the program, a music technology company called Common Edits came to Galvanize with a coding challenge. "I had planned to learn the framework beforehand," Tosin recalled, "but I was too busy with other school projects. I ended up sending them a ninety-minute video of myself learning the framework. They watched the video and said, 'We want him.'" Tosin stepped out of a Galvanize workshop on how to negotiate your job offer to take the call from Common Edits. The initial offer was part-time, with lower pay than Tosin wanted. He negotiated a week-by-week contract for a higher amount. Two days after the contract started, Common Edits management offered Tosin a full-time position. "I couldn't have dreamed of anything better than combining music with my new skill set in software engineering," he said.

Tosin started his new job three days after graduation from Galvanize, within weeks bought a new car, and a few months later secured an apartment for his family.

After eight months of working at Common Edits, Tosin said he used skills he learned at Galvanize every day. Not just the technical skills but learning how to learn, work in teams, break projects down, and problem solve. "My job title is Senior React Developer," Tosin said. "React is a library that helps build websites. That isn't a program that Galvanize taught, but I taught it to myself for my final project. At Galvanize, I developed the skillset of, 'How do I learn to do something that no one has done before, when it's not something I can Google, or copy and paste?' Right now, I'm learning how to create the functionality of programs such as Pro-tools and Ableton in a browser-app that can work on a phone. Galvanize taught me how to deal with the moments of frustration when it feels impossible and like no one can help me, how to break the problem down into small pieces, and to persevere."

Tosin's view on college is that its one-size-fits-all approach doesn't work. "College is good at critically thinking about things in a vacuum but bad at solving real-world problems or preparing you for real-world experiences," he said. "People fall through the cracks."

• • •

While bootcamps are most prevalent in coding, there are a variety of boot-camps or immersives in other areas. PrepMD is a last-mile training pathway to careers in the medical device industry. Companies like Medtronic and Boston Scientific that produce cardiac implantable electronic devices must provide trained clinical specialists to be present during implanting (i.e., testing whether the location of the electrode is electrically optimized) and to provide ongoing device support to patients and doctors. As with coding, no college or university provides the combination of anatomy and physiol-ogy, along with simulations and clinical training, that employers require for the approximately five thousand clinical specialists currently employed in the United States.

PrepMD has established itself as the leading pathway into this profession. Based in Boston, the PrepMD program encourages but does not require a bachelor's degree, and although admission is selective, a STEM background is not required. Other admissions criteria include geographic flexibility. The training includes thirty hours of online training and then on-ground train-ing for five months, including ten weeks of clinical rotations. PrepMD has a 94 percent placement rate ninety days after graduation, and graduates aver-age $90,000 starting salary plus bonus. Tuition is $30,000, but it's lower risk than a year at college given the placement record. There's also an option that's even lower risk: students who opt to work for PrepMD's partner employers for one year after graduation receive a significant tuition discount.

Founder Bob Mattioli is proud of PrepMD but is quick to note that PrepMD is not an institution of higher education—unless, of course, "you spell 'higher' like 'hire.'"

• • •

I absolutely love what I do; I learn something new every day, it's never boring, and 90 percent of people I see in my work wouldn't be alive without it.

—Christina DiMartino, PrepMD

Christina DiMartino's parents didn't pressure her to go to college, but when she graduated from high school in Franklin, Massachusetts (on the border of Rhode Island), she had no idea what she wanted to do. She got mediocre grades and had worked as a waitress. A friend of Christina's attended Community College of Rhode Island, so Christina decided to go there too and study business management. She thought it would be good overall preparation for something. She just wasn't sure what.

In college Christina brought her grades up but still wasn't sure it was for her. "I mostly kept to myself," she said. "I commuted and didn't live on campus, and I'm not a social butterfly. Partying wasn't my scene, and I didn't want to hang out. I'd rather work and hang out with my dog." About her classes, Christina said, "I learned some good study habits for success in the classes that I liked. English helped with writing professional emails. But it was hard to apply the world history course to my life."

Two main factors led Christina to leave college. First, she had to pay out-of-state tuition—$10,000 per year, expensive for a community college. After one year, she transferred to Bridgewater, a Massachusetts community college, which brought tuition down. But the second factor was harder to solve: Christina couldn't stand math. "Math is my devil subject," she said. "Even with tutoring I couldn't pass math. I couldn't fathom struggling with math in business school for another year."

While searching for alternatives, Christina found a cardiac medical assistant certificate program with no math requirement at Lincoln Tech, a for-profit college. Christina excelled, ending up with a 4.0 GPA and a job as a medical assistant at a hospital. One day, a nurse practitioner asked Christina to prepare information for patients with pacemakers. "When she thanked me, she asked if I was interested in learning more about medical devices," Christina recalled. "She told me she used to teach at PrepMD in the cardiac device specialist program. She said, 'Why don't you go to the program? And your job here will be waiting for you.'"

Christina researched the program and liked what she saw. She applied and was accepted with her medical assistant certificate. She started in May 2016.

The first four weeks of the program were online and included basic anatomy and physiology. Then students spent two months in the classroom. Christina explained, "We went through pacemakers, defibrillators, and CRT (cardiac resynchronization therapy, a treatment with three wires in the heart that beats both ventricles at the same time). Everything was broken down into weeks and it was all about the heart. There was no extra stuff that you wouldn't need to know."

PrepMD concludes with three months of clinical training. Christina opted to train in a clinical outpatient setting rather than with a single device manufacturer and then returned to her hospital where she was rewarded with a salary increase from $20 to $30 per hour. "I had waitressed at night during PrepMD," she said. "I finally quit waitressing after the raise."

"I'm happy here," Christina continued. "I'm in the clinical outpatient setting at the hospital. I have a set schedule, and I work with all the devices. I love my set schedule."

Christina is happy she never earned a degree. She sees some of her friends who had a great time for four years and are now struggling. "They have crippling debt, they can't afford to move out of their parents' house, and they're working jobs they don't even like," she said. "I feel sorry for them."

● ● ●

Kash Shaikh spent nearly a decade working at consumer packaged goods leader Procter & Gamble in Cincinnati, where he ended up leading social marketing in developing markets for P&G's $9 billion fabric care business. While at P&G, he developed the idea for Besomebody, a mobile app that would connect people with learning experiences in areas such as sports, art, or cooking. Besomebody matched students with instructors and took a cut.

After cashing out his 401(k) and raising $2 million in funding from investors, Shaikh appeared on ABC's *Shark Tank* and got bit. "This is a lot of talking," Mark Cuban told him. "You aren't getting anywhere right now. You know what's going to screw you up, Kash? The fact you're believing your own nonsense."

With no offer forthcoming from any Shark, Shaikh revisited his business plan and decided to focus on a second product he had been mulling over: Besomebody Paths. From now on, Besomebody would identify employers facing skill gaps, work with them to identify necessary skills for entry-level jobs, then create bespoke hands-on, four- to eight-week skills-based training programs that could guarantee at least one hundred jobs to graduates.

Shaikh's first stop was Kroger, America's largest grocery chain that is also based in Cincinnati. Kroger operates thousands of pharmacies and Shaikh had learned that although students often spend tens of thousands of dollars to earn a pharmacy tech degree, most pharmacies don't require degrees. Plus, Kroger had told Shaikh that they had to retrain every single graduate of a pharmacy tech program. Shaikh's vision was to custom-build an eight-week pharmacy tech training program for Kroger where graduates wouldn't have to be retrained.

Kroger was intrigued but wanted to start smaller. They envisioned a new position in their grocery stores: nutrition technician. Directed by a registered dietitian, nutrition technicians would serve as in-store resources to promote and market products consistent with Kroger's health and nutrition programs. Kroger worked with Shaikh on the training program and guaranteed jobs in Ohio at a starting salary of $32,000. Shaikh took the challenge head-on and within a few months had recruited, screened, and run three cohorts of students at Kroger's headquarters in Cincinnati, all of whom graduated and were placed.

Besomebody has now done the same thing with MassMutual for financial sales reps (starting salary $55,000) as well as with University Dental for dental assistants (starting salary $30,000). Besomebody is looking at other areas like automotive repair and culinary. In all cases, degrees are not required, the paths last no more than eight weeks, and jobs are guaranteed. The cost of enrolling in a Besomebody's path: $2,990.

With that kind of value proposition, you'd expect a big reaction. And you'd be right. Besomebody has had eight hundred applications to date for forty slots in its three programs—a 5 percent acceptance rate. Applicants are assessed for cognitive skills and then undergo video interviews. To date, 60 percent of applicants have college degrees, but Shaikh expects the number to fall as Besomebody becomes an established faster + cheaper alternative pathway to good first jobs.

• • •

It's ironic looking back, knowing I could have gotten this job without the college experience. It makes me second guess it a bit.

—*Morgan Combs, Besomebody*

Morgan Combs was the first person in her family to graduate from college, but after earning a degree in psychology, the best job she could find was working in a restaurant. "Once I graduated," she said, "I knew I needed more school to do anything with psychology, but I didn't have money to go back to school right away."

After a year of waiting tables, Morgan thought, *I want to use my degree.* She started scrolling around the internet for job opportunities. "I had always been into health and wellness and the connection between body and mind," she said. "I was always an athlete. I found the nutrition technician job post-ing with Kroger. It required a high school GED and to do the Besomebody training pathway. I contacted Besomebody to get details. It sounded way too good to be true."

Morgan completed an online survey and got a rating to see if her per-sonality was a match for the job. She then interviewed with Besomebody at a Kroger store. She got all the details, like the fees, the job guarantee and pay, and the schedule: four four-hour training sessions a week for a month. "I was able to keep working throughout the training," she said. "It was a long month, but it was completely worth it."

The five trainees in Morgan's cohort met in a Kroger conference room, which served as their classroom. "We started with introductions and went over the curriculum," Morgan said. "Everyone wore business casual clothes; they taught us to dress for the job you want. Every day we'd recap the previous day, then spend thirty minutes going over nutritional informa-tion and preparing for questions we might get from customers: how to read labels, vitamins, and macronutrients. Then we'd go on the floor and work with customers. They want us to be the face of the store. We had to walk up to strangers and talk to them. That's the job. They trained us to be comfortable with that. We handed out recipes and fliers for events, ran lots of samplings. We learned how to use the kitchen and set up displays, the logistical, nitty-gritty stuff."

The training also emphasized getting to know coworkers. "It's impor-tant to know everyone's name, to explain why we were there, what we were doing," Morgan explained. "They made sure we were comfortable and con-fident enough to insert ourselves into new stores. Besomebody goes to the source, the employer, and works backwards. The training was hands-on, exactly what I'd be doing when I started the job. You don't get that in a college classroom."

Morgan is now the nutrition tech at the Kroger Marketplace in Leba-non, Ohio. "My family asks if I want to keep working for Kroger forever," she said. "Honestly, it's an option. If there are growth opportunities in Kroger, I could stay. We've been working with dietitians. I might go back to school one day for that kind of degree, but right now I'm very happy where I'm at."

Her student loan debt for her psychology degree floats around $35,000. She's on track to pay it off in fifteen years. Morgan makes a set payment each month. "I treat it like an electric bill," she said. "That size of debt can cause stress and anxiety. I try not to think about it."

Despite her student loans, Morgan said she wouldn't do anything differently: "I'd love to remove the debt, but it would also erase all the friends I made and experiences I had. But to a high school graduate now, I'd say choose a more direct path and avoid college, unless it's taking away a dream you've always had."

• • •

Sales associate is the most common job for new college graduates in large part because every employer has a sales function.[14] Gabe Moncayo noticed that technology companies seeking salespeople expect entry-level candidates to already have sales experience and particularly experience on the Salesforce CRM platform—something colleges and universities don't teach. He found it odd that talented graduates from UC Berkeley were unable to secure employment at these companies. In response, he started a San Francisco bootcamp for technology sales called AlwaysHired.

The AlwaysHired curriculum includes training on technology and sales, and then technology sales strategies followed by a rotation through a real sales environment where students cold call on behalf of a client and log calls in Salesforce. Although the AlwaysHired training is a relatively brief forty hours, Gabe notes that the program is a "huge differentiator for new graduates who don't understand the difference between a Series A and Series B company, let alone how to sell technology to each type."[15]

AlwaysHired also boasts a 90 percent placement rate and further reduces risk by only requiring that students pay a $200 deposit. Always-Hired gets paid when students are hired, by taking either 6 percent of the student's first-year salary or less if students are hired by a company in the AlwaysHired network.

• • •

I got so overwhelmed with offers and second interviews that I
cut the process short. I didn't want to wait; I wanted to start work
right away.

—*Mark Anthony Robles, AlwaysHired*

Mark Anthony Robles always thought he'd go to college. He had a 4.0 GPA
in high school and won a bunch of awards. He was born in San Francisco
and raised by a single father. "He had me when he was young, straight out
of high school," Mark said. "For the first five years of my life, I traveled with
my uncle, my father's brother, who was in the Air Force. My father took me
back as soon as he was able to support me."

When Mark was thirteen years old, his father was diagnosed with can-
cer. Mark spent high school balancing his school work, helping his dad,
and taking care of their home. Mark was accepted to UCLA, but when his
father sadly passed away during Mark's senior year of high school, he had
a big decision to make. He decided to stay home with his family. "It was
too late to apply to a state school in San Francisco," he said, "so I enrolled
in City College."

Mark inherited some money from his father but needed to support
himself in an expensive city. He found a job in sales and discovered he was
pretty good at it. "Ever since I was a kid I helped my dad with his own business," Mark said. "He owned a restaurant in San Francisco, and I worked as
a host and delivered pizzas. It was my nature to be face-to-face interacting
with people." But supporting himself wasn't easy. "The cost of living in San
Francisco was astronomical. My pay covered rent, car payments, food, and
that's it. A studio apartment costs $2,100 a month." Then Mark got a much
better job as a mortgage broker. In no time he was making six figures.
Unfortunately, his timing wasn't great; it wasn't long before the bottom
dropped out of the mortgage market—the Great Recession.

He kept thinking about college and was accepted to a bridge program
to UC Berkeley but couldn't figure out how to pay for it. He believed he
had made too much money from his sales jobs to qualify for federal loans
and his credit wasn't good enough for private loans. At the same time, he
was aware of how much new college grads made: much less than he made
the prior year. "I was used to adult living by then," he said. "So given that
I'm in the Bay Area, I decided I would look into tech sales. I kept applying
to tech companies for sales and getting rejected. When I started looking

into how to interview better, I found AlwaysHired. I realized that's what I needed."

Mark describes his experience at AlwaysHired as eye-opening. "I learned how to have a better online presence and how to interview," he said. "I sharpened my sales skills in managing leads, creating leads, opening and closing sales. In any industry, the sales techniques are the same: cold calling, managing relationships, generating leads, and being efficient during the sales process."

Mark also learned about the tech industry: the culture, the big players, the language. "Before the bootcamp, I would read the newspaper but didn't go into depth," he recalled. "If you are in the tech industry, you need to know what's on the rise, what the newest innovations are. I learned what was going on in the industry and that it was essential to stay up to date."

Mark completed fifty interviews and received six job offers: one from Yelp, one from Xerox, and four from smaller companies. He accepted an account executive position at Yelp.

Mark also appreciates the alumni community that AlwaysHired is developing. "It's been going for two years," he said. "Two hundred plus AlwaysHired grads are scattered around the industry. If I ever wanted to switch jobs, I could contact alumni and they could help with advice on how to get in."

•   •   •

Medical Sales College (MSC) is a bootcamp that trains technical sales representatives for medical device companies, focusing on orthopedic devices relating to the spine and orthopedic reconstruction such as artificial hips and knees, arthroscopic products used in ACL or rotator cuff repairs, or plates and screws used in spinal fusions. The program runs from six to ten weeks on three campuses—Memphis, Tampa, and Austin—and provides last-mile training not only on sales and devices but also on anatomy, pathology, and biomechanics, as well as noncognitive skill training so students can be effective in a hospital environment. After all, medical device sales reps sell to a fairly sophisticated clientele: surgeons.

MSC is selective, accepting about 25 percent of applicants. Since its founding in 2008, MSC has placed more than 900 graduates across the top ten spinal and orthopedic companies, such as Smith & Nephew and Medtronic, achieving a 95 percent graduate placement rate. More than three hundred employers have registered with MSC to recruit graduates. MSC does not require a bachelor's degree but says if candidates don't have a degree, they will need a strong sales or clinical background to be accepted into the program.

Employers are enthusiastic. According to one spinal device distributor who relies on MSC for sales talent, "Unlike big companies like Medtronic, we don't have the ability to recruit directly from colleges." An orthopedics distributor added that, "MSC is a brilliant idea in a space where everybody's scratching their head." Another employer said MSC candidates show seriousness and purpose: "They're not just kicking tires. They've spent their own time and money to distinguish themselves from the general applicant pool." Not surprisingly, employers report lower turnover from MSC.

● ● ●

There's no college degree for this job, no medical sales option in universities that I've seen. There's a gap. Medical Sales College is honed in, right on the money. I don't think there's anything that could have gotten me more prepared.

—*Matthew Theisen, Medical Sales College*

Matthew Theisen played football in college and started his career in sales. While he had many friends, former football players, who had gone into medical device sales and were doing well, Matthew had been a business major with no medical or STEM background. He began trying to figure out how to break in.

Matthew found MSC online and reached out to the admissions person. "I picked her brain and it felt like something I wanted to do," he said. He relocated to Denver for the six-week-long program.

"The course went well," says Matthew. "I learned tons. We spent 8 AM to 5 PM Monday through Friday in a classroom or lab setting. It was almost like a college course, but the profs are former sales reps, each with their own specialty: sports medicine, reconstruction, extremities, spine, trauma. It gives them credibility because they did the job and were successful." The classes had five to ten people each and involved lots of small-group work and one-on-one role plays. "The instructor would play the surgeon and someone from the class would play the rep and have to talk about the product. It's a technique I use now when I train employees."

For Matthew, the program was both interactive and applied. "You're not just sitting there," he said. "In labs, the instructors would bring in Striker's ACL equipment and fake tibia and femur bones and joints and simulate an actual surgery. Everyone participates, asks questions, and gets called on to answer technical questions. You do video role plays so you can watch yourself and learn from what you've done wrong. It has the intensity of a college course but with a very low teacher-to-student ratio." The small, specialized groups would join for classes like anatomy and operating room procedure that were relevant to all specializations.

At night, Matthew and the other MSC students staying at the hotel would study together and test their retention of the day's material. "I'm still in touch with my friends from the program," he said. "I was even able to get one of them a job. It's similar to college in that respect."

MSC also helped with interview preparation. Even though Matthew had sales experience, he needed the help. "In this industry, selling is different from other fields," he said. "You're selling to surgeons, as well as hospital CEOs, CFOs, and chief clinical officers. You need to be able to relate to all of them. At MSC, we learned to separate ourselves from all the putzes who assume everyone golfs, and they ask about the client's golf game and the conversation dies there. I do my research. I learn where they grew up, what they specialized in, their hobbies, and read their past publications to create talking points. If you say to a surgeon, 'I read that article you wrote on back in 2005. I'd love to chat about it,' they'll be excited to talk to you."

At MSC, Matthew decided on sport medicine. His football background made it a good fit, and he likes the schedule. "I know people in trauma who haven't had a Christmas day off in five years," he said. "In sport, ACL, and rotator cuff, surgeries are almost always planned, so you're not getting calls in the middle of the night, and they are usually scheduled Monday to Friday. I almost never have to work a surgery on a weekend."

After completing MSC, Matthew landed a second interview with market leader Smith & Nephew. In preparation, Matthew put together a thirty-six-page business plan on how to grow the territory. He profiled surgeons and materials managers at fifty-two different facilities. "I wanted to impress them," he said, "and I wanted to know who everyone was so I could hit the ground running if I got the job."

Now Matthew is a territory retail manager for Smith & Nephew. "I hire, and unfortunately have to fire, employees," he said. "Sometimes people are missing something. I often recommend MSC in those cases. They get hired after."

• • •

Of course, good last-mile programs aren't cheap. The average coding bootcamp costs $11,400.[16] If $11,400 sounds like a lot, it's worse for an underemployed college graduate struggling with $40,000 in student loans. As a result, some last-mile programs have taken to offering money-back guarantees. Flatiron School and Code Fellows tell students they'll refund tuition if they don't get good jobs. At the same time, two federal programs have begun providing a small amount of funding to bootcamps. Flatiron School is participating in the government's EQUIP pilot program, which will allow a small number of Flatiron students to qualify for federal financial aid. And in the summer of 2017, the Forever GI Bill set aside $15 million per year over five years for a "high-technology" pilot program to train veterans for careers in tech sectors.[17] But neither money-back guarantees nor limited federal funding solves the cost problem for the average student.

What about loans? Unfortunately, federal student loans aren't generally available for last-mile programs. Traditional private student loans are based on credit scores, which are problematic for many students because they're young and haven't established sufficient credit history or because, like Mark, they've made some missteps. The result is that standard private loans aren't a great solution either. Going to a bank for a loan to pay for a last-mile program will likely result in denial or an unacceptable interest rate, either of which might reflect an inaccurate risk assessment on the part of the lender. Credit scores are simply a poor measure of credit risk for an investment in education, the purpose of which is to materially increase earning power.

Think about two borrowers, Student A and Student B. They're both college seniors and need a private loan to supplement their federal loans. Student A has a 4.0 GPA at a selective school's engineering program and is on track to graduate in a year. However, she's only had a credit card for two years, made one late payment, and has a current balance of $500. Student

B has a 2.5 GPA in American Studies at a nonselective college and is not on track to graduate next year. But he does have a credit card with a higher limit and no late payments. Most credit score-based lenders would lend to Student B at around 9 percent, while Student A would either be rejected or charged an interest rate above 12 percent.

Credit scores are a particularly bad measure of risk for last-mile programs that increase income in a relatively short period of time. But last-mile programs like Galvanize have been able to identify new funding sources that are specifically not lending based on credit scores. Galvanize has two partners, Climb Credit and Skills Fund, that allow students to borrow not only the cost of tuition but also living expenses and even a laptop. At Galvanize, a poor or nonexistent credit score is unlikely to pose a problem. Galvanize's employment outcomes are so strong, interest rates are lower than you'd see on a typical private loan. Finally, because most students are able to repay within a couple of years, there's less total interest owed than on a comparable longer-term private loan for a four-year degree.

Meritize is another new provider of financing for last-mile programs. Meritize uses quantified academic success factors and other alternative underwriting methods as a basis for making its loans. Founder Chris Keaveney believes that "high performing students who are going to graduate and get good jobs should get loans with lower interest rates." In other words, Meritize cares less about where you've been and more about where you're going. In 2017, Meritize made loans to approximately two thousand students at fifty different programs. Like Climb Credit and Skills Fund, Meritize requires last-mile programs to share the risk by holding back a percentage of the loan until students begin making payments.

Following the emergence of Meritize, Climb Credit, and Skills Fund, most last-mile programs have financing options for students—options that benefit students not only by allowing them to attend the program but also by ensuring that the last-mile programs themselves have "skin in the game" with regards to the graduates' employment.

CHAPTER 5 • KEY POINTS

- Tuition-pay coding bootcamps were the first last-mile programs, remain the most prominent, and tend to produce strong employment outcomes.

- Bootcamps are now preparing students for a range of entry-level positions beyond coding: sales, medical devices, nutrition technicians.

- Most bootcamps remain "top-up" programs: programs for under-employed, indebted college graduates.

- Financing is increasingly available for these programs with qualification determined by likely future income rather than credit history.

CHAPTER 6

The College MVP

THORNTON: When I used to dream about going to college . . . this is the way I always pictured it.

JASON: Wait a minute. When did you dream about going to college?

THORNTON: When I used to fall asleep in high school.

—*Back to School (1986)*

I n college, I was a member of the Yale Political Union, a poor facsimile of a real debating society, the Oxford Union. Yale's version existed as a political game of Dungeons & Dragons, providing reasonably good training for a career in government. But instead of killing monsters, the object was to run for one of a panoply of meaningless PU offices.

I headed the Progressive Party, a group that nominally followed the teachings of Teddy Roosevelt but in reality existed to play pranks on the serious parties like the knee-jerk Liberal Party and the fascists in the Party of the Right. For our social action project one semester, we took on the graffiti painted on New Haven's East Rock by painting it "rock color" (amazingly, the Parks Department provided the paint; they had no better—or more cost-effective—solution).

When uninspiring and visionless candidates for PU offices sought the endorsement of the Progressive Party, we had a sophisticated system for screening candidates, like ordering a foot-long sandwich at Subway with

every ingredient, with "extra" for each one of the sauces, and then inform-
ing them they needed to eat the "sandwich of life." (I'm told that, after our
graduation, the hazing progressed to blindfolding candidates, sticking them
in the back of a U-Haul, and driving them around New Haven at breakneck
speed. Perhaps similar treatment would improve our decisions in more
important elections.)

There were also less disgusting and dangerous screening mechanisms.
A favorite was dumb dichotomies, requiring the candidate to select the
preferred (or more likely, less objectionable) option, such as:

- "Lee Harvey Oswald or Oswald Mosley?"
- "Light of my life or fire of my loins?"
- "Han Solo or Luke Skywalker?"
- "ABBA or Wings?"
- "Au jus or sans jus?"
- Or my favorite: "MSG—Madison Square Garden or monosodium
  glutamate?"

If the Progs existed today (they died, likely as a result of lack of serious
debate), I imagine a hot dichotomy would be this: MVP—most valuable
player or minimum viable product? While the former is familiar to any
sports fan, the latter emerged out of Silicon Valley in the past decade. A
minimum viable product is the simplest, smallest product that provides
enough value for consumers to adopt and actually pay for it. It is also the
minimal product that allows producers to receive valuable feedback, iterate,
and improve. A minimum viable product is one of the core tenets of the
"lean start-up" and explains why many technology entrepreneurs are now
able to launch businesses with practically no investment at all.

College as we know it is the polar opposite of a minimum viable product. A bachelor's degree is neither simple nor small. It's not designed to
allow colleges and universities to iterate and improve, and it's certainly not
minimizing anyone's investment. That is why the most important development in higher education in the next decade will be a college MVP.

• • •

At what point does a last-mile program become a viable alternative to college? That's what Galvanize was for Tommy Gaessler. Galvanize CEO Al

Rosabal sees a huge need. He says he's tired of seeing candidates whom Galvanize could benefit but who are struggling with $50,000+ in student loan debt from college.

"We're seeing too many students with too much debt but without work-ready skills," he said. Rosabal has begun speaking out on the issue of college affordability, and Galvanize is now promoting the nontechnical skills that students gain in its six-month web development immersive program, as well as its twelve-week data science program. Meanwhile, AlwaysHired's Gabe Moncayo says he welcomes all students seeking a career in sales: "Degrees are not a prerequisite for our program, and our placement rate is steady at 90 percent."

Last-mile programs already attract many students without college degrees. According to *Course Report,* about 24 percent of students enter without a bachelor's degree.[1] Individual programs report comparable numbers. To date, about 20 percent of AlwaysHired students enter without a college background. General Assembly (GA) estimates that across all of its programs 13 percent of students enroll without a college degree. But of its four hundred students receiving some level of financial assistance, the number is 42 percent. Both percentages are increasing. Bloc, an online coding last-mile program, estimates two-thirds of its students enter without a college degree.

In 2017, GA launched its first program targeting students without college degrees in partnership with Per Scholas, a job training program, and La Guardia Community College in New York. The program provides technical and noncognitive skill development during a six-week bridge program along with support during the last-mile program itself. "The bridge program is about developing the right mindset for General Assembly," said GA program head Tom Ogletree. GA has run four cohorts of fifteen students through so far. "They're getting good jobs," said Ogletree.

•   •   •

I learned a lot that I wouldn't have learned on my own. Prior to entering the program, I studied basic HTML for six months. When I couldn't grasp concepts, I had no one to ask. In the program, teachers and other students helped me. It was a great opportunity.

—*Anthony Pegues, General Assembly*

Born and raised in New York, Anthony Pegues was on track for two possible careers: custodian at the local junior high school or professional boxer.

His mother always pushed Anthony to go to college. It worked for his brother; he got a bachelor's degree in business and now works as a marketer for a wine distribution company. "Mom thought college would be the best thing for me," Anthony said. "She said to go, get a nice degree, and get a good job."

When Anthony graduated from high school in 2007, he went directly to Westchester Community College. His goal was to get into a program in audio engineering. "Going right into college from high school, maybe I wasn't prepared," he admitted. "I didn't have the mindset or the focus, I was ignorant about what I needed to do to pursue a career in audio engineering. In the end, I didn't get the classes I wanted to take and I wasn't interested in the basic liberal arts curriculum of psychology, calculus, and basic algebra. It was just like high school. I was not feeling it."

When his grades weren't good enough to get into audio engineering, Anthony dropped out. "Mom thought it was a stupid decision," he said. "I had no plan."

Anthony divided his time between the gym and the local middle school where he worked as a part-time custodian. "I realized I didn't enjoy being a custodian anymore, and boxing wasn't a great long-term career. I started to think, do I want to be successful using my body? Or doing manual labor? The answer was neither. I wanted to be successful using my mind."

With new motivation, Anthony began studying web development on his own. He also applied to bootcamps, thinking it would get him trained faster than on his own and would be easier and quicker than traditional college. Anthony found General Assembly and applied for a scholarship called the Opportunity Fund. "I got the nod," he said. "They referred me to Per Scholas, a bridge program into GA. I was ecstatic. Classes are funded by a Department of Labor grant. You apply and take a few tests and if you pass, you get to go to the program for free!" Anthony started at Per Scholas in December 2016.

In one month at Per Scholas, Anthony learned basic JavaScript. Per Scholas also offered career development training. Anthony was assigned a career development coach to help prepare him for a job search. "I didn't have a résumé or a LinkedIn profile going in," he said. "I wouldn't have been prepared for a business or office setting. That preparation really helped me out."

Per Scholas also helped with Anthony's work ethic. "It wasn't easy," he said. "I had to decide if I really wanted to do this or not. Assignments had to be handed in every day; if they weren't turned in it would jeopardize getting into GA. I had to lock down on work and focus. I had to get stuff done. I learned how to ask other classmates for help, how to put pride aside."

Anthony got through the Per Scholas bridge program and was admitted to GA. Once at General Assembly, everything went twice as fast. The technical skills were more advanced.

"I learned more about JavaScript, front end and back end, and cool frameworks like React and Express," Anthony said. "I learned how to work with databases, sequencing and processing data. I learned to venture out into a completely different programming language. I dabbled in Elixir. Overall, it sharpened my ability to learn new technical skills. Things I'm doing in my job right now I can do because of GA."

GA also coached Anthony on how to organize his résumé and LinkedIn profile, how to approach industry recruiters, and how to network. "The career development coach at GA used to work for a start-up as a recruiter," he said. "She had great experience and told me to use LinkedIn to reach out to other GA alumni who are already employed." She helped Anthony format and write professional emails and gave him a better understanding of how to reach out to people.

"From the beginning to the end of the program, your confidence grows," Anthony said. "At the beginning you're scared, you're unsure of your technical skills, unsure of your career skills. You gain confidence in yourself, more confidence in your skills, in who you are."

Anthony graduated from GA in April 2017 as the valedictorian of his class. Within a few months he was hired to work on the web development team at MM.LaFleur, a start-up that sells personalized clothing for women. Anthony's mom is ecstatic, his brothers too. "They're very proud of me," he said. "They saw all the energy I put into the program and they're happy it worked out. This whole path has been a blessing."

• • •

Like GA, most last-mile providers are now considering how to shift from top-up programs to full-on college MVPs. As with the GA bridge program, the key is to add curriculum ahead of the last-mile technical training as the first stage of a comprehensive pathway to a good job.

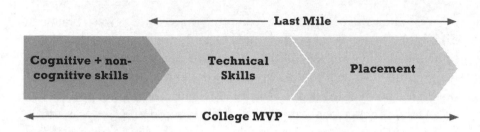

This added curriculum is intended to equip students with cognitive and noncognitive skills at a level comparable to a college graduate, as quickly and inexpensively as possible in order to get to the last mile.

All college MVPs aim to provide faster + cheaper pathways to good jobs than the colleges and universities they hope to displace. But, by definition, college MVPs are slower and more expensive than last-mile programs. Not every program can rely on a Department of Labor grant, so are students willing to pay more? Fortunately, a new financing mechanism is propelling the growth of college MVPs: income share agreements (ISAs). ISAs are income-linked repayment contracts in which programs front funds for student tuition and fees—either from their operating budgets, or external sources. Then programs (or their funders) receive repayment following graduation as a percentage of student income.

When I talk to people about income share agreements, a common reaction is that they sound like indentured servitude. But I always tell them this: Federal student loans, the primary form of financing for traditional higher education, require students to make defined monthly payments. Failure to do so results in impairment of credit and wage garnishment. And of course, student loans can't be discharged in bankruptcy. Now compare this to income share agreements: contracts between the program and the student that can only be enforced like any other contract (i.e., no impairment of credit or wage garnishment) and that would not survive bankruptcy. I'm not aware of an income share program that asks for more than a 20 percent share for a handful of years (typically three or four). And all income share agreements are capped in terms of total dollars repaid. Most important, income share agreements have an income floor below which students aren't required to pay. And as of fall 2017, there are two bills in Congress—one in the Senate and a companion bill in House—to clarify the legal status of income share agreements. All things considered, student loans feel a lot more like indentured servitude than income share agreements.

What income share agreements are, in effect, is insurance: if you don't get a job, you won't have to pay; and if you don't get a good job, you won't have to pay as much. While many defenders of the status quo argue that the current system works for the average college graduate, as we have seen, that's probably no longer true today. Moreover, since when do we judge success based on average outcomes, particularly when the stakes are so high? Cars aren't allowed on the road if they only protect the "average" driver or passenger in the event of a crash. Doctors don't win malpractice suits by claiming that their treatment would have saved the "average" patient. Even auditors that allow companies to cook the books aren't permitted to remain in business because their work would have been sufficient for the "average" client.

Income share agreements are a new approach to the financing of higher education, one that protects not only the average student but exactly those students who have been experiencing the worst possible outcomes. Like all insurance, income share agreements redistribute from customers with good outcomes to those with poor outcomes: income share graduates who do well are likely to pay more than they might have paid on a student loan, while income share graduates with poor outcomes will pay less or nothing at all.

Purdue and other universities have already launched income share agreement programs for exactly these reasons. In 2017 the American Enterprise Institute released findings from a survey of students and parents to ascertain interest in ISAs. Although awareness of ISAs was limited at the outset, once respondents were educated about repayment scenarios, 53 percent preferred ISAs, while only 29 percent preferred student loans.[2]

College MVPs fit well with the income share model. Whereas Purdue's "Back-a-Boiler" income share program has only been made available to college seniors and some juniors—meaning participants are taking on income share agreements on top of student loan debt—college MVPs are easily financed with an income share model.

• • •

In the past few years, several income share programs have emerged as college MVPs. Holberton School is a San Francisco–based coding program, named after Frances Elizabeth "Betty" Holberton, one of the six programmers of ENIAC, that is open to anyone, even students without a high school diploma. It is a self-proclaimed "college alternative" that aims to recruit and train a much more diverse set of software engineers than top colleges and universities. While the program lasts two years, students are finding great jobs after a year at Holberton. Holberton's backers include Jerry Yang (founder of Yahoo!), Pierre Omidyar (founder of eBay), and Grammy award–winning R&B star Ne-Yo.

Holberton was founded in 2015 by Sylvain Kalache and Julien Barbier, French technology entrepreneurs who were struggling to find technology talent (and when qualified, too often burdened by student loans). Like coding bootcamps, Holberton is project-based, with many projects from employer partners, all guided by instructors. Its curriculum fosters "improved communication and interpersonal/social skills, enhanced leadership skills, and increased creativity."[3] Holberton gives students "increasingly difficult programming challenges to solve, with minimal initial directions on how to solve them. As a result, students naturally learn to look for the theory and tools they need, how to understand them and use them, and how to work together and help each other."[4] One interesting twist is that Holberton will intentionally break students' projects so students learn how to troubleshoot and fix. Holberton also focuses on writing skills: students are required to write at least one technical blog post each week.

Holberton selects applicants on criteria such as problem solving, perseverance, and teamwork—but like other coding bootcamps, no computer science background is required. The program is attracting a diverse student base—35 percent female, 50 percent minority.

Holberton has enrolled more than 200 students to date and many have already found internships or jobs at top Silicon Valley companies such as Apple, NASA, Tesla, and LinkedIn. Students can choose to complete the Holberton program part time after they begin working. Holberton's income share model is 17 percent for three years after they leave the program but only once they earn at least $40,000 per year. So if a Holberton graduate fails to make $40,000 for three years after graduating (not counting returning to formal postsecondary education, in which case the clock stops), then their Holberton education is free.[5]

Holberton's value proposition has attracted thousands of applicants to date. Due to its small size, it has only been able to accept 3%. But this College MVP has just moved to a new campus capable of enrolling 500 students a year. So Holberton's founders expect to serve many more diverse students interested in digital careers.

• • •

Not everyone has the money to pay for education. Holberton provides opportunities to people who have the ability but not the money.

—*Justin Marsh, Holberton*

Justin Marsh grew up in a small town west of Chicago. He had lots of friends, enjoyed outdoor activities, sports, and video games. But near the end of high school, when Justin started looking at colleges, it was hard to choose what he wanted to do. He remembers when a high school guidance counselor came to his class and administered career planning and personality tests. Justin's test results were inconclusive. He asked the counselor, "What does this mean?"

The counselor said, "It means you have too many interests."

One thing Justin knew was that he spent a lot of time on computers. He was interested in how computers work and figuring out how could they work differently. He decided to attend University of Illinois to study computer science.

The first year at university was challenging. It took Justin a while to make new friends and he found the classes fairly boring. "My learning style is applied," he said. "I like breaking things apart and putting them back together. But long lectures and rigid, academic, not-very-explorative content didn't work for me." After a year, Justin wasn't sure that computer science was the right place for him. "The way it was presented at school didn't interest me."

He remembers the moment he decided to leave school. One of the software engineering courses brought in a professional every week to talk about their work. "Every week, I heard about jobs I didn't want," Justin said. "I liked computers because they're complex and involve problem solving. But listening to one of the speakers, I realized he was just doing things other people told him to do, which was the opposite of why I was studying computers. It made me question my decision to study computer science. I didn't want to finish a degree just for the sake of a degree."

Justin left but didn't have much of a plan. He went back to work at his parents' restaurant where he had worked part-time during high school.

His parents were less than pleased. "They worked really hard to give me the opportunity to go to college," he said, "and it seemed to them like I was throwing it away. They didn't understand my decision and couldn't imagine that it would bring about success."

Justin's first taste of success also didn't thrill his parents; he began playing poker online and got pretty good at it. Once he was making more money from poker than from the restaurant, he decided to become a professional poker player. He was just turning twenty and knew it wasn't a long-term career, but it afforded a lot of flexibility. He got to set his own hours and play where he wanted. He thought it would give him the opportunity to figure out what he really wanted to do. Through poker, Justin supported himself for eleven years.

But as the years passed, Justin's love of computers endured. He developed computer programs to help make poker easier to play and worked on complicated equations. By the final two years of his poker career, he was spending half his time developing these programs. He realized he was developing transferable skills. He also realized that he still had a passion for computer science. In June 2016, Justin officially retired from poker.

That was when Justin found Holberton; their two-year program stood out. "It takes a decent amount of time to learn anything worth learning," he said. "Two years seemed like a decent amount of time." It also seemed like the teachers believed in learning by doing, something he wished he'd experienced at university. Justin applied to the two-year software engineering program at Holberton and was accepted.

Another aspect of Holberton that Justin liked was the income share model. "A lot of schools make you pay a lot of money upfront, which divorces education from its outcome," he said. "Holberton lets you pay nothing upfront, and you pay it back once you have a job." This structure aligned Holberton with Justin's goal: to get a good job. Justin also thought this model proved the school's confidence that they could take people with no real experience or education and get them great jobs within two years.

"At Holberton, learning is based on projects," Justin explained. "Assignments are simple but broad. Each project is designed to teach a skill that the next project builds on. We covered specific program languages and algorithms and those are helpful, but it's at the points when you don't know the answer that you learn the most. If I got stuck on a problem, I'd take a break, come back to it, and try to look at it from a different angle. I spent a lot of time asking questions—to teachers, to other students, and to the school founders themselves. The learning model is, if you get stuck, can you find your answer yourself? If not, ask a peer. If they don't know, ask another peer. Through this chain of working with people, you are learning and teaching others. If you're not able to explain something to someone, you probably don't really understand it. This is a core concept at Holberton."

Beyond simply learning and teaching others, however, Justin thinks "the most important thing that's taught at Holberton is the ability to teach yourself." He said, "You aren't ever going to know all the answers. You need to be able to think through the problem and know where to go to find the information to solve it. Do I go to the library? Do I go to Google? Do I already know more than I think? Do I ask a peer? In the workforce, it's the same. You get presented with difficult problems. You're not expected to know the answer; you're expected to be able to find the answers."

Justin got a job at LinkedIn after only six months of the two-year program. "This shows the effectiveness of the model," Justin said. Many of his peers found great jobs a year into the program.

Justin recognizes his career path has been unorthodox but thinks he's learned an important lesson that's relevant for high school students who are trying to figure it out. "It's okay to not know what you want to do with your life," he said. "But try to find a connection between what you like to do and how you'll spend your time working. I found that connection and went into software engineering."

● ● ●

There are two reasons why college MVPs like Holberton may be able to achieve targeted levels of cognitive and noncognitive skills in much less time. The first is selectivity; if motivated and talented students are attracted to the college MVP's faster + cheaper value proposition, the baseline capabilities of entering students will give college MVPs a significant head start.

The second—and one you're not likely to hear about from college MVPs themselves—is that technology may be lowering the cognitive and noncognitive skill target for many entry-level jobs. So what employers are seeking may not be as distant as colleges and universities might like to think. This is due to the proliferation of SaaS platforms to manage practically every business function across every industry. SaaS platforms tend to define and even restrict the span of responsibility and decision making compared to the more general and freewheeling entry-level jobs of 10 or more years ago.

According to Bob LaBombard, cofounder of Avenica and entry-level career thought-leader:

> When I started in sales, I was the CRM. I decided who to call on, how often, when to drop a prospect, and when to add new leads. I knew my contact list inside and out. Much of this is automated now. These systems tend to discourage independent thinking. You have more leads, but much less familiarity and ownership. You just call the next lead scheduled by the system.[10]

This is not the case for all entry-level jobs. In some of the largest job categories—nursing, teaching, social workers, even software developers and engineers—entry-level jobs continue to require as many cognitive and noncognitive skills as they ever have (and probably more). But my rough estimate is that half of the top thirty jobs are at risk of SaaS mediation and restricted decision making.[11] If that's true for all jobs, it's likely that more than half of entry-level jobs fall into this category.

It may even be true for some coding jobs. A recent article in *Wired* titled "The Next Big Blue Collar Job Is Coding," noted that Silicon Valley only employs 8 percent of all coders. Most of the other 92 percent "won't have the deep knowledge to craft wild new algorithms for flash trading or neural networks. Why would they need to? That level of expertise is rarely necessary at a job. But any blue-collar coder will be plenty qualified to sling JavaScript for their local bank. That's a solidly middle-class job."[12]

Economic Strategy Institute's Robert Cohen has concluded that given the technical skills gap, "employers are probably very willing to hire professionals with a more narrowly defined range of skills for early-stage positions. Employees taking these jobs would then acquire new skills so they could move on to more skilled intermediate and senior posts."[13]

While *Wired* calls these jobs blue collar, they don't involve risking life or limb or even getting one's hands dirty. So IBM has proposed a better term: "new collar."[14] New collar jobs are middle-skill jobs that call for advanced digital skills (which Burning Glass defines as "more sophisticated than spreadsheets or word processing, but not as specialized as programming"[15]). These jobs are the first jobs that most college grads are trying to get, unsuccessfully in most cases.

New collar jobs don't require the level of numerical reasoning, critical thinking, creative thinking, or problem-solving skills that colleges and

universities are aiming at when they prepare students for their fifth job
(not their first). As a result, candidates with mid- to high levels of motivation and aptitude don't require four years of formal education beyond
high school to do these first jobs well. By putting a greater focus on SaaS
platforms themselves and less on hard-to-measure cognitive skills, they'll
require less time—perhaps by an order of magnitude.

To be sure, no employer is jazzed about the prospect of hiring less-
skilled workers. Aren't skills and education an unmitigated good? But in
keeping with the SaaS theme, it didn't take long for enterprises, including colleges and universities, to acclimate to buying exactly the software
functionality they need when they need it (in stark contrast to the massive
enterprise software deployments of the 1990s and 2000s that included a
great deal of functionality they didn't need and massive expense). SaaS
products are much more efficient. Similarly, there's reason to believe many
employers will opt for the talent that fits the need.

When the talent better fits the need, employers may see benefits. Better-
fit employees may perform better and churn less. And if the postsecondary
education required for the job costs less and requires less debt, employers
should be able to pay a bit less. They certainly won't be asked for benefits
like student loan repayment.[16]

Large tech employers are fiercely rational and not snobs. Burning Glass's
list of the top ten employers with entry-level tech openings isn't a "who's
who" of elite Silicon Valley or San Francisco companies but rather includes
systems integrators like Accenture, Deloitte, and Booz Allen Hamilton, as
well as top health care companies Anthem Blue Cross and United Health.
In fact, there's not a single Silicon Valley company on the list (Seattle-based
Amazon is on there).[17] These large employers are highly motivated by cost
savings and more likely to begin hiring for the skills they need when they
need them. Moreover, the new "reshoring" trend for outsourced tech jobs
that might have gone to India but that now are going to American consul-
tancies large and small will only increase the number of these jobs.[18]

● ● ●

Do new faster + cheaper alternatives to college have the potential to "disrupt" American higher education per Clayton Christensen's definition of
"disruptive technologies"? Last year the Christensen Institute produced a
disruption checklist for a College MVP. Here's what they concluded:[19]

Does [the college MVP] target people whose only alternative is to buy nothing at all (nonconsumers) or who are overserved by existing offerings in the market?	**Yes.** The target audience is eighteen- to twenty-nine-year-old undergraduates who feel that the traditional four-year degree is too expensive and bloated—but who want to make sure they get a high-paying job. It's unlikely that these students would otherwise be nonconsumers, but choosing [the College MVP] is a clear signal they want something that is simpler, cheaper, and faster.
Is the offering not as good as existing offerings as judged by historical measures of performance?	**Yes.** [The College MVP] has minimal physical infrastructure, one major (Data Analytics + Business Intelligence), no research faculty, no degree, and no accreditation. For now, the program is only available to those willing to relocate to within fifty miles of San Francisco. Overall, the offering is significantly less comprehensive than that of traditional institutions, by design.
Does the offering have a technology that enables it to improve and move upmarket?	**TBD.** In disruption theory, "technology" means the processes that companies use to create value. [The College MVP] generates value by getting its graduates hired. It works closely with employer partners to calibrate its curriculum, keeping it cutting-edge and based on real-world problems. These partners then gain early preferred access to the . . . talent pipeline for hiring.
Is the technology paired with a business model innovation that allows it to be sustainable?	**Yes.** The employer-driven curriculum is paired with an ISA revenue model, which aligns the incentives of [the College MVP] and its students. [The College MVP] is motivated to ensure that students learn what they need to get into solid, high-paying jobs, and can scale efficiently with its lack of a physical campus.
Are existing providers motivated to ignore the new innovation and not feel threatened by it at the outset?	**Yes.** [The College MVP] cuts out several traditional elements of higher education that existing institutions cherish. Some may be distantly wary, but no colleges have shown signs of changing their game plan yet.

As college MVPs emerge in every large metropolitan area, across a range of technical entry-level job functions, colleges and universities will finally get practical experience of the disruption that's been taught at Harvard Business School for the past twenty years.

CHAPTER 6 • KEY POINTS

- Bootcamps are morphing from top-up programs to full-on college degree replacements.

- College MVPs add requisite cognitive and noncognitive skill development curriculum to last-mile programs.

- College MVPs are being financed and powered by the rise of income share agreements.

- College MVPs are the textbook definition of "disruption" and will lead the faster + cheaper revolution.

CHAPTER 7

Get to Work

He ain't exactly what you'd call "college material," so don't you
go fillin' his simple head with all those crazy dreams . . . of
school and college and things of that sort.

—The Waterboy (1998)

Last fall I attended the twenty-fifth anniversary of the founding of
Rumpus, Yale's tabloid and source of the "50 Most Beautiful People."
Rumpus had asked Yale's President to speak to the assembled alumni,
but since he was out of town, he sent a written congratulatory greeting and
thanked *Rumpus* "for still publishing in paper form. It is reassuring that I
can rely on you to provide tinder for my fireplace."

Learning that no real representative of the university was slated to
kick off the reunion, some alumni pranksters took it upon themselves to
hire an eighty-six-year-old local actor via Craigslist to portray former Yale
Associate Dean "Jonathan James" (a Google-proof name) and write a speech
welcoming the group.

The speech started out plausibly. Dean James had been Deputy Dean
of Yale College for Student Affairs in the early 1990s. He had helped
various Yale Presidents with special projects, such as dealing with the
unions, preventing grad students from unionizing, and keeping the new
campus tabloid from causing too much trouble. Then the speech began
to get uncomfortable. Dean James handled municipal officials who "had

their hands out"; his job was to keep former Yale President Benno Schmidt "clean." He talked in graphic detail about his time in Vietnam and his subsequent experience with Vietnamese students. And then he told the story of how *Rumpus* upset a wealthy donor by running an article titled "Three Men and a Courtyard," which reported on an early-morning courtyard tryst that concluded with the participants standing up and waking the entire college by loudly singing the Turkish national anthem (which could not possibly be true, Dean James surmised, because "who the heck would recognize the Turkish national anthem?").

Through it all, *Rumpus* alumni nodded and laughed nervously. But everyone believed he was a former dean representing the university. That is, until "Dean James" concluded by telling us that as a result of the Turkish story and the upset donor, Yale terminated his employment. As a result, he hasn't had a steady paycheck in years, can no longer afford his medication, and given the tabloid's causal role, planned to visit with "each and every one of you" over the course of the reunion to see "what you can afford."

He added, "I'll gladly take checks or whatever cash you have on hand."

Unemployment and employment are often game-changers. This explains why no faster + cheaper alternative is getting as much attention as the one where students get hired first.

• • •

It seems as if everyone's talking about apprenticeships; they were the Trump Administration's first postsecondary education initiative; in June 2017, President Trump signed an executive order aiming to use apprenticeships to train five million Americans who would otherwise be disconnected from the labor market. Currently, there are only about half a million apprentices in the United States.

Research shows that apprenticeships provide students with a remarkable return on investment: students who complete apprenticeships earn nearly $250,000 more over the course of their careers than comparable students who don't complete an apprenticeship.[1] And notably, apprenticeships are in the upper-right quadrant of our matrix: rather than paying upfront for an uncertain outcome, you learn while already in a job.

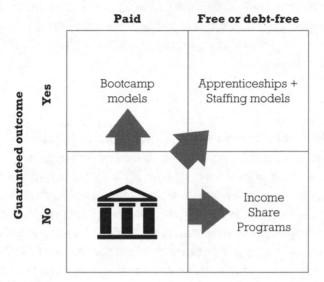

While many more people may believe they have had "apprenticeships"—including contestants on the President's former reality show—technically an apprenticeship is an employer-sponsored training program registered with the U.S. Department of Labor. Apprentices are employees, hired by the employer. The difference between apprentices and other new employees is that apprentices receive on-the-job training from an experienced mentor plus a prescribed program of related technical instruction (RTI) to move the apprentice to full occupational proficiency over a period of one to six years. In return, employers may start apprentices at a lower wage ($15 per hour, on average).[2]

While apprenticeships are more common than you think—more than 150,000 companies have programs—one reason you may not have considered them is that 80 percent of American apprenticeships are in the traditional building and industrial trades, with a significant percentage sponsored by unions rather than employers. The most common apprenticeships in the United States are for electricians, plumbers, carpenters, and iron and steel workers.

Herein lies the problem. Policy makers love to talk about training welders, but few parents who attended college and work in white-collar jobs are excited about sending their child down an apprenticeship path that's

historically been blue collar, involving manual labor and union membership. But this is proving to be a false choice. Emerging digital apprenticeships provide pathways for exactly the same entry-level jobs in growing
sectors of the economy as bootcamps or income share programs or even
four-year colleges.

• • •

While the countries most identified with successful apprenticeship programs are in Central Europe (Germany and Switzerland), it's unlikely
America will be able to copy this model. The German apprenticeship
model—generally viewed as a major contributor to Germany's low levels of
youth unemployment, as well as manufacturing strength—is a unique product of an ecosystem of government support and engagement by employers, chambers of commerce (membership is mandatory for employers and
membership fees are high), trade unions, and vocational tracking starting
in high school that seems impossible to replicate here. Nearly half of all German high school students graduate into apprenticeship programs instead
of pursuing a university degree.[3]

But about fifteen years ago, with apprentices about the same percentage of the workforce as the United States, the UK found itself asking how
it could expand apprenticeships beyond traditional building and industrial
trades—specifically looking at growing sectors of the economy like technology, media, health care, and financial services. The government pro-
mulgated apprenticeship standards for 1,500 different occupations. Today
approximately 400,000 apprentices are at work across the UK—nearly five
times the rate of the United States—in a wide range of industries, with
strong growth in technology.

How did the UK do it? One of the keys has been clarifying how the
training gets funded; employers aren't excited about paying for the cost
of training in addition to apprentice wages. Another is the emergence of
apprenticeship service providers (ASPs)—intermediaries that establish,
manage, and deliver apprenticeship programs on behalf of employers,
standing between the employer, the apprentice, and the government and
"hiding the wiring" for all. There are nearly eight hundred such intermediaries in the UK.

If ASPs sound like last-mile providers, that's because they are. ASPs
supply last-mile training to candidates, but placement is even easier because

candidates are in the job from day one. This is why Euan Blair, son of former UK Prime Minister Tony Blair, has spent several years creating WhiteHat, a London-based ASP that is creating the "Ivy League of apprenticeships."[4]

"If [apprenticeships are] going to be taken seriously, they can't just be seen as the option for kids who aren't that academically bright, who were never going to go to university anyway," said Blair. "We want a situation where smart kids, who could go to Oxbridge or [other top] universities, have to make a difficult decision: 'Do I go down that route, or do I join this incredible apprenticeship scheme at a top UK corporate or really exciting tech start-up?'"[5]

WhiteHat calls itself a "talent accelerator for future leaders" and to the extent it uses the term *apprentices*, it applies the prefix *digital*. WhiteHat works with 120 leading employers such as Burberry, Nomura, and the pharmaceutical company Wellcome. Applicants go through a lengthy admissions process before being matched with an employer and starting work in a range of digital apprenticeships: digital marketing, finance, HR, and business development. While working, students participate in WhiteHat-led RTI for five to ten hours per week—typically onsite at the employer with the support of an online platform. After a minimum period of twelve months, employers are expected to hire apprentices as regular employees with a commensurate salary bump.

Employers are keen to have WhiteHat manage their digital apprenticeships because WhiteHat handles everything: recruitment, training, securing government funds to cover the training, and managing the paperwork that is part and parcel of dealing with the government. Plus, according to Blair, apprentices stay with employers twice as long as entry-level university graduates. To date, WhiteHat has brought on more than two hundred apprentices.

● ● ●

At university, I was just going through the motions. Now I feel like I'm progressing, really moving in the right direction.

—*Chrish Kumar, WhiteHat*

Chrish Kumar is a bright young Londoner who learned easily in high school and planned to pursue a career as an accountant. But he abandoned that plan when he dropped out of his accounting program at Brunel University, London.

Why did he drop out? First, finances. Since his older brother had gone to university a few years prior, annual tuition had risen from £3,000 to £9,000 ($4,000 to $12,000) per year. "In addition to that, I attempted to live away from home and property prices are ridiculous," said Chrish. "My room cost £130 ($175) per week. I was trying to sustain myself off money from a part-time job at a gas station. It didn't seem worth it."

Second, when Chrish picked economics, he thought it would be different. In high school he loved economics—the theory, the history, the social ramifications. He still reads *The Economist* every day. It promised a wide range of prospects and directions. "But in first-year economics," he said, "we didn't study the theory behind it or anything interesting. We just looked at modules and plugged in equations. It was quite dry."

Third, Chrish wanted real work experience. His older brother had a challenging time finding a job. Employers wanted experience and technical knowledge. Chrish feared racking up more debt in university and having the same problems as his brother.

At school, Chrish heard mention of apprenticeship programs. Intrigued, he started investigating online, filled out the WhiteHat application, and was invited to an assessment day. He completed math and English assessments, then moved on to the personality and field assessments. "I sat face to face with the WhiteHat interviewer who asked questions about the way I work, how I like to work, my previous work experiences," he said. "They wanted to figure out what would be a good fit."

WhiteHat began looking for placements and setting up interviews with employers. "They spend a lot of time prepping you for an interview," Chrish recalled. "They taught us how to research a company, gave a list of possible questions, and helped show me the methodology behind giving a good answer. After the interview, WhiteHat spoke with the employer and debriefed me on how I did so I could use the feedback to improve next time."

After his second interview through WhiteHat, Chrish was offered an apprenticeship in the accounting department of an advertising agency. He's now a full-time apprentice there and his plan to become an accountant has been reactivated. The WhiteHat training is preparing him to obtain his qualification for the Association of Accounting Technicians (AAT), a UK qualification and professional organization for vocational accountants.

Through his apprenticeship, Chrish has learned a lot about organizational skills, time management, and attention to detail. "When you make a mistake in this role, it will come back to bite you later," he said. "Time management is not about getting things done as fast as possible; it's about taking your time and getting things done right the first time. Then you don't have to spend time fixing mistakes later. I didn't learn any of this at university. University was about getting stuff done at the last minute."

Reflecting on his decisions, and despite student loans he hasn't begun to pay back yet, Chrish has no regrets. "White Hat was a great opportunity," he said. "I'm getting a lot out of it. I made a good move. They helped me figure out what was a good fit for me and encouraged me to be picky, to find a job I'd really enjoy. Meanwhile, my brother, who now works as an analyst, is facing full loan payback for four years. Part of him wishes he did what I'm doing now."

●　●　●

You can pay for a university degree and put in the work, but you can't pay for experience.

—*Sami Mustafa, WhiteHat*

Unlike Chrish, Sami Mustafa bypassed university completely. But when he was in high school, Sami was obsessed with going to university. No one in his family had a degree. He dreamed of attending the University of Kent to study business and finance. "I was so set on going that when I didn't get in, I repeated my A-levels to bring up my grades," he said. "I took a whole year out of my life just so I could get in."

It worked. Sami was accepted to Kent on his second attempt. But then something happened that Sami can barely explain: he changed his mind. "I can only call it a hunch," he said. "An idea hit me that I could do what I want to do without university. Too many people go for the wrong reasons. Schools have too many people to cater to, the teachers don't have practical skillsets. University degrees aren't respected as much as they were twenty years ago." On this hunch, Sami deferred his acceptance to Kent for a year and started applying to entry-level finance jobs.

On getmyfirstjob.co.uk, Sami kept seeing advertisements for White-Hat. He filled out a short, interactive form and the next day received a call inviting him in for assessments. His first interview through WhiteHat was with Portland, a communications consulting and PR firm. He wasn't a fit for the open position, but they liked Sami so much they created a position for him as a junior finance assistant.

"I couldn't believe they created a job for me," Sami said. "I was so nervous before the interview that I called WhiteHat. They coached me through the whole thing. I had done other interviews before, not through WhiteHat, and I wasn't offered any jobs, then my first one through White Hat was a success."

Sami is eight months into his contract and he doesn't dream about going to Kent anymore. "For the first few months I did," he said. "I thought, 'What if?' But now I know I love my job. I have no debt. To get a degree, I would be £50,000 ($67,500) plus in debt, and I'd lose out on the experience. There are some skills you can only learn from experience. When I started, I was so scared to pick up a phone and chase people for money. You can't learn that in a classroom. As an apprentice, you're thrown into the deep end.

"I think I am a bit more skilled than someone who chose university," Sami continued. "I'll already have three or four years' experience on the job while they're looking for their first job. I hope to have a promotion and three specific professional qualifications by then."

• • •

The United States remains well behind the UK in terms of digital apprenticeships, primarily because of confusion around who funds the training, and a lack of independent (i.e., nonunion, nongovernment) ASPs with an incentive to scale. Nonetheless, digital apprenticeships are emerging in a range of new sectors, driven by a combination of state governments, nonprofit organizations, and employers themselves.

America's biggest apprenticeship success story is in South Carolina, where Brad Neese leads a state-sponsored program called Apprenticeship Carolina, affiliated with the South Carolina Technical College system. Starting about a decade ago, the goal of Apprenticeship Carolina was to develop digital apprenticeships in advanced manufacturing, health care, pharmacy, and IT. Today, more than five thousand apprentices work at nearly one thousand companies throughout South Carolina while receiving RTI through a technical college.[6] Most students secure financial aid to cover the cost of the training.

Another factor in the growth of apprenticeships in South Carolina is, actually, Germany. South Carolina is the US base for many large German companies such as BMW and Bosch. These employers don't need to be convinced of the value of apprenticeships; they already operate major apprenticeship programs back home.

There is also Opportunity@Work, a nonprofit organization dedicated to closing the skills gap. Opportunity@Work is the force behind TechHire, an effort to foster "apprenticeships" in technology by finding grants to cover the cost of training. (TechHire programs aren't registered apprenticeships, but they provide a similar structure of technical training connected to paid employment.)

In Eastern Kentucky, TechHire secured a $2.7 million grant from the Appalachian Regional Commission to fund a six-month software development training program. Seeing a source of qualified candidates, employers flocked to sign up, paying apprentices like Nichole Clark $400 per week. After a four-month training program and two months of work at Interapt, a software development and consulting firm, Nichole was hired into a $40,000 per year job—about twice what she made working at Pizza Hut.[7] There are TechHire programs in seventy-two communities across thirty-three states. In less than three years, TechHire has placed more than five thousand workers into jobs.

In the absence of intermediaries like Apprenticeship Carolina or TechHire, a handful of employers have such a shortage of technical talent that they're stepping up themselves. Many of these American pioneers are divisions of German companies. Siemens has launched programs in four states (Alabama, California, Georgia, and North Carolina) and has plans for Louisiana, Pennsylvania, South Carolina, and Texas. The Siemens programs are advanced manufacturing apprenticeships (e.g., building gas turbines), typically in partnership with local community colleges. At the end of four years, apprentices receive an associate's degree, a journeyman's certificate, and a job making $50,000. According to Judy Marks, President of Siemens in the United States, apprenticeship programs are a "strategic investment in people and talent and our future"—and not an inconsiderable one considering that Siemens is paying for the cost of the training.[8] In Chicago, the German American Chamber of Commerce helped create an apprenticeship program for thirty employers, half of which are German subsidiaries. The Chamber itself performs a part of the role of an ASP.[9]

One surprising industry where employers have taken the initiative on digital apprenticeships is insurance—or maybe not surprising because few young people dream of careers in insurance. But Aon, the Hartford, and Zurich all operate apprenticeship programs. Aon offers apprenticeships in insurance, technology, and human resources in partnership with a Chicago community college while paying a salary of $35,000. Bridget Gainer, VP for global public affairs at Aon, said the program originated after the company realized it was experiencing a "distracting" level of turnover in certain entry-level positions. Believing that overqualified people would take the jobs and then leave in eighteen months, Aon abandoned its degree requirement and launched its apprenticeship program to "fill positions and reduce turnover . . . It is neither [a] charity nor a job creation program."[10]

Like Siemens, Aon covers the cost of tuition as long as apprentices remain at the company. Two evenings each week, Aon apprentices head over to the college campus for insurance industry–specific classes. Once a week, apprentices receive counseling from a coach to help balance work, school, and their personal lives. At the end of two years, Aon apprentices receive an associate's degree in business management with a concentration in insurance, technology, or HR—not to mention a great job. Apprentices who complete the program are guaranteed full-time positions.[11] Aon received 285 applicants for its first class of twenty-five apprentices and plans to start new classes every year.[12]

The Hartford is expanding its new insurance claims apprenticeship program to two hundred participants by 2020. The Hartford has obtained grant funding for its program and its insurance curriculum is delivered online by Rio Salado College.[13] Zurich North America also received grant funding to cover the cost of its training, which is delivered by a local community college. Zurich's apprenticeships are in both claims and underwriting and involve weekly classes at the community college. To provide apprentices with an incentive to complete the program, any apprentice who drops out or leaves within a year of completing the program is contractually obliged to repay the cost of tuition.[14]

Enthusiasm for apprenticeships in insurance appears to be spilling over to other financial services. Wells Fargo has launched an apprenticeship program initially targeting military veterans (GI Bill benefits cover the cost of training). Apprenticeships are available for financial crimes specialist, collections manager, and branch manager. Once participants complete the program, they can expect an average starting salary of $60,000.[15] JP Morgan Chase, as well, has launched a small program in Houston with plans to hire forty apprentices in tech-related jobs.[16]

Another new area for apprenticeships is for pharmacy technicians—yes, the same job for which Besomebody is planning brief bootcamps. CVS Health, the pharmacy giant, is offering pharm tech apprenticeships in Arkansas, Michigan, Missouri, Rhode Island, Texas, and Wisconsin in partnership with local community colleges. President Obama recognized the CVS apprenticeship program in his 2015 State of the Union Address.[17] Finally, in an auspicious sign for apprenticeships, Accenture and Amazon have launched apprenticeships for technology positions such as data center technicians and cloud support associates.[18]

While the connection between apprenticeship training and government funding will likely become clearer in the next few years—allowing for broader deployment beyond what piecemeal grants or community college partnerships can support—another possibility is that students are willing to pay for the cost of apprenticeship training themselves. As more employers consider launching their own apprenticeship programs in the next few years, Meritize—the innovative student lending company—is talking to employers and emerging ASPs about providing loans for apprenticeship training. Meritize's Apprenticeship Financing Program provides a loan for tuition and cost of living that is cosigned by the apprentice and employer. For as long as the apprentice remains employed, employers make payments on the loan. This provides a major retention benefit for the employer: paying off the cost of apprenticeship training for employees who stay five years or more is a good investment.

The CEO of Aon acknowledges that apprenticeships "definitely work . . . the question is whether we can scale it effectively."[19] All the new energy around apprenticeships is actually spawning the first ASPs in the United States. Like WhiteHat, Franklin Apprenticeships aims to help dozens or hundreds of employers launch digital apprenticeships. Founded by a couple of experienced apprenticeship executives from Britain, Franklin has contracts with several large US employers, as well as with CompTIA, the IT industry association, and plans to launch programs beginning in 2018. Another ASP, Elite Apprentices, a subsidiary of UK ASP Middleton Murray, has just launched in San Francisco, targeting technology companies. Both

Franklin and Elite hope to convince US employers that, with their support, apprenticeships are worth a try. As Kimberly Nichols, CEO of Franklin, said, "Apprenticeships are sold, not bought."[20]

We're also seeing the launch of apprenticeships on an outsourced basis. Techtonic Group is a Boulder-based software development shop that is simultaneously a registered apprenticeship program. Techtonic hires and trains apprentices and, by week five or six, apprentices shadow more experienced software developers. After a few months, apprentices are billing meaningful hours on meaningful client projects. A year later, Techtonic clients are invited to hire the software apprentices they've been working with and whose work they've seen, which radically reduces the risk of entry-level hiring.

Outsourced apprenticeships are a promising model for achieving scale. Every employer outsources services. A wide range of IT services are commonly outsourced, as are accounting, payroll, legal, insurance, real estate, sales, customer support, human resources, staffing, consulting, marketing, public relations, and design. While midsize and large companies are likely to have employees in these functions, most also contract with providers for these services.

Though many service providers are accustomed to having their talent poached by clients, few have built a business model around it; Techtonic has done so, and others will follow. Think of a call center providing a range of customer support and inside sales functions for your firm. You probably have employees in sales and customer service roles but with a clear division as to what functions are outsourced. What you're less clear about is how or who to hire for these internal roles, and how much to rely on (lower-cost) entry-level employees as opposed to (higher-cost) employees with experience. When your call center provider also becomes a provider of outsourced apprenticeships, it will continue to charge you for providing customer service and sales and now also charge you a placement fee for hiring the purpose-trained and proven entry-level talent that's been working for you for the past year or two. That's highly attractive for employers, and replicable across a range of industries. American employers have led the world in outsourcing non-core business functions. Entry-level hiring—via outsourced apprenticeships—could be next.

● ● ●

While apprenticeships are an increasingly popular alternative to college, several staffing companies—firms that hire workers and then staff them out to clients—are facilitating smoother pathways to good jobs, allowing young Americans to get to work in growing industries more easily than before. As with bootcamps, the initial focus of staffing firms has been college graduates. But within a few years staffing companies that incorporate last-mile training will be providing faster + cheaper alternatives to college for tens of thousands of students. These emerging staffing models should be on everyone's radar.

You probably don't realize it, but staffing is a gigantic business. Staffing firms like Manpower, Allegis, Adecco, Randstad, and Kelly Services hire about 14 percent of the nation's workforce. In 2015, US staffing firms hired a total of 15.6 million temporary and contract employees and generated about $150 billion in revenue. In the past decade, staffing employment has grown twice as fast as the economy and six times faster than overall employment.[21] Perhaps as many as 20 million Americans earn a living via a staffing firm. Many of these staffed jobs are temporary or seasonal, but most are effectively full-time work. The *Wall Street Journal* has reported that Google has roughly the same number of staffed resources as full-time employees. Other large employers such as Bank of America, Verizon, and FedEx also engage thousands of contractors.[22]

Employers are going to great lengths to avoid hiring, and staffing has become a primary alternative workforce strategy for finding employees. Accenture has predicted that within a decade, one of the two thousand largest companies in the world will have "no full-time employees outside of the C-suite."[23]

Deciding to source labor through a staffing firm can be strategic. Outsourcing noncore jobs allows employers to focus on what they do best. But for most companies it's about cost. Full-time employees require benefits; they may be unionized; they may also expect higher compensation when being hired by IBM as opposed to by Allegis. Outsourcing allows companies to limit their commitment. Projects and products are increasingly viewed like Hollywood movies where talent is hired for the duration of the project, then disbanded so studios have no further financial obligations.

But staffing can also be about talent. Staffing companies have established recruitment channels and strategies that may be able to produce talent of greater quantity or quality for a particular industry and job function.

This is where last-mile training comes into play. In areas of talent shortages, staffing firms are increasingly taking on responsibility for last-mile training themselves.

From the standpoint of underemployed Millennials, staffing is also a promising strategy for closing the skills gap. In a completely efficient market, everyone would be hired immediately into a job that perfectly suits current competencies and future potential. But that's not the way it works in real life where there's a lot of friction. The paperwork required to hire employees, add them to benefits programs, arrange for direct deposit, etc., is substantial. One recent estimate is that the preliminary work involved in hiring an employee takes up to six weeks and costs $4,000.[24] The paperwork involved in terminating a bad hire is even worse. According to one expert, bad hires can cost employers as much as $240,000—a petrifying sum.[25]

The primary source of hiring friction isn't imperfect information but rather cost and risk. In other words, employers aren't merely looking for someone to stand up and vouch that candidate A is a good match for a given open position, although sometimes that suffices (i.e., referral from current employer). Hiring friction won't be materially reduced unless and until that someone offers to bear some/most of the cost and risk of hiring. This is what staffing companies do when they provide skilled, hand-picked (and often trained) candidates on an evaluation-to-hire basis. This means employers aren't hiring until candidates have proven they can do the job over a trial period that typically lasts multiple months. Staffing companies reduce hiring friction because they bear the risk and cost of training and hiring.

Revature is a great example. Srikanth Ramachandran grew up in Chennai, India, where he demonstrated an entrepreneurial bent at an early age. In high school, he built a business assembling and selling computers. He majored in computer science at the University of Madras and moved to the United States in the late 1990s. In 2003, he started Revature, an IT staffing company that hired experienced software developers and staffed them out to clients. Revature grew each year for the next decade, becoming a 250-person, $30 million business.

Around 2011, Ramachandran recognized that many of Revature's clients also had a need for entry-level software developers. He had a simple and powerful idea: recruit high-aptitude college graduates with basic coding skills and provide free training on the specific skills his clients were seeking. Initially the demand was modest and Ramachandran turned a single office at Revature's Herndon, Virginia, headquarters into a classroom. But before long, he recognized he had a tiger by the tail. His clients loved the purpose-trained candidates he was supplying. Revature candidates were young, motivated, relatively inexpensive, and they "hadn't learned the wrong things." More offices became classrooms, and more of Revature's business shifted to entry-level candidates. Revature even hired a recruiter to visit local Virginia campuses.

Fast forward to today: Revature has recruited, trained, and hired more than four thousand college students or recent graduates. The company has partnerships with universities such as the City University of New York, Arizona State, University of South Florida, Florida State, University of North Carolina at Charlotte, University of Virginia, University of Texas at Arlington, University of Missouri, Davidson College, and University of Maryland University College. Revature offers free ten- to twelve-week advanced training programs on campus for qualified applicants. The deal for students is the opposite of traditional college: a guaranteed outcome, free training, and students are hired before they start training (they also receive housing). Once they complete the training, Revature staffs students out to any one of hundreds of clients.

Students qualify by demonstrating basic coding aptitude. They can do this through an undergraduate computer science major, by showing relevant coursework, or through completing an online project or two. It's important that students know Java before starting the training program, because Revature's training is advanced and based on precisely the technologies or languages clients are seeking. One client may want twenty new DevOps engineers. Another may want fifteen new engineers who have mastered AngularJS. Revature takes orders from clients and starts cohorts almost every week across its training centers at university partners, and at its office in Virginia. Clients hire Revature engineers about 90 percent of the time, so Revature provides a pathway not only to a good first job but also to a good second job.

● ● ●

I probably wouldn't have gotten this position at Capital One just from going to the university I went to.

—*Yasmine Sadid, Revature*

Yasmine Sadid took accelerated and honors courses through high school. She achieved a high enough GPA and ACT score that she was accepted into a program where she took university courses during her last two years of high school. But even with this head start, when she graduated from Kent State University with a degree in computer science, she couldn't find a job.

"In general, I viewed computer science as a good degree to have," she said, "but the curriculum wasn't exactly what employers were looking for." The core language was C++. All the projects used C++. The program provided a "good theoretical understanding of computing in general"—but not much hands-on experience. "We did projects," she said, "but usually they were not very practical and didn't apply to everyday work situations. Under certain professors, I felt a gap between what I was doing in class and real-life application." Getting a job wasn't really emphasized in her program.

Yasmine graduated in May 2015 and started looking for jobs. She received some responses, landed a few interviews, and then would hear they'd chosen a different candidate. She never received any feedback about what she was lacking. She took a part-time job working as a realtor's assistant while continuing to search.

"I underestimated how difficult it would be to get a job," she said. "C++ is focused around the outward-oriented paradigm, but Java and C# are what companies are looking for. They are also looking for web development skills and experience; I wasn't strong in that. There were no Java courses at Kent State. I never took a course in web development, but I used HTML and JavaScript in some projects, and I didn't think I would need more than that."

A year into her job search she saw a posting on Glassdoor for Revature. She completed an assessment. "It wasn't technically difficult," she said. "It had questions that people who know something about coding should be able to answer." She passed and submitted her résumé. "The same day, I got a call from a recruiter, had an in-person interview, and the interviewer said they thought I'd fit their program well."

Yasmine decided to go for it. She relocated to Richmond, Virginia, and started the three-month training program. "I learned a lot in three months. I didn't have any formal training in Java. Conceptually, it was like what I learned in university but in a different, more widely used language. In the first two weeks, we covered core Java and SQL. After that we covered server-sized Java and JavaScript in more depth than I had covered in school. Then we covered some frameworks—Hibernate and Spring, frameworks I hadn't heard of."

A framework is an extension of the language that is used to simplify a task. It's something coders use regularly to streamline the web development process. "In university, there was no talk of frameworks," Yasmine said. "We learned how to write everything out from scratch. But at a job, there's no need to write out everything from scratch because someone's already done that. If you wrote out everything from scratch in the job world, things that get released in a couple of months would take a couple of years."

Comparing her twelve weeks at Revature to her experience at Kent State, Yasmine said, "Revature was stressful in a different way than school is stressful. It was a whole lot of information packed into a small time window. It was enjoyable in the sense that I knew I would use the skills at my job, and that if I got comfortable with the material I would be more comfortable in my job. In school, there was an underlying question as to whether a project would apply to anything real. I didn't really know what developers did in the job world when I was at Kent State."

After she finished her training at Revature and passed the final comprehensive interview, Revature helped Yasmine build her résumé and send it out to various clients. They call this the marketing stage. "Within two weeks I had an interview with Capital One," she said. "It was shorter than I thought—only twenty minutes long with two middle developers—but high-pressure. It was a technically oriented interview with no behavioral questions." A week later, she found out she had passed the interview and would be starting her contract at Capital One.

Yasmine describes Capital One as her ideal working environment. "I didn't know about the company, beyond the fact that it was a bank, until I started working there," she said. "It's like a college campus atmosphere—ten buildings four levels high, gardens, sports complexes, a wildlife preserve—a beautiful environment to work in. The work is inspired. We're constantly pressing to make advancements, but at the same time it's not an oppressive atmosphere. There are a lot of exciting, collaborative projects going on. We don't work in cubicles; we work in open desk spaces. You can go for a walk or work in a different seating area. You're not expected to sit at your desk for hours on end."

Yasmine is thrilled with how Revature jump-started her career. "Revature gave me a lot more confidence," she said. "I believe it took me longer to get a job out of school because I lost confidence in myself after my initial job search. Being rejected was disheartening. I knew I needed to improve my performance in a measurable way, because clearly my degree wasn't enough."

• • •

Cook Systems is another IT staffing company that has launched its own bootcamp program. Founder Wayne Cook had previously been CIO at a bank and had run a successful hardware training program for new hires. He thought such a model could work for his new company.

Cook's last-mile training program is called FastTrack'D. It's a free eight-week program for Java and .Net software development. Like Revature, FastTrack'D provides students with a place to live while they're learning. Cook has run FastTrack'D programs in Memphis, Dallas, Atlanta, and Jacksonville. While Cook doesn't guarantee jobs to those who complete the training program, the company has hired 85 percent of all graduates. COO Brad Weeks reports hundreds of graduates, with over 90 percent completing their contract with Cook and moving on to the client or other coding positions.

Unlike Revature, Cook's program doesn't require prior coding experience. Candidates must only demonstrate aptitude. Cook also doesn't require that candidates have degrees. Weeks estimates that nearly half of FastTrack'D students have entered without college degrees.

• • •

I love the path I took. I envisioned what I wanted to do for my career, and once I got to the program I knew I was there. I get to solve problems and do puzzles all day.

—*Quinton Bolt, Cook Systems*

Quinton Bolt did not expect much from his computer science program at North West Mississippi Community College. That was the school he chose after dropping out of high school, trying home schooling, and then getting a GED. His goal was to transfer to Mississippi State University and get a degree in computer science. But by second semester, Quinton had enough.

"It was demotivating," he said. "The classes were boring. I already knew a bit about programming and computer science in general. I started browsing LinkedIn and found Cook Systems' FastTrack'D program. They didn't require much educational background, it was free, local, and provided a good chance of getting a job after. I had nothing to lose."

His application to FastTrack'D involved an online logic quiz, a programming assessment, a technical interview, and an interpersonal interview. He got in and decided to drop out of college. His decision was soon validated.

"In the first week, they covered all I'd learned about web design in two semesters of college and on my own," Quinton said. "I loved how passionate the instructors were. They were insanely good developers. And they had gone through the FastTrack'D program too and experienced real-world challenges and problems, as opposed to college professors who went to college and then taught without having any development experience."

Quinton's cohort of fifteen students met in a conference room-turned-classroom for eight hours a day, Monday through Friday, for eight weeks. The first half of the day involved a lecture, the other half a technical assignment. "We covered core Java, Java Enterprise, Spring, Hibernate related to Java, HTML, CSS, JavaScript, and Angular," Quinton said. "They cover everything you need to know for full-stack Java development, using Angular for front end."

Students had to complete three assessments. The first involved designing a server where clients could chat back and forth. The second was a back end for a Twitter-like service. The third, the front end for the same. "Assessments lasted two to three days," Quinton explained. "The final assessment was in groups. We developed skills you need to work as a team and to collaborate with other developers, both technically and interpersonally. The instructors stepped back initially and let us try to figure it out ourselves. It was trial by fire. Later they provided some guidance on how to work together, how to communicate, how to keep track of what needs to be done when you're working on a problem with a group." People were cut from the program after each assessment. In the end, ten out of the initial fifteen students graduated. Sound harsh? Quinton actually liked the competitive nature of the program. "I see it as a positive," he said. "That drew me in. It presented as a challenge and I took it seriously."

FastTrack'D also helped Quinton with soft skills and interview preparation. "Throughout the course, instructors monitor interpersonal development," he said. "They were always watching, noticing how students acted, and the skills they had—like handling pressure and working in teams."

They spent time on mock interviews and practicing interview skills. But Quinton was offered a contract with FedEx without any interview. "FedEx trusts Cook Systems."

Quinton is seven months into an eleven-month contract with FedEx, which he expects will be renewed. "I use all the skills I learned in the FastTrack'D program at FedEx," he said. "I helped them transition from older technology to newer technology using the skills and content I learned in the course."

Reflecting on his path, Quinton said, "If I hadn't found this program, I'd be starting my third year at North West or transferring to Mississippi State, paying for it with student loans. I have one friend who is at college studying computer science. He's former military, so he gets money for college and he doesn't want to throw it away. But he saw the projects I did in FastTrack'D and wishes he could do the same."

• • •

Staffing models can be so helpful at creating clear pathways to good first jobs that some firms flourish even before adding last-mile training. Avenica is one such example. Founded almost twenty years ago as GradStaff, Avenica now has seven offices located around the country. Avenica bridges the gap from college to career for thousands of new graduates each year by soliciting résumés from seniors and new college graduates, analyzing their competencies according to a rubric developed at the University of Minnesota, and matching candidates to posted entry-level jobs (including jobs where Avenica has convinced clients to try entry-level candidates). Avenica matches candidates to positions and prepares and schedules them for interviews. When employers nod in the direction of Avenica candidates, Avenica hires them and staffs them out for a four-month evaluation period. Employers love the ability to evaluate candidates on a trial basis before committing to hire. And more than 85 percent of the time, that's exactly what they do.

In 2017, Avenica placed students from nearly four hundred universities. The service is free of charge to students. According to CEO Brian Weed, "Millennials are struggling under the weight of student loan debt and persistently high levels of underemployment. Avenica helps provide pathways to good careers for new college graduates."

Avenica plans to launch a series of last-mile training programs across a range of industries. Starting in 2018, following an assessment of their competencies, students may be invited to participate in a free last-mile train-ing program, which will increase their chances of being placed by Avenica.

● ● ●

I must have applied to 50 positions . . . I didn't get one interview.

—*Trinae Adebayo, Avenica*

Trinae Adebayo graduated from Arizona State University in 2014 with a degree in sociology. She started applying for jobs a couple of months before graduation. Since Trinae had worked as a test proctor at ASU, she started her job search close to home. She applied for every position at the university that she thought she was qualified for. "I tried for TA jobs, desk jobs, admin-istrative jobs, jobs in the financial aid department," she said. She sought help on her résumé from career services but still didn't get any responses.

Next up was Monster and other job sites. She applied to anything she thought might fit. "I just needed something to pay the bills," she said. She got a few calls, but mostly no feedback at all. As her job search plodded on, she found a link to Avenica on ASU's career site portal.

Jessica from Avenica's Phoenix office called Trinae back immediately to schedule an interview. "I interviewed with Jessica on the day of my gradu-ation," Trinae said. "It was a chaotic day, getting to the interview and back in time, but Jessica gave me helpful feedback. We discussed my strengths and worked on how to highlight them on my résumé. She told me to add my high school experience working at my parents' restaurant. I didn't think it was relevant so I had left it out. And she helped me prepare for interviews by giving me common questions and advising me on how to look professional. I was grateful for her help and told her I'd take anything."

Avenica matched Trinae to an open account associate position with the Doctors Company, a medical malpractice insurance firm. Jessica submitted Trinae's updated résumé and sent Trinae information about the Doctors Company so she could prepare for the interview. "Jessica gave me lots of information on the company and the job description," Trinae said. "I had a breakdown of tasks the job required so I was prepared to talk about my relevant skills from past work experiences."

On the day of the interview, Trinae felt nervous but prepared. "I left the interview thinking that I answered everything properly and as I had rehearsed," she said. "No questions caught me off guard." Trinae got the job and started in June 2014. A year later, she was promoted to account manager. She got along well with her coworkers and was earning more than her friends from college.

Although Trinae wasn't passionate about insurance, her good first job with the Doctor's Company allowed her to make her loan payments while completing a master's in sociology at ASU. She now works with a nonprofit organization running workshops for third and fourth graders on physical and sexual abuse.

"I didn't think the job in insurance would help me get my current job," she said. "But once I started, someone on the hiring committee disclosed to me that the reason they pushed my résumé forward was because they needed help with budgeting and desk work. They thought that I'd be good with Excel and strong in email communications because of my experience working in insurance. The job I got through Avenica helped me stand out."

CHAPTER 7 • KEY POINTS

- Faster + cheaper alternatives with guaranteed employment outcomes may be even more attractive than college MVPs.
- Digital apprenticeships—organized by employers and emerging apprenticeship service providers—provide relevant training for new collar careers as students are paid.
- Staffing and placement models incorporating last-mile training provide a similarly attractive value proposition and are scaling rapidly.
- Not only do these pathways provide guaranteed employment outcomes, they're entirely free to students.

CHAPTER 8

Online Bootcamps (an Oxymoron) and Competency Marketplaces

GRIFF: I want to go to college.

RICHARD: College? You got to be . . . I'm sorry. Listen, Griff, I'll make you a deal. You help me get these kids to learn and I promise you, I will do everything in my power to get you into college.

GRIFF: Don't try to play me, Mr. Clark. I've been promised stuff before that hasn't come true. I'm saying, where would I get the money for college from?

RICHARD: You ever hear of scholarships? Well . . . you probably won't get any of those. But there are plenty of other ways. I promise you.

—*High School High (1996)*

M y first exposure to the power of technology in higher education occurred junior year. The gray-box security phones placed
around campus buildings were upgraded. The new phones were
superior in several respects. First, they were Yale blue. Second, they featured
a big red alarm button. Third, instead of a receiver, they had a speaker that
operated at high volume. The complete package screamed security.

My roommates and I had great affection for the gray-box phone outside
our dormitory. Someone had written the phone's five-digit number inside
the box and we spent countless hours calling the phone to see if a passerby
might pick up. If someone did, we'd pretend to be campus security and ask
what was in their backpack, or we'd be trying to deliver a pizza, or we'd
casually offer some Grey Poupon. We would compete to keep ambulating
interlocutors on the phone as long as possible.

On the day our gray box was replaced with a gleaming new blue phone,
we dialed the five-digit number. Lo and behold, the phone picked up automatically, providing a booming megaphone for a group of sophomores on
the cusp of redefining sophomoric.

Naturally, we felt compelled to share our discovery through *Rumpus,*
the college tabloid we'd recently founded. So we found one of the few phones
on campus with caller ID and divided Yale into quadrants—each of us
charged with running or biking from blue phone to blue phone and calling
into the central number with our coordinates. A friend at central wrote
down each number and location. By the end of the night, everyone was
exhausted.

The resulting product was a Blue Phone Map we published for the entire
campus as a Valentine's Day present. Ostensibly for security purposes (i.e.,
follow your friend as she walks back to her room), students immediately
began exploring the many different ways of playing the "Hey, I'm stuck in
this blue box" joke. Predictably, we were stuck for some time in the Dean's
office, attempting to explain ourselves.

• • •

Technology has always had the potential to upend the academic enterprise.
In the late 1990s, as I began working in higher education, the *New York
Times* mused about the transformative potential of online education: "Just
by doing what he does every day, a teacher potentially could grow rich
instructing a class consisting of a million students . . . 'Faculty are dreaming

of returns that are probably multiples of their lifetime net worth,' said Kim Clark, dean of the Harvard Business School."[1]

As anyone who has taken an online course will tell you, none of this came to pass. Nearly twenty years ago a company called UNext—founded by disgraced junk bond king Michael Milken—spent $180 million to build simulation-based business courses with schools like Columbia, Stanford, and the University of Chicago, only to disappear several years later. No one has really tried to do this since. Why bother, when more than 3 million students are enrolled in online degree programs that are largely text-based, translated from traditional on-ground college courses in such a literal manner that it's almost robotic: read material, participate in discussion, submit weekly assignment. And the faculty who deliver these courses are about as far from rich and famous as you can get.

About five years ago, two Silicon Valley companies, Coursera and Udacity, made new waves with big-name tech founders, mountains of venture capital, and a goal of revolutionizing learning. Their model was Massive Open Online Courses (MOOCs)—free self-paced courses, open to everyone. When it turned out that few learners completed the MOOCs, and that it was difficult to build a viable business model on a foundation of free anything, both companies pivoted to tuition-based novel credentials: Udacity nanodegrees with curriculum from brand-name companies like Google and Apple; Coursera specializations with curriculum from brand-name universities like Yale and Stanford but with additional content from some of the same brand-name companies (e.g., Google, Splunk, Yelp, Qualcomm).

One of the challenges facing online providers is the question of efficacy. It turned out that the online education revolution wasn't in quality or outcomes but rather access—allowing millions of Americans to pursue degrees on their own time. Completion rates remain low and prominent researchers have questioned the return on investment of online programs.[2]

Concerns about quality may explain why none of the major employers associated with Coursera and Udacity have committed to hire or even interview graduates of these novel online programs. No one was surprised at VentureBeat's report from mid-2017 that of the 10,000 nanodegree graduates, "more than 1,000 participants have found jobs"—a roughly 10 percent placement rate that should spell the demise of any last-mile program.[3] As a result, Udacity has resorted to a series of money-back guarantees for graduates who don't find jobs. But of course, money-back guarantees don't address the real guarantee students are seeking: a job. Udacity may give you back your money, but who's going to give you back your time?

Udacity's latest initiative is more promising. In partnership with the city of Reno, Nevada, Udacity announced Udacity Connect: Reno-Tahoe, a program that combines a three-month nanodegree with "in-person collaboration for projects and mentoring . . . specifically designed to prepare graduates for employment."[4]

The lesson Udacity, Coursera, and other companies are learning is that developing skills-based online courses and credentials is the easy part. The hard part is getting employers to pay attention.

●   ●   ●

One thing all last-mile programs have in common is that they're intensive. Many are eager to embrace the bootcamp moniker. In contrast, Coursera and Udacity online skills-based offerings are self-paced and might lead one to believe that an "online bootcamp" is an oxymoron. There's simply no way to guarantee intensity in an asynchronous online program. At any moment online students are likely to surf to another site, turn away from the screen, or simply drop out. Based on the completion rates of these courses, that's often what happens.

These online platforms are in stark contrast to programs like Galvanize where employers are present in the same physical environment, come into contact with students, and appreciate the high intensity. Demonstrating confidence in Galvanize's model, WeWork, the leading coworking space company, recently acquired coding bootcamp Flatiron School with the objective of integrating Flatiron's programs into some of WeWork's 170 global offices—an acquisition which, according to *Axios*, "would further test the growing idea of bypassing college, at least in the US tech world."[5] Even Amazon, which knows a thing or two about online delivery, has launched a bootcamp to help Amazon World Services clients close the skills gap in machine learning. The ML Solutions Lab Express program is "a four-week intensive program involving a one-week 'bootcamp' at Amazon, and followed by three weeks of intensive problem-solving and machine learning model building with Amazon machine learning experts."[6] While employers show great interest in physical proximity, they're less interested in engaging with online programs and graduates of such programs. As a result, expect continued inferior placement outcomes for online programs, which defeats the purpose of last-mile training.

There are ways to use technology to bridge the skills gap, but they're more nuanced than throwing a bunch of courses online, hoping employers will bite. MIT's experience is instructive. Several years ago, MIT began offering a MOOC through its partnership with edX, a nonprofit version of Coursera: Entrepreneurship 101, which aimed to teach the "essential skills needed to effectively identify and target customers."[7] As is usually the case, tens of thousands of students enrolled in the free course, but only a small percentage completed.

In thinking about the MOOC's purpose, MIT lecturer Erdin Beshimov had the idea of inviting successful students to apply for a one-week on-ground bootcamp that would challenge students to start a company in five days. A single email to students who completed the MOOC generated 500 applicants interested in paying $6,000 for the bootcamp. Forty-seven students enrolled in MIT's first entrepreneurship bootcamp and had a transformative experience based on the following principles: (1) a meaningful goal (e.g., launch a new business); (2) intensity (according to Beshimov, the typical student slept only ten hours that week); (3) team-based active learning (leading to bonding and a typical "hero's journey," i.e., adventure-crisis-victory); and (4) exposure to employers. Employers judged the final competition and met with students.

One student in that initial bootcamp, David Anderton from the UK, described the program as superintensive. "The first day we formed groups and ideas for projects, and we had the week to develop the project before a final pitch," he said. "Every night our team worked till 3 or 4 AM. There was lots of problem solving and team arguments."

David's team experienced major stress the night before the presentation. "I remember one guy was writing an idea on the board, and right behind him another person was erasing it. The lesson I learned was to respect each other, and we hadn't done that. We put on professional faces for the presentation, but when we got a real offer, nobody from our team wanted to talk to each other. Another team that didn't win got a half-million dollar offer from Verizon."

Since that first bootcamp, MIT has gone on to extend MOOCs into bootcamps for food innovation (large food companies provide the challenge and judge) and Internet of Things. Bootcamps have run not only in the United States but also in South Korea and Australia, attracting students from more than thirty countries. Beshimov says that the bootcamps appear to be producing strong outcomes for students. "In just two years," he said, "bootcamp graduates have raised tens of millions of dollars for their ventures." Moreover, MIT's MOOCs "command convening power for latent talent from every corner of the globe." Unlike many other last-mile programs, MIT spends zero on marketing.

• • •

The staffing company Revature has decided to do the same thing: utilize online learning to qualify candidates for its immersive last-mile program. Like MIT's MOOCs, RevaturePro is available for free exclusively to students at Revature's partner universities. Students with no coding background but who are interested in learning the basics of JavaScript are invited to learn and demonstrate basic coding proficiency with more than four thousand hours of technical learning and project development. RevaturePro introduces students to coding, like differentiating between procedural programming and object-oriented programming, through a combination of video lectures and projects. Students who complete three projects in RevaturePro automatically qualify for Revature's immersive training program.

Revature's university partners are excited about RevaturePro's potential to create pathways to great entry-level coding jobs for students from every discipline. RevaturePro helps democratize good entry-level jobs in technology for students who may not have been as career-minded in selecting their program of study.

• • •

> I've spoken to computer science undergrads and told them the languages I was learning on RevaturePro, and they hadn't learned them or even heard of them.
>
> —*Haisam Elkewidy, RevaturePro*

RevaturePro worked for Haisam Elkewidy. He graduated from Texas A&M in 2015 with a bachelor's degree in petroleum engineering. The plan was for Haisam to follow in his father's footsteps as a petroleum engineer. Haisam is complimentary about his experience at A&M. The in-class learning was directly relevant to the field. But it didn't work out because Haisam graduated at a time of record-low oil prices, which meant poor employment opportunities. "I looked for sixteen months but didn't get any offers," said Haisam. "Some classmates had jobs lined up, then their offers were revoked. Two people I know relocated for jobs and, once they got there, were immediately laid off. It was shocking."

Haisam looked for advice on LinkedIn and considered his options. "I thought about going back to school for a master's," he said, "but that takes time, a year or two, and I didn't have $15,000 to do that. So I decided to shift careers." The trick, according to Haisam, is to figure out what skills you have and find an intersection with other fields. He decided coding could work.

Haisam started applying for entry-level software developer jobs, like software testing, but they wanted someone with a computer science degree or equivalent. He called more than eighty companies in Texas but didn't have the degree, background, or experience they were looking for. Haisam decided to study coding on his own. But without any direction, he worried that he would waste time. He needed to find a mentor.

That was when Haisam found Revature. Within thirty minutes of his initial contact with the company, he received a call back from a recruiter. Revature offered Haisam the opportunity to demonstrate aptitude and learn basic coding skills on RevaturePro.

"Video lectures teach the basics to get you up and running," Haisam said. "Then to assess your progress, you choose from five major projects, each divided into three or four smaller ones." Haisam picked an online bookstore. The module after that involved creating a shopping cart. By the time he was done, he had created a complete app on RevaturePro. As a result, he was admitted to Revature's free immersive training program.

"My friends who studied computer science in college learned about programming, but complained that it wasn't hands-on enough," said Haisam. "They weren't actually fixing bugs and writing codes. RevaturePro, which got me into Revature's immersive training program, was a drastic shortcut—saving time and money."

● ● ●

Beyond using online learning to screen or qualify students for last-mile programs, a few new providers have launched online-only models that are showing promise in connecting students to good jobs. What they have in common is that, unlike Coursera and Udacity, they don't believe the value is in the online content. That's not what the tuition's for. Rather, the most important element of these programs is intensive real-time coaching sessions with an industry-connected mentor.

Designlab provides last-mile training across a range of design professions, starting with UX design, UI design, interaction design, and branding. Its six-month online intensive, UX Academy, provides 480 hours of learning, fifty hands-on projects, and thirty-four synchronous mentoring sessions with a professional working in the field. Designlab has more than four hundred part-time mentors to help reinforce learning, check on progress, and, critically, coach students through a successful job search. To date, 94 percent of the 500+ students who have completed Designlab's UX Academy have found employment in UX design.

• • •

On the long list of choices I've made in my life, taking Designlab is at the top.

—*Wendy Pei, Designlab*

Wendy Pei's degree from San Francisco State University was followed by ten years of working in restaurants and retail before she decided she wanted to be a product designer.

"I took a course on Treehouse and Lynda," she said, "then started looking at bootcamps. My partner had just done an engineering bootcamp where you don't have to pay upfront. I liked that model because it meant that the providers were investing in their students. I thought there must be a design bootcamp like that by now."

That was how Wendy found Designlab. "I was attracted to Designlab's values," she said. "They prioritized the growth of their students and getting them jobs. The point isn't just to collect money and provide information; it's about providing mentors and getting jobs for their students. The fee was $3,500, but they guaranteed that if you complete the program and don't get a job, they refund the whole tuition. Having the guarantee helped me accept the fact that I would be a guinea pig in the first cohort."

A care package with a few books arrived shortly after Wendy registered. She was invited to a Slack group with the mentors and other members of the cohort, had a video chat orientation, and was given access to a student portal with all the course material. Students were expected to dive into the material and had meetings scheduled with their assigned mentors.

The first phase of the program develops basic tools and resources integral to the field of product design—like Sketch, a program designers use to create mock-ups for drop-down menus and icons without having to code.

"We started with Design 101—how to look at design, how to describe and critique it, different elements and principles of design," Wendy said. "Then it moved into a research portion, which was new to most of us. Part of what we do as designers is identify the problem, then provide solutions. Then the goal was to complete three capstone projects. Each student develops an app from the idea stage through to the design stage in one week. Wendy said, "The mentors provided design briefs, two-page descriptions of a fictitious company with an app they want designed, or a problem they want to solve, like low usage of an app, or people not coming into their shop. We could choose from five different design briefs or come up with our own ideas."

Wendy's first project involved designing an app that responds to an asthma sensor. "I interviewed people who had experienced asthma attacks and learned about terms and symptoms," she said. "One of the goals of a product designer is to become knowledgeable in the industry and topic they're designing for. The app I designed would contact EMS and monitor oxygen levels and heart rate." Her second app was a food waste prevention app that connected people with "public pantries," solar-powered community fridges where people could donate and access food. For her third project, Wendy designed an app to help someone brewing kombucha, a health drink.

For Wendy, mentorship was the best aspect of the course. "Having access to industry leaders and their support was crucial to building confidence in my own skills," she said. "I learned that asking for help is important and necessary when doing a career change. Angel was my mentor and her mentoring style completely matched what I needed. When I showed her my projects, she went right to the core of the issue and gave me straightforward, clear feedback to improve my work. When I asked her for career advice or for info on industry standards, she would go beyond just the typical one sentence answer and really gave me deep insight about how things are now, how they've been, and how they might be in the future."

With a strong portfolio, Wendy's job search went quickly. She received competing offers and had to choose between a job at a small agency that was looking for a founding designer and an entry-level product design position at Microsoft. "It was a hard decision because I'm used to working with smaller companies," she said, "but the promise of a career path and other benefits—including that Microsoft donates money for every hour their employees volunteer at nonprofit organizations—influenced my decision."

Wendy uses her Designlab training every day at Microsoft. "I'm the designer on my team that communicates with researchers because of all my research experience from the program," she said. "Also, now I facilitate critique sessions with Designlab students. It's great to be able to give back to the program."

• • •

Bloc is a last-mile program for coding that runs entirely online. Like Designlab, Bloc relies on intensive mentorship to boost completion and placement outcomes from the online norm. Bloc calls its model a "remote apprenticeship" and encourages students of all backgrounds; only about a third of all Bloc students enter with a college degree. Students must choose the desired pace: sprinting (forty hours per week with three synchronous video mentor meetings of thirty to sixty minutes per week; jogging (twenty hours with two meetings); or walking (twelve hours with one meeting).

Bloc's online program is rigorous and ensures each graduate has a "robust profile—between three and eight projects you've built yourself," said founder Clint Schmidt. Students must demonstrate mastery via a series of assessments. If they can't, they're asked to leave, which amounts to about half of all students who undertake the program. But noncompleters aren't on the hook for the full cost of the program; they pay only for the portion they've successfully completed.

All Bloc mentors are experienced coders. "Some have decided to take a break from shipping code every day and are mentoring full time," said Schmidt. "But just as many are full-time software developers and designers who are mentoring on the side." Mentors also focus on interview skills and other soft skills to increase placement rates. In fact, Bloc compensates mentors based on the placement of their students.

• • •

My college degree failed me. No one should graduate from math
or engineering programs without knowing how to code.

—Jeffrey King, Bloc

Jeffrey King went back to school at the age of forty-two. In his twenties,
he completed an associate's degree at a junior college in California then
worked as a waiter. "Once my kids were school-age," he said, "working
evenings at restaurants didn't work. Going back to school seemed like the
right thing to do."

Jeffrey decided to pursue a bachelor's degree in actuarial science at the
University of Nevada, Las Vegas (UNLV). "I loved math, probabilities, and
stats," he said, "so it seemed like a career I would enjoy. The only problem
was that UNLV didn't actually prepare me to be an actuary." After graduating, Jeffrey applied for lots of jobs and "landed some interviews," but the
consistent feedback was that while his math skills were great, his coding
wasn't up to par. "We need people who can model math, not just understand
it," is what Jeffrey heard.

Jeffrey chose Bloc's "sprint" option not only because he could learn
online but also because of the mentorship. He recognized that he'd hit
roadblocks if he relied only on online classes. "It's really hard to learn from
scratch what you need to be a full-stack developer," he said. "You need the
mentorship. The mentorship is really what you're paying for at Bloc."

When he began working with his mentor, Jeffrey felt he had gotten
lucky. "Ben was a good teacher, cared about his students, and invested the
time in me," he said. "He spent way more than the requisite ninety minutes
a week. Usually you are assigned a different mentor for each quarter, but
I had such a good relationship with Ben that I requested to stay with him.
The curriculum got me to where I needed to be, but Ben made the whole
program worth it."

Ben also supported Jeffrey as he approached the end of the program
and began applying for jobs. Even before he could complete his portfolio,
he received responses from four companies and interviewed with two. He
received an offer from Trinity Integrated Solutions, where he feels his work
is like what he'd done for recreation his entire life—"games, puzzles, math
problems," he said. "My job is a form of entertainment."

For Jeffrey, the most profound thing he got out of Bloc was learning how to learn in a new way. "I'd always been good at learning," he said, "but web technology changes every day. By the time someone writes a book, you're onto the next version. Traditional learning methods don't apply. You need a new way of getting information, searching and digging around the internet. My mentor helped me through that. Ben gave me the confidence that I could learn whatever I needed to know to work on a project or solve any problem."

● ● ●

There's one more online approach that shows real promise. Rather than focusing on mentorship, it uses an accessible online experience to orient students to possible career paths and ensure they develop a portfolio of relevant work to showcase in their job search.

One company with this approach is Yellowbrick. Yellowbrick works with top universities on career discovery courses in areas Millennials are passionate about. The first online certificate was Fashion Industry Essentials with Parsons School of Design. Students are taught by industry insiders from Parsons, as well as *Teen Vogue* magazine, GILT, and designer Rebecca Minkoff. They develop an understanding of different entry-level jobs available in the fashion world and then build an e-portfolio of work. The program also prepares students for job interviews.

In the last year, Yellowbrick has launched an online certificate in sports industry essentials (SIE) with Columbia University (taught by Columbia faculty and executives from the NFL, NHL, and Nike), as well as a new program called beauty industry essentials (BIE) from the Fashion Institute of Technology (with professionals from Bobbi Brown, Shiseido, and MAC Cosmetics). For a relatively low cost, graduates are more informed and directed in finding a good first job in the field they love.

● ● ●

I fell in love with the sports environment and I knew that's what I wanted to do. But I couldn't figure out where I fit into the industry with my communications degree.

—*Maria Rodriguez, Yellowbrick*

Maria Rodriguez graduated with a degree in communications studies from Texas Christian University. She knew she wanted to work in the sports industry and understood she would need experience, so she completed an internship in the athletic department at the university. But even with the internship, Maria found herself underqualified.

"I landed a few interviews," she said, "but if I got an offer the pay was too low, or it wasn't a job I wanted to do, or there wasn't any potential for growth. Sometimes they hired other candidates with more experience, even for entry-level positions. I didn't have enough experience for entry-level positions! The employers I wanted to work for were looking for candidates with a clear understanding of the sports industry, with lots of teamwork experience, and who knew what everyone in the organization is doing. I needed to know more than just my field. My internship didn't give me the experience they wanted."

Six months into her job search, Maria decided she needed to be more proactive. "I didn't want to start an MBA program yet because I didn't have the money," she said, "but I started to research it. While I was searching graduate programs, sports management certificates popped up, and that's when I found the online sports industry essentials course from Columbia. I was so excited. They had a payment plan, it was easy, the lectures were awesome, and it offered just what I needed to learn about working in different areas of sports."

Maria focused all her attention on the Columbia program and finished it in six weeks. The certificate consisted of five courses, all online, that she could complete in any order. Each course has eight thirty-minute videos covering a variety of topics, including event planning, stadium operations, sponsorships, digital media and stats, sports operations within teams and with fans, public relations issues, and the industry in general beyond teams, such as apparel and financing. The videos include lectures from faculty and industry professionals. Following each video is a list of readings and an assignment. To complete each course, Maria had to submit the assignment for assessment.

"The assignments were challenging," she said. "If you needed help you could reach out to the faculty. You could do everything on your own time, watch each lecture as many times as you wanted. There were transcripts available for lectures so you could read the lectures too. After I completed my final assignment, I received a certificate of completion from Columbia."

In college, Maria learned general communications strategies for social media, press releases, and marketing strategies, how to understand markets and audiences, how to handle crises, and some content-creation technology skills, like Photoshop. SIE filled in the industry specifics.

"There were lots of little things I didn't know about digital media and PR in sports," Maria said. "For example, if I want to write an article about a player, I need to go to the scouts and get the stats and understand what the numbers mean, and I need to be able to communicate with people in various roles in the organizations. I learned how sponsorships and media releases work, how to help the organization save money, and how to work with the people in sales, marketing, and sponsorships so everyone meets their goals."

Equally important were tips on how to get an entry-level job. The program provided a wealth of advice on how to reach out to industry professionals. Maria learned about sports industry communities on LinkedIn and Facebook. "I applied for three jobs from a website I learned about through the program," she said.

Six months later, Maria works in the marketing department for the Pittsburgh Steelers, helping to grow their international market using social media. "They noticed international growth is bigger than domestic growth for the NFL," she said, "so I joined their international department. Global expansion was one of the chapters in the course." In the job interview with the franchise, the interviewers asked Maria, "What was the most valuable thing you learned in the program?"

She answered, "How to speak to a global audience."

Maria said, "I don't believe I would have gotten the interview for this job without the SIE course, and I was able to answer interview questions perfectly because of it."

● ● ●

Despite the promise of new mentorship-focused online models, no online models have proven to be game-changing pathways to good jobs. Still, it may be that technology's transformation of higher education lies not in the transformation of learning but rather in the advent of a new digital language that connects education and employers and, in so doing, exerts profound changes on both.

The historic disconnect between higher education and employer needs is a data problem. Employers haven't been clear on the skills they require and educators haven't been particularly interested in finding out. So hiring managers have been content to rely on signals supported by anecdotal evidence at best—for example, assuming that philosophy majors from Brown make terrific analysts or that teachers with master's degrees will perform better in the classroom.

Technology has begun to change this in three distinct ways, first via the increasing availability of competency data: e-portfolios, microcredentials, microassessments, and simulations are surfacing student competencies beneath the level of the degree. Second, "people analytics" technologies are allowing employers to track employee performance with a feedback loop to job descriptions. As a result, job descriptions are improving, moving from vague and data-poor to precise, data-rich renderings of top performers. Third, advances in applicant tracking systems will allow employers to take advantage of the fruits of their people analytics investments. Vendors like Oracle will add functionality to applicant tracking system products to proactively search for candidates with competencies that are most predictive of performance and retention in open jobs.

Ultimately, these technological developments will complete the faster + cheaper revolution. The resulting "competency marketplaces" will help students understand the jobs and careers they're most likely to match and help employers identify students who are on track (or on a trajectory to match in the future) and manage long talent funnels in an automated way. For students, competency marketplaces will inform postsecondary education decisions by providing a human capital "GPS" to help them select the pathways that will move them most efficiently toward target professions or employers. By emphasizing skills, competency marketplaces will accelerate the trend away from pedigree and degrees.

Specifically, competency marketplaces will tell:

- students which jobs/employers they match today based on skills.
- employers which students match today.
- students which future jobs/employers they should target based on their learning trajectories, velocities, and zones of proximal development.
- employers which students are on a trajectory to match in the future.

- students which assessments/projects/virtual internships might advance their cause with specific employers.
- students which educational programs provide the most efficient and effective path to matching target jobs/employers.
- educational providers which students are good targets for specific programs based on target jobs/employers and competency gaps.

What does a competency marketplace look like? If you're a student or job-seeker, think of your LinkedIn profile shifting from a recitation of your education and experience to a long list of competencies and levels. This list may be unintelligible to you, but it won't be unintelligible to the algorithms sitting atop the applicant tracking systems and HR information systems that employers will use to engage in competency-based hiring and predictive hiring.

It will be irresistible for employers to use competency marketplaces to meet hiring needs. Your firm has to hire 100 entry-level salespeople every year? No problem. Your next-generation ATS has already identified 250 nineteen- and twenty-year-olds whose demonstrated curricular, cocurricular, or extracurricular competencies correlate to sales success in your company, and either advised them to take a course in business statistics or invited them to participate in a short online course, the result of which will be an invitation to interview for a summer job.

The transformative potential of competency marketplaces undoubtedly played a role in Microsoft's decision to pay a 50 percent premium to acquire LinkedIn for $26.2 billion.[8] LinkedIn boasts by far the largest collection of candidate profiles and integrates with many applicant tracking systems. Moreover, LinkedIn CEO Jeff Weiner's vision for an "economic graph" is the clearest expression by any technology company of the competency marketplace future.

• • •

Just like faster + cheaper alternatives to college, competency marketplaces require both students and employers to think differently. For students, it's about making their competencies visible. The most obvious way is to show their work. Research demonstrates that work samples are more predictive of job performance than any other factor—about five times more predictive than years of education, three times more predictive than job experience, and 50 percent more effective than unstructured interviews.[9]

Fortunately, technology is making it easier to show work. Coding repositories like GitHub help employers evaluate programming talent—an imperative in a sector where top employees may be more productive by an order of magnitude.[10] But you don't have to be a software developer to show your work; all 18 million students enrolled in US colleges and universities produce work for every course they take (or at least those they pass). Student work takes various forms: papers, projects, models, designs, drawings, videos—any and all of which can be showcased for employers in e-portfolios. Students also gain competencies from their many extracurricular activities, and this work can be showcased as well.

Portfolium is an e-portfolio network that allows students to make their work (and the competencies demonstrated therein) visible to employers. It had grown to more than 2,500 colleges and universities and 5 million-plus students and alumni in just over two years after its founding in 2014. Portfolium derives competencies from work product and matches students to entry-level jobs. Employers across a range of industries, not simply IT, are now utilizing Portfolium to identify and recruit talent. Portfolium is the most advanced competency marketplace for entry-level jobs.

Another way students can make competencies visible is by sharing microcredentials or badges. Driven by many of the same forces propelling the faster + cheaper movement, microcredentialing involves education or training providers ("issuers" in credential-speak) providing microcredentials or badges to students ("earners") for each competency demonstrated. Like the boy or girl scouts they once may have been, earners can collect hundreds of badges, each representing a discrete competency.

The microcredentialing revolution is already underway in IT, as evidenced by millions of Cisco-certified and .NET-certified technology workers. Many universities are eager to issue microcredentials in IT and other fields; hundreds of institutions have either launched or are in the process of launching competency-based programs, which, once designed around competencies, are easy to microcredential. Employers are also enthusiastic about microcredentialing training and employee performance to improve engagement and retention. Industry associations also see microcredentialing as a new way to provide value to members. Credly is the market leader in microcredentialing. More than 12,000 educational institutions, employers, and industry associations issue microcredentials through Credly, including AICPA, Mozilla, IBM, and Harvard. Microcredentials issued through Credly are secure, accessible, and portable to social media platforms. Issuers find that when their microcredentials are exported to LinkedIn and Facebook, it can be valuable marketing for their credentials and their organizations more broadly. It won't be long before applicant tracking systems begin searching for Credly badges.

According to Credly founder Jonathan Finkelstein:

> Many employers and associations now view micro-credentials as more precise indicators of knowledge and skills than traditional degrees and companies are already seeing them drive better hiring and promotion decisions as well as improved employee retention. They are looking to educational institutions to scale up their use of micro-credentials so that individuals can navigate the labor market with a common currency and a more transparent signal of what they know and can do.

A third strategy is microassessments. As I've noted, several top employers have integrated microassessments into their hiring funnels. These microassessments tend to test for distinct cognitive skills like reading comprehension, numerical literacy, or locating information to provide employers with a sense of general ability. Some also use situational judgment tests (SJTs) that apply knowledge and skills to real-world settings across a wide range of professions, and that also test soft skills like teamwork and empathy. In deploying microassessments, employers aren't primarily focused on technical or vocational skills but rather on executive function skills without which employees are unlikely to be successful. Ernst & Young, Nestlé, and other companies have integrated microassessments into their applicant tracking systems. Candidates who cannot pass these assessments will not be considered.

A final way to use technology to make employers aware of competencies is games or simulations. Last year, the *New York Times* breathlessly declared that you should "start solving puzzles" if you want to work for Jaguar Land Rover. While Jaguar will still consider the pedigrees of "traditional" applicants, those who are able to assemble a virtual sports car and then complete several code-breaking puzzles will "fast-track their way into employment."[11]

If you've ever been online and seen a window asking if you can code better than an Uber engineer, you've just been challenged to a CodeFight. The San Francisco company is gamifying hiring by providing thousands of coding challenges across dozens of coding competencies to experienced and first-time hackers alike. Candidates compete against bots or against each other in timed competitions. Challenge, competition, and immediate gratification (the "achievement-dopamine cycle")—seminal elements of every video game you've ever played—are deployed for the purpose of educating, sourcing, and filtering candidates. Employers like Uber, Asana, Dropbox, Thumbtack, and Evernote have already hired through CodeFights.

Games and simulations actually help level the playing field. Eighty percent of candidates placed by CodeFights did not attend an elite university or come from a major tech city like San Francisco or New York. Moreover, 30 percent of candidates placed to date are women—three times higher than the Silicon Valley average.

CodeFights founder Tigran Sloyan believes games and simulations represent the future of sourcing and filtering for any objectively measured skill. This includes fields like accounting and finance and any regulated or licensed field where there's a qualifying exam (watch out, health care!). It also includes skills that may not be at once objectively measurable but where crowdsourcing can quickly yield an accurate judgment on performance (e.g., design).

According to Sloyan, "While using pedigree as a proxy for skill was reasonable thirty years ago, it's unnecessary today because excellent postsecondary education is available from a wide variety of institutions and sources. In the twenty-first century, we hope to say farewell to pedigree and usher in an era of skill-based recruiting."[12]

● ● ●

Stock trading is a supremely measurable skill that is determined by the value of the trader's portfolio. Two years ago, Justin Ling, a dynamic recent graduate of Canada's Simon Fraser University, with a few years' experience in asset management, saw this opportunity and created EquitySim, a simulation platform for trading stocks, bonds, currencies, and other securities. His intended target: college students. So once the initial platform was built,

Ling began calling college finance clubs and finance professors, offering his platform as a resource.

Unlike pure learning-oriented simulation portals, EquitySim has been designed to record the "why" behind investment and trading decisions (e.g., risk management capability, market research). It also captures behavioral data points (e.g., order of steps followed, duration of time spent, etc.)—more than 100,000 data points per student. The company provides top entry-level candidates to asset management firms globally, effectively functioning as a recruitment company.

To date, the platform has been adopted by faculty at more than 250 universities, producing over 60,000 student users. Like staffing and placement businesses, EquitySim is paid by employers for every student placed into an entry-level position at an investment bank or fund. Employers are excited about EquitySim because it helps them identify top talent at schools where they don't recruit.

"While EquitySim is starting with trading," said Ling, "there is a large number of professions where entry-level work can be simulated and assessed in a way that will give employers broader access to talent while opening up exciting new employment pathways for students."

Ling says he named his company EquitySim not because of equity trading but because he strongly believes that simulations can create a more equitable playing field for students regardless of background. So far, 48 percent of hired students are female and 68 percent come from schools where employers are not actively recruiting.

• • •

Most top finance professionals are male, white, and attended an Ivy League school. For candidates outside the traditional background it's important to be confident and to push yourself to get these sorts of roles. It requires digging deeper, getting creative with the application process, going past school career centers and LinkedIn. Think outside the box.

—*Jennie Cheung, EquitySim*

Jennie Cheung always wanted to work in finance. She double-majored in economics and math at a liberal arts college in the Northeast but knew it would be challenging to break in. "The major employers don't recruit at my school," she said. "They just go to the Ivy League schools."

Jennie's parents grew up China, and when they came to the United States, her dad delivered Chinese food. "Wall Street is a big nothing to them," Jennie said. "So when I started my job search I knew I had to try anything. I have to succeed." To find the job she wanted, Jennie reached out to alumni or anyone she could find for a connection to the finance industry. Nothing popped for her until she found EquitySim.

Jennie got started right away with EquitySim's trading simulation. "It's a way to experience what it's like to trade," she said. "You can apply financial concepts to the simulated trades you're making and explain the rationale behind your trades. It evaluates your Sharpe ratio—a measure of how well you're doing related to risk you're taking, your max drawdown, and other measures of returns."

One day, Jennie received an email from EquitySim that said Credit Suisse was looking at high-performing candidates on the simulation. Once the interview with Credit Suisse was set up, EquitySim helped her to prepare. "EquitySim walked me through various markets and taught me to flag my industry-specific skills," Jennie said. Her interview was successful and she was invited to a month-long training program in New York. She ended up with the top scores on all the tests and was offered her dream job.

"Without EquitySim, Credit Suisse never would have found me, and I never would have gotten their attention," she said. "EquitySim helps draw candidates from different backgrounds, not just Princeton and Stanford. In HR, it's the talk of the town."

Jennie has since heard from Credit Suisse human resources that they're planning to hire all their intern class from EquitySim. They like the platform because candidates have to explain the rationale for trading decisions.

● ● ●

With the coming competency marketplace, betting on a faster + cheaper route to a good first job makes even more sense because there's less risk a subsequent employer gets hung up on a formal credential. In a world where competencies are archived and accessible digitally, the second employer is likely to care less about a degree than demonstrable skills and achievements in the first job. Once you start seeing signs of the competency marketplace, you're well beyond "Peak Credential."

CHAPTER 8 • KEY POINTS

- What makes last-mile programs work is the intensive bootcamp or real-work setting.
- An online bootcamp is an oxymoron, which explains why online skill-building programs tend to have poor employment outcomes.
- Online programs can achieve positive employment outcomes if there's extensive synchronous coaching through placement; they can also be effective for screening candidates for last-mile training and for career discovery programs.
- Technology will transform education not through online skills training, but rather through online competency marketplaces and enabling competency-based hiring.
- Competency marketplaces will accelerate the shift to faster + cheaper alternatives.
- Faster + cheaper pathways to good first jobs, along with the ability to archive competencies digitally, are diminishing the importance of traditional credentials.

PART III

Graduating
from College

CHAPTER 9

The Road I Didn't Take

SCHMIDT: You all right?

JENKO: Yeah. It's just . . . I'm the first person in my family to pretend to go to college.

—22 Jump Street (2014)

One of my favorite features of *Rumpus,* the tabloid newspaper we started in college, was Captain Da. Captain Da was the pseudonym my roommate Dave used to make prank phone calls, and the Captain Da column in *Rumpus* was a transcript of his greatest hits. Here's a good example from when Dave called the esteemed literary publication the *Yale Review.*

YALE REVIEW: Hello, *Yale Review.*

DAVE: Yes, I wrote some poetry that I'd like to submit, but before I bother putting a stamp on it, I'm just wondering if I could read it to you.

YR: Oh . . . you know, I don't . . .

DAVE: Okay, here it is. I call it "The Road I Didn't Take."

> Two roads diverged in a yellow wood
> And sorry I could not travel both
> And be one traveler long I stood
> And looked down one as far as I could
> To where it bent in the undergrowth
> Then took the other as just as fair
> And having perhaps the better claim
> Because it was grassy and wanted wear
> Though as for that the passing there
> Had worn them really about the same

Well, what do you think of it so far?

YR: (laughter) I think it sounds a lot like Robert Frost.

DAVE: Well he's really been, I'd say, the biggest influence on my work, and I can't say that I haven't read his stuff. But I'm just wondering what you think of it. Is it up to snuff.

YR: The reason I was demurring at even having you bother to take the time to read it to me is that my job doesn't influence what goes into the *Review*. They would have published Frost, in fact they did, before . . .

DAVE: But this isn't Frost. This is me. Okay. I think I've got one that fits what you're looking for. I call it "Taking a Little Break in the Orchard on a Very Stormy Evening."

YR: (laughter)

If you're approaching the end of high school, or if you have a family member who is, you're probably concerned about "The Road I Didn't Take." For young Americans, the road they choose—college or a faster + cheaper alternative—will leave one road not taken. As a result of the emergence of faster + cheaper alternatives, over the next few years an increasing number of high school graduates will realize they have a choice to make rather than simply blindly applying to and enrolling in traditional colleges and universities. The question is which road to take.

There's no question that a college degree will remain the default choice for the foreseeable future. But it's clear that the conditions under which the default should and will be rejected are multiplying.

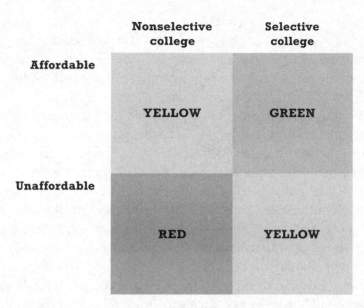

Recall how we started off: green quadrant (selective college, affordable package) means go; red quadrant (nonselective, unaffordable) means stop. Yellow means it depends. Now that we've seen viable alternatives to college, it's time for definitions.

The Lumina Foundation, one of the most respected philanthropies focused on higher education, has put a name on college affordability. Lumina calls it the "Rule of 10." The Rule of 10 states that students should pay no more for college than the savings their families have generated through 10 percent of discretionary income for the past ten years, plus the earnings from working ten hours a week while in school.[1] Arguing that families should not be expected to contribute anything to college unless they're able to support themselves, the Rule of 10 provides an exclusion for all household income up to 200 percent of the poverty level.

For example, a family of four with a household income of $100,000 should have been able to save $429 per month for a decade, or $51,500. Add to this an estimated $3,625 that the student could earn by working ten hours per week for four years and the family should not be expected to contribute more than $65,000 in total—whether out-of-pocket or by taking out student loans. And a family of four with a household income of $50,000? They'd contribute $1,500 out of savings plus $3,625 per year from student earnings, or not more than $16,000. Any college or university that expects that the family should contribute more than that to tuition, fees, room and board—whether out-of-pocket or via loans—is unaffordable.[2]

Unfortunately, that's nearly all colleges and universities. Which means there are very few schools at which a family near the median household income would find themselves with a green light for college. On the other hand, if your family is very well off, then the red quadrant—in fact, the entire bottom half of the matrix—will be foreign to you.

As to the difference between selective and nonselective, Jeff Selingo points out there are only about two hundred colleges and universities that can properly be called selective (i.e., less than 50 percent acceptance rate).[3] Although selective institutions enroll less than 10 percent of all undergraduates, they play an outsized role in American life. They include the top private research universities and liberal arts colleges, but only a surprisingly small number of public flagships (about a dozen) including Berkeley, University of Texas at Austin, University of North Carolina at Chapel Hill, University of Virginia, and University of Michigan. These schools graduate many of the most talented and motivated students, primarily because they attract many of the most talented students. They're the lens through which American culture views higher education. If you go to any prominent company or organization, you'll be hard-pressed to find anyone in a leadership role who hasn't attended one of these schools. So selective schools have proven vitally important to America and are likely to continue to play this role.

They're also a lot wealthier than nonselective schools. According to Moody's Investor Service, the twenty richest private universities have 70 percent of the wealth of all private universities.[4] This means more spending on students, like Yale's two new residential colleges on which the university spent $500 million for 800 new beds, including intricate stonework and stained glass windows that epitomize F. Scott Fitzgerald's famous phrase, "Let me tell you about the very rich. They are different from you and me."

Selective universities pay dividends decades later through alumni networks and connections and pay off immediately in the form of higher starting salaries. Recent graduates of Stanford earn an average salary of $86,000 while recent graduates of Northern Kentucky University make $36,000.[5] Some of this relates to an actual talent gap, and some stems from a gap in signaling value: employers have a pretty good sense of what a Stanford degree means, but much less so for a degree from NKU.

As a result, if you can get into a selective school, you really ought to try and go. To define selective, the 50 percent acceptance is as good a marker as any. While yield rate (the percentage of accepted students who actually enroll) is also a key element of selectivity, schools with lower yield rates must admit more students to fill the class, making it less likely that they'll stay under the 50 percent acceptance threshold. Keep it simple by focusing on acceptance rate.

For all these reasons, if you find yourself in the bottom-right yellow quadrant—selective college, unaffordable—you'll want to view affordability much more flexibly than you would for a nonselective college. My suggestion is to consider taking on more debt, or even significantly more debt, than the Rule of 10 allows if you have three or more of the following "go to college indicators":

Go to College Indicators

✓   I never stopped or dropped out of college before.
✓   I have a network of family and friends to support and encourage me to complete college.
✓   I live in the Northeast.
✓   I'm a woman or a minority.
✓   If I major in business, it will be in finance or accounting rather than general business or marketing.
✓   I might want to work in a field that requires a license (e.g., medicine, law, education).
✓   I'm hopeless with or not interested in technology.

The first two indicators relate to the likelihood of completing college—by far the single biggest risk when deciding to embark on a four-year journey.

The Northeast is a college-going indicator because a degree continues to carry more social status there than it does in other regions of the country. This explains why in 2017 Massachusetts became the first state where more than half of all working adults had a bachelor's degree.[6] It also explains why Northeast families spend an average of 70 percent more on college than families from the South, Midwest, and West.[7] If you're a woman or a minority, returns on a college degree appear to have held up better than for white males, so your investment is more likely to pay off.[8]

The question of major is an important one. Business is the most common major, so it's a good litmus test: students who major in general business or marketing are much more likely to have negative employment outcomes than students who major in "math-focused" business majors like finance and accounting.[9]

If you might want to work in a licensed profession, most require a bachelor's degree (and are likely to continue to require them long after you complete your postsecondary education). Professions like medicine and law operate like guilds and utilize degree requirements and accreditation of degree programs to limit the supply of new entrants. So you'll have higher career risk without a college degree.

Finally, although some faster + cheaper alternative pathways involve little or no technology, the majority are technical. So if you're avowedly nontechnical, traditional college is a relatively better bet (and also, good luck to you).

The upshot is that if you've been admitted to a selective university and have three or more of these go-to-college indicators, I suggest thinking of the Rule of 10 as a Rule of 20: double the amount you're willing to pay net of scholarships and grants. For a family making $100,000 per year, that's $130,000, or in the ballpark of what selective universities will expect.

At the same time, I wouldn't scale the Rule of 10 depending on how highly the institution in question ranks in *US News & World Report,* or whatever ranking you might happen to see. Rankings are not only deleterious to the entire higher education enterprise—contributing to high tuition and the student debt crisis—they're entirely arbitrary. Rankings are the product of data that is easily available to editors, as well as their best guesses as to how to weight different categories to produce a list that gets attention and sells magazines. Moreover, only a couple of new (and less recognized) rankings even attempt to incorporate student outcome data like average income of graduates. No rankings attempt to measure placement rates, let alone underemployment of recent graduates. So don't waste your money paying for rankings. Best to stick with a hard-and-fast rule: if the university admits fewer than 50 percent of applicants, be prepared to double the Rule of 10.

One final note on selective schools. As a result of declining enrollment, acceptance rates are creeping up at many of our top two hundred institutions (although not at the Ivies, Stanford, MIT, and the very elite). Kenyon College's acceptance rate has increased from 24 percent three years ago to 33 percent in 2017, while Grinnell College's increased from 20 percent to 29 percent in 2017.[10] So the universe of selective schools could well shrink. Get into those schools while they're still worth getting into.

• • •

For the other yellow quadrant—an affordable ride at a nonselective school—I suggest a different approach. In the 2017 book *Law Mart: Justice, Access and For-Profit Law Schools,* Riaz Tejani, an assistant professor at University of Illinois Springfield, makes the point that in legal education there's a gulf between selective and nonselective schools. Nonselective schools "try to downplay the significance of that hierarchy," he says. According to Tejani:

> What's striking to me is the lengths to which a [nonselective] school . . . will say, "Hierarchy and prestige don't matter—it's whatever you want to be." So suddenly, the students are somehow themselves set free, unleashed, to be whatever they want to be and their destinies are unfettered by sociology, when, in fact, it's just not true. It's nice and it's aspirational but the reality if you're being perfectly honest with students is that they will face obstacles on the way out.[11]

Nonselective schools want you to believe a degree from their institution is the same as a degree from anywhere—even Harvard or Stanford—Tejani argues, because "the downplaying of the significance of those things allows the institution to charge premium tuition."[12]

While *Yale's 50 Most Beautiful People* was a parody, it rings true in the context of universities: "In the world, there are those that have, and those that have not . . . we are not all equal . . ." Many nonselective colleges and universities remind me of Olive Garden. You've undoubtedly experienced Olive Garden. It's a facsimile of a nice Italian restaurant, typically with mood lighting and art on the walls. Customers are seated, attended by servers, and given wine lists. Superficially, it's everything you'd expect of a fancy Italian place. Except that the company's not Italian; it's based in Orlando. And there are a lot of salty breadsticks on the table. And the food isn't very good. Visiting Olive Garden, it's hard to believe that this is what Americans think pasta is supposed to taste like: overcooked and tasteless, as if they had stopped salting the water (the cardinal rule of cooking pasta). The menu includes burgers, fries, and Spanish tapas, along with "authentic" Italian items like fried lasagna bites, alongside fried foods of every variety. Perhaps to compensate, Olive Garden has made up Italian-sounding dishes like "pastachetti" and "soffateli." Then there's the mind-boggling vegetable lasagna topped with chicken (for vegetarians?) or the classic spaghetti with meatballs that, according to *CNN Money*, "smell a little like cat food."[13]

All of which raises the question: why do people keep going to the eight hundred Olive Garden restaurants in the United States, particularly those who buy the "Never Ending Pasta Pass" that the company markets periodically? That's like a pie-eating contest where first prize is more pie, except that entering costs $99 and the pie is soggy. The answer, I think, is the same as why students keep enrolling at nonselective colleges: Olive Garden has the accoutrements of excellence but little of the quality.

Nonselective schools have the same accoutrements as our most selective institutions. There are campuses and quads, presidents or chancellors and boards of trustees, academic departments, department chairs, faculty governance, varsity football and basketball, and don't forget career services (cough cough). But the level and quality of academic programs, courses, and instruction at nonselective institutions are uneven at best. Yes, there are excellent, caring faculty at every college and university. There are talented and diligent students at every school. But finding pockets of quality is much harder at nonselective schools; many nonselective schools resemble the anarchic environments profiled by Craig Brandon in *The Five-Year Party*: an academic Olive Garden.

All of which raises the question: if nonselective institutions are ruining the reputation of college, why don't selective schools do more to point out that their institutions are quantitatively and qualitatively different? Jonathan Barnett of the University of Southern California Gould School of Law has a theory derived from the world of fashion. While consumers clearly value brand-name luxury goods, billions of dollars of low-quality knockoff bags, shoes, watches, and jewelry are sold annually. So why do luxury goods companies like LVMH continue to invest in production and development of new products when—often mere blocks from their stores—knockoff bags are sold at a fraction of the cost? While one would think that LVMH would be irate about counterfeits and insist on strict enforcement, that's not what's happening.

In his paper "Shopping for Gucci on Canal Street," Barnett posits that Gucci and LVMH allow counterfeits because they signal desirability, provide free advertising, and ultimately boost sales. But luxury goods companies only benefit from low-quality counterfeits under the following conditions: (1) when goods (or services) confer significant status benefits—with counterfeits signaling desirability of the original item and providing free advertising for the producers; (2) when producers can't introduce imperfect grades of the original without significantly depleting accumulated brand capital; and (3) when imitators produce imitations of the original that are *obviously* imperfect—for example, via poor workmanship, lower-quality materials, or misprinted or missing labels. As a result, counterfeits may result in increased revenue for producers of luxury goods.[14]

As a luxury good, a degree from a selective college or university meets Barnett's first condition. While a degree from Harvard confers significant status benefits, Harvard has benefited from the college-going culture that thousands of nonselective institutions have fostered. Instead of occupying the apex of an obscure corner of American education, the twentieth-century evolution of college as the sole socially acceptable path to a successful career has magnified Harvard's importance. Harvard and its selective brethren are quite happy at the top of this much larger $500 billion industry, and their presidents and trustees are equally happy as prominent spokespeople for the more prominent enterprise of higher education.

A Harvard degree also meets Barnett's second condition: Harvard can't easily introduce lower-quality versions of Harvard without harming its own brand. We know this because for more than twenty years Harvard and other selective institutions have resisted launching online bachelor's degrees—limiting online activities to executive education and obscure professional programs.

It's Barnett's third condition that makes the relationships between selective and nonselective institutions less stable and sustainable than the luxury-knockoff ecosystem in fashion. The distinguishing marks of an elite education aren't as easily identifiable when consumers judge based on appearances: quads, academic departments and programs, sports teams, and, yes, high tuition prices. But as the employment imperative has caused the market to shift, and with an increasing amount of employment and graduate income data available to prospective students, Barnett's third condition starts to break down in the higher education context. While Barnett points out that courts have noted that, in fashion, there "does not seem to be any significant problem of purchasers who mistakenly purchase fakes when intending to purchase the original," that's clearly no longer the case in higher education. Students who purchase degrees from nonselective institutions expecting to achieve selective-like outcomes are experiencing significant harm.

So while selective institutions have heretofore resisted calling out nonselective institutions for poor student outcomes—to the point that not a single top college or university has taken a position on the many low-quality institutions that have recently closed their doors under regulatory pressure—expect this to change. Selective colleges and universities will have no choice but to begin publicly supporting meaningful accountability and outcome measures that will allow students to more readily distinguish low-quality knockoffs. We're starting to see this in the UK, as elite "Russell Group" universities have been lobbying the government to force less-selective universities to lower their fees.[15]

This coming bifurcation will make it easier for prospective students and families to strictly adhere to the Rule of 10 affordability benchmark for nonselective colleges and universities. If you find yourself deciding on a nonselective college or university—if you're in the top-left quadrant—you'll need to be firm. The go-to-college indicators simply don't factor in; they're largely irrelevant for nonselective schools. If nonselective schools expect you to contribute more (net of grants and scholarships) than the Rule of 10 allows—and it's likely they will because these tuition-dependent schools are less able to offer generous financial aid—you'll be better off with a faster + cheaper alternative. Here's the bottom line: if your goal is a great first job, choose an alternative over a nonselective college unless you're getting a great deal (i.e., unless it meets the Rule of 10).

The argument for a faster + cheaper alternative may be even stronger at this early stage in the revolution. While every hiring manager has seen hundreds, if not thousands of applicants with bachelor's degrees from nonselective universities, few have seen graduates from faster + cheaper alternatives. Because we're still early, these pathways will differentiate you in the hiring process. Many hiring managers will be interested in learning more about the program you attended, and how and why college became the road you didn't take. As Laszlo Bock remarked when he was with Google, "People who don't go to school and make their way in the world . . . are exceptional human beings."[16]

Such a hard-and-fast distinction between selective and nonselective institutions naturally elicits this question: aren't there good schools that no one applies to? Perhaps, although by today's definition a "good school" must produce strong employment outcomes for its graduates. So in the event there are any good schools experiencing this kind of market failure, I suggest they do a better job of tracking and promoting employment outcomes, particularly for first jobs. That's the only surefire path to moving from nonselective to selective in the era of the employment imperative.

• • •

Deciding not to go to (a nonselective) college is hard. But if you do opt for a faster + cheaper alternative, you'll be at the leading edge of a wave that will have employers' attention. As faster + cheaper alternatives become more numerous and prominent, their superior value propositions will attract more talented and motivated students. Employers will see a high level of talent coming from these programs and add them to their recruitment processes. As graduates from faster + cheaper alternatives achieve strong employment outcomes, expect to see a snowball effect as more young people opt for faster + cheaper options over traditional colleges.

It could tip faster than anyone thinks possible. Look what's happened in the world of credit cards. According to the *New York Times,* it took only seven months for American Express—the credit card that for generations has "defined ostentatious luxury and capitalist striving" and charged cardholders up to $7,500 annually—to lose its status among Millennials. Following its launch in August 2016, the competing Chase Sapphire Reserve card signed up more than a million cardholders, half of whom are under thirty-five. Why? Sapphire Reserve provides a sign-up bonus of 100,000 points, $300 in travel credits, a TSA Pre✓® credit, lounge access, and a higher rewards points levels. It also only charges $450 a year (vs. $550 for Amex's flagship platinum card). It's faster + cheaper.[17]

It's also less ostentatious. As the *Times* pointed out, while American Express has essentially sold snob appeal for decades ("Membership Has Its Privileges"—sound familiar, colleges and universities?), "For Millennials, snobbery isn't quite as appealing as it once was. Or more precisely, snobbery has to be hidden and camouflaged as something else, like an Instagram post from your Iceland spelunking adventure or a lament about how hard it is to find a charging station near Burning Man for your electric sports car."[18]

One of the strengths of American Express over the years has been its bundled travel services. Cardholders can access Amex concierges to book travel and restaurants and even receive help "if you leave your reading glasses inside a hotel room in Budapest."[19] But as the *Times* noted, "Millennials don't really need travel agents or concierges: They have Priceline and Yelp. Nor are they traditionally fans of opera, ballet, Dom Pérignon tastings, or the other high-culture events Amex can get cardholders into. If you leave your reading glasses in Budapest, it's probably faster to order new ones from Warby Parker, which is pretty cheap to begin with."[20]

According to the creator of Sapphire Reserve, "The message we send is, this isn't your father's credit card. For Millennials, travel might mean taking an Uber to a hole-in-the-wall restaurant in Chinatown, and then riding the subway to karaoke, and then catching a taxi home. So we're going to give you accelerated travel points on all that. This is a card for accumulating experiences."[21]

One focus group respondent quoted in the *Times* said, "An Amex says you're rich, but [Sapphire Reserve] says you're interesting." Similarly, graduating from an unaffordable nonselective college says you're rich, but a faster + cheaper alternative says you're interesting. Hiring managers like Laszlo Bock who are aware of faster + cheaper alternatives already believe this to be true.[22]

The logic that leads public opinion to disregard alternatives to college today is pretty much tautological: If every student with the requisite talent and grit to do well in the twenty-first-century market economy chooses an Amex, then by definition American Express cardholders will have higher incomes than other cardholders. It's the same thing with bachelor's degrees: by definition alternatives have had inferior results to date. The question we should be asking is what faster + cheaper pathways will achieve when, like Sapphire Reserve, they gain status equal to Amex-like colleges and universities and attract comparable talent.

We're about to find out. It wouldn't surprise me if Millennials and Gen Z-ers who begin opting for alternatives in order to be interesting and gain experience, become richer as well. (They'll certainly be less indebted, not to mention more informed and motivated when it comes to deciding on additional postsecondary education beyond their entry-level job.) The rapid emergence of Sapphire Reserve demonstrates that status is mutable and always mutating. While disregarded today by constituencies as varied as parents, guidance counselors, and policy makers, faster + cheaper pathways to good first jobs are on their way to becoming a Sapphire-like status symbol.

• • •

If the idea of not choosing college is still hard to process, you may want to consider a gap year. Gap years evolved in the seventies and eighties as a way for young people to gain life experience, maturity, and direction before launching into years of formal postsecondary education.

In 2016, President Obama's daughter Malia announced she would take a gap year before starting at Harvard, bringing additional attention to the phenomenon. The *New York Times* reported on Malia's gap year as "part of a growing and expensive trend,"[23] but that's not necessarily the case. Early gap year participants were primarily engaged in travel and recreation; there are now an increasing number of organized gap year programs oriented around social impact projects as well as personal and career discovery. If a gap year results in a more targeted, better informed decision on postsecondary education, it could yield major dividends.

Year On is one such program. In the spirit of "try before you buy," students are signing up for Year On's three-phase program. First, students have a ten-week volunteer experience in India, Indonesia, Mexico, Peru, or Tanzania. Projects involve environmental conservation, youth development, women's empowerment, construction and renovation, or teaching English. Phase two is a twelve-week bootcamp-like program in San Francisco, where students collaborate on projects and develop an e-portfolio for employers. Then students do a twelve-week internship with an employer partner.

Matthew Bal participated in a Year On program in Indonesia teaching computer skills to grade-school children. Combined with the San Francisco program and internship, Matthew calls Year On some of the most important learning of his entire life. "I finally had a space where I could create and fail and learn without any fear," he said. "When considering what to do after high school, I hope students everywhere remember that they matter—that their goals, interests, and lives matter beyond what clubs they join or college they get into. Making the decision to take a gap year can bring that sense of purpose and belonging into clear view."[24]

Applications to Year On increased by a factor of four in 2016. More students and families are sensing that it might be a good idea to take a step back and assess before committing to a six-figure investment over four years or more.

• • •

Today, young Americans choose among colleges. Tomorrow, they'll choose between college and faster + cheaper alternatives. If you're considering a faster + cheaper option, you'd do well to keep four things in mind.

First, just because you're not going to college, it doesn't mean you're choosing a blue collar career. Too many people confuse faster + cheaper with the idea of traditional vocational education, which tends to be associated with sawdust-covered memories of middle or high school shop classes. America may well need more tradespeople, and working with one's hands is intrinsically and financially rewarding for many people. But most students considering college aren't interested in heading down that road. What you are choosing is a new collar first job, one that's going to require a moderate to high level of technical training on specific software, but probably not the same level of other skills that employers expect of a college graduate.

Second, if these alternatives seem cheap today, they'll be even cheaper tomorrow. Given their risk-return profile, tuition-pay bootcamp models are likely to be crowded out by no-tuition-upfront models: either employer-pay or income share. Nearly all quality faster + cheaper alternatives—and certainly those that are twelve months or less—are capable of being financed by income share agreements. Within a few years, charging tuition (and requiring students to take on debt) for any postsecondary program that's twelve months or fewer will be viewed as a negative market signal and anachronistic. ("What? No one's willing to back an ISA for this program? Forget it.")

Third, unless you performed at or near the top of your class in high school, the fastest + cheapest alternatives are unlikely to work for you. These brief programs simply don't have much time to further develop your cognitive and noncognitive skills. So look at programs that are at least six months in length but expect a year or two, along the lines of something like Holberton School.

Fourth, recognize that the way you'll be purchasing higher education will be akin to the way we now purchase software. Back in the day, companies used to buy software via enterprise licenses, which cost a lot and gave companies access to a whole lot of functionality, much of which wasn't required. Equally punishing was the implementation: extensive and expensive. Some enterprise software products became infamous for multiyear implementations that ultimately failed. Enterprise software companies had lots of unhappy customers.

We no longer buy enterprise software. Now we buy SaaS products—immediately available and configurable online, and we pay for what we need when we need it. If more functionality is required, it can typically be added immediately for an additional monthly charge.

SaaS products are more efficient than enterprise software in the same way that faster + cheaper alternatives are more efficient than degree programs: At the age of eighteen or nineteen, rather than trying to antici-pate all the higher education you'll need for the rest of your life, why not opt for what you need right now to get a great first job, then go from there?

By opting for faster + cheaper, you'll be staging your postsecondary edu-cation—not getting it all in one greedy gulp. Opting for a faster + cheaper path doesn't mean that's all the postsecondary education you'll get or need. What it does mean is that when it comes time for more, you'll be better informed as to what you need. And given that the average Millennial is on track for four career changes before the age of thirty-two, the more infor-mation you get, the better.[25]

With time also comes perspective and maturity, meaning it's likely that you'll put more in and get more out of your education. The adage "education is wasted on the young" may not be correct, but it's probably true that education is less likely to be wasted on the young than on the very young (so argued a 2017 *New York Times* column: "Let's Waste College on the Old").[26] Perhaps most important, without tens of thousands of dollars of student loan debt, you'll be much better positioned to afford whatever further education you need.

Finally, if your family is upper-income, while the bottom of the matrix may not be a concern, I urge you to think about helping to blaze the trail of faster + cheaper alternatives to college. The more families like yours that opt for alternatives to college, the faster the market will tip. Financial matters may not be a concern for you, but the health of our democracy should be.

CHAPTER 9 • KEY POINTS

- As faster + cheaper alternatives emerge, students will have a real choice in postsecondary education.
- It's probably worth stretching the definition of "affordable" to attend a selective college, but it will make sense to maintain a strict definition of "affordable" for nonselective colleges.
- Millions of students will opt for a faster + cheaper alternative instead, and perhaps sooner than anyone thinks.

CHAPTER 10

The Importance
of Being Faster
+ Cheaper

Seven years of college down the drain.

—*Animal House (1978)*

At the end of college, I had a final interview for a job with a national consulting firm that reserved guest rooms at a hotel near campus. The rooms were tiny and, unfathomably, had no chairs. So, in the most awkward half-hour of my nascent professional life, both the interviewer and I sat uncomfortably on the king-size bed. The other notable thing about that interview—albeit dwarfed by the louche setting—was that we talked about little of substance other than the fact that a forty-something man and a twenty-something man were sitting together on a bed (which was so weird that nothing else seemed remotely as substantial).

It was only later, once I had begun working at another consulting firm, I learned that the primary purpose of these final interviews was to administer the "Pittsburgh Airport Test" to candidates. The Pittsburgh Airport Test demanded that the interviewer imagine being stuck in the Pittsburgh Airport for eight hours and ascertain whether it would be bearable to be stuck with the interviewee. Of course, this Pittsburgh Airport Test isn't a

test any more than having drinks with Bunny and Digby at the country
club is a test. Or as my industrial-organization psychologist and psychome-
trician friends would say, it has no validity. But it is how many employers
continue to hire.

J. D. Vance came to the same conclusion in his best-selling book *Hillbilly Elegy*:

> I had always thought that when you need a job, you look online for
> job postings. And then you submit a dozen resumes. And then you
> hope that someone calls you back. If you're lucky, maybe a friend
> puts your resume at the top of the pile . . . The problem is, virtually
> everyone who plays by those rules fails. The week of interviews
> showed me that successful people are playing an entirely different
> game. They don't flood the job market with resumes, hoping that
> some employer will grace them with an interview. They network.
> They email a friend of a friend to make sure their name gets the
> look it deserves. They have their uncles call old college buddies.[1]

With employers playing the Pittsburgh Airport Test with college grads
on king-size beds in university-adjacent hotels, it's not unreasonable to con-
clude that our current pedigree- and degree-based system is rigged against
working class Americans. Recent surveys show that's exactly what's happening. A 2017 poll of white working class voters by a Democratic political
action committee found that 57 percent believed a college degree "would
result in more debt and little likelihood of landing a good-paying job."[2] This
seems to be contributing to a rapid deterioration in trust by conservatives.
Between 2016 and 2017, the percentage of self-identified Republicans who
said colleges and universities are having a negative effect on the country
increased from 45 percent to 58 percent—virtually the same percentage as
white working class voters who are down on higher education.[3]

The causes of this loss of confidence are easy to identify: the employ-
ment imperative coupled with poor employment outcomes, skyrocketing
student loan debt, and the sense that four-year degrees are out of reach. In
Hillbilly Elegy, Vance wrote of talking to a Kentucky teacher who told him,
"It's like our politicians think college is the only way . . . For many, it's great.
But a lot of our kids have no realistic shot of getting a college degree."[4]

Working class students are caught between the rock of perceived
employer expectations and the hard place of affordability and completion

reality. The pollster who conducted the survey of white working class voters concluded, "When these voters hear people tell them that the answer to their concerns is college, their reaction is to essentially say—don't force your version of the American dream on me."[5] And so we can also apportion blame to policy makers and employers who have encouraged and accepted the cult of the bachelor's degree. How this came about is entirely understandable: well-intentioned but misguided educational paternalism (i.e., having had the benefit of a four-year college education, everyone should have the same opportunity). But the upshot is that college and its primary product—the four-year bachelor's degree—have become synonymous with elites and elitism.

This is highly ironic for two reasons. First, despite the relatively recent emergence of a mass market for higher education, it's a return to college's roots. This is what college was back in the day: a way for the merchant elite to distinguish their sons in society. Second, degrees are producing much less "elite" employment outcomes than they were a decade ago. Irony aside, there's truth to the charge that degrees equal elitism. American society is increasingly stratified by degrees more than anything else. According to Harry Holzer, former chief economist for the US Department of Labor, below the top 1 percent, inequality in the bottom 99 percent is explained entirely by credentials.[6] As Brit Kirwan, former chancellor of the University of Maryland has said, "We are creating a permanent underclass in America based on education—something we've never had before."[7]

The elites in the mainstream media have—probably unwittingly—deepened the association between college and elitism by showcasing faster + cheaper alternatives that lead to blue collar careers. While I'm as keen as anyone on young people learning trades and becoming plumbers and electricians, and while there's surely a skill gap in the skilled trades, these jobs aren't growing as quickly as technology-centric new collar jobs. More important, few upper-middle class parents are excited about the prospect of their children pursuing such careers (i.e., we didn't invest in our child's education so she could become a plumber). As a result, the incessant identification of anything less than a bachelor's degree with blue collar work acts as a brake on the faster + cheaper revolution; the revolution only happens when upwardly mobile families feel confident that choosing nondegree pathways won't relegate their children to a life of working with their hands.

Nevertheless, 2016 was the year the backlash began. As Condoleeza Rice said in a May 2017 interview, "One of the things that broke down and one of the reasons we got the election we did—as my friend calls it, the 'Do You Hear Me Now' election—is too many people have felt that the American Dream isn't there for them." Rice recommended a national project on education and job skills because "when people have the sense that they have control of their future, they are then really a part of this democracy."[8]

On one side, higher education's failures may be prompting Millennials to give up on capitalism, or at least to say they are. In "Why Young Voters Love Old Socialists," Sarah Leonard, a twenty-nine-year-old editor at *The Nation,* wrote in the *New York Times* that "Millennials are worse off than their parents were . . . they are loaded with college debt (or far less likely to be employed without a college degree)."[9] She concluded that "the post-Cold War capitalist order has failed us." But fear not, there's a great alternative: "Because we came to political consciousness after 1989, we're not instinctively freaked out by socialism." She went on to cite a 2016 Harvard poll that showed 51 percent of eighteen- to twenty-nine-year-olds rejected capitalism.[10] According to Richard Wolff, a professor of economics at the New School University and one of America's few remaining Marxist economists, due to growing awareness that wages have been unable to keep up with the cost of living, younger Americans "are getting closer and closer to understanding that they live in an economic system that is not working for them, and will not work for their kids."[11]

On the other end of the political spectrum, Donald Trump was prescient enough to exploit this vulnerability. In polls leading up to the election, support for Trump from those without a bachelor's degree was up to 20 percent higher than for Americans with them, leading to his memorable line following his win in the Nevada Republican caucus: "I love the poorly educated." He ended up winning a whopping 72 percent of white males without degrees and 62 percent of white women without degrees.[12]

Ali Lapp, executive director of a Democratic political action committee, has reviewed recent polling data and concluded:

> When Democrats go and talk to working-class voters, we think talking to them about how we can help their children go to college, they have a better life, is great. [But] they are not interested . . . It's a problem when you have a growing bloc in the electorate think that college is not good, and they actually disdain folks that go to college.[13]

As a result, *Politico* has concluded that free college is not a winner for Democrats: "The call for free college tuition fosters both resentment at ivory tower elitism and regret from people who have degrees but are now buried under debt."[14] President Trump's top priority in higher education seems to have more popular support: "We must embrace new and effective job-training approaches . . . These kinds of options can be a positive alternative to a four-year degree."[15]

Boosting alternatives to college is on the way to becoming Republican Party doctrine. In June 2017, Rep. Virginia Foxx (R–North Carolina), a former college president who is now Chair of the House Committee on Education and the Workforce, wrote:

> Too many Americans have come to believe that the pathway to a successful career lies solely on a college campus, and in a baccalaureate degree. For many Americans, this is not the case, and not the best path they can take to find the skills needed to ultimately lead them to the overall goal of an education—a good paying job and a successful life.[16]

This disenchantment with higher education manifested itself in the initial 2017 Republican House tax reform bill, which amounted to a broadside attack on colleges and universities: reducing incentives for charitable giving; eliminating the deduction for student loan interest; eliminating the Lifetime Learning Credit; taxing employer tuition assistance; taxing wealthy endowments; taxing graduate school stipends; and restricting access to the tax-exempt bond market.

While it is disturbing that those most in need of social mobility seem to have declared war on what once was America's engine of social mobility, what's really dangerous is that the backlash against college seems to have sideswiped something even more important, and perhaps existential. Colleges and universities have long been America's primary source of expertise. But as higher education has become identified with elitism for a significant percentage of the population, the expertise resident in university faculty and researchers has been undermined in the minds of far too many.

As a result, while college and university experts in areas like climate change, trade, and immigration are vocal and nearly unanimous with regard to certain policy positions, they've never had less impact than they have today and, in fact, could be causing conservative policy makers to adopt opposing positions simply because it's "good politics"—a product of the creeping sense that higher education demarcates the line between the elite and the "real" America.

• • •

Across the pond, the United Kingdom experienced a similar backlash in the summer of 2016: the vote to exit the European Union. With elites (degree holders all) telling Britons to vote one way—according to *The Economist*, "The more qualifications someone has, the more pro-European he or she is likely to be"—too many working class voters went the other way.[17] The country is still struggling with the Brexit result. In response, during the 2017 general election, the Conservative Party platform aimed at shifting away from traditional universities toward new institutes of technology, which would specialize in technical disciplines and provide "higher level apprenticeships" and "bespoke courses" for employers.[18]

Singapore is also ahead of the curve. The Singapore government has begun actively discouraging families from enrolling their children in bachelor's degree programs. The prime minister has encouraged students to work for a few years or start their own business before making the decision to enroll in a university program: "You will gain experience and understand yourself better and then be better able to decide what the next step will be," he said. The National Development Minister was even more blunt: "You own a degree, but so what? You can't eat it . . . Can you have a whole country where 100 percent are graduates? I am not so sure."[19]

South Korea appears to be next up. *The Economist* suggests that "South Korea is losing faith in an elitist education system," pointing to student protests to reject universities, "trying to persuade people to boycott the whole process."[20] In 2017, legislation was introduced to extend the government's exam-based blind hiring process (where a student's academic record is not considered) to state-owned firms as well.

• • •

The importance of being faster + cheaper is clear: improved social and economic mobility and inclusion, reduced inequality, and greater political stability. But as faster + cheaper alternatives to college continue to proliferate and grow in popularity, it's also important to question what might be at risk. Which products or values of the current college-centric system will we miss once a proportion of students vote for faster + cheaper?

I'll start with the most common objection: economic growth. Over the past century, economic growth has been driven by new technology and improvements in how we allocate physical and financial capital. But we have not gotten much better at allocating human capital. The emergence of faster + cheaper alternatives to college will help, not hurt. Rather than making a four-plus-year and six-figure investment before beginning to think about a career path, more young people will be able to "try before they buy" and, as a result, more people will find occupations (faster + cheaper) where they're happy and more productive—resulting in improved productivity and economic growth. Faster + cheaper alternatives to college are an important tonic for the slower growth that has ailed the American and other developed economies over the past fifteen years.

Still, critics will point to data suggesting that students who take shorter, more focused postsecondary programs may see better employment outcomes in the first few years but are surpassed five to ten years out of school—and typically by a large margin.[21] I have three responses to these concerns. First, this literature is entirely focused on traditional vocational or trade programs, which may not be representative of new collar faster + cheaper models. Second, there are studies that directly contradict these findings, such as University of Chicago economist Ofer Malamud's longitudinal model comparing English university (early specialization) vs. Scottish university (later specialization) outcomes and concluding that wage differences don't persist over time.[22]

More important, economic gains or losses hinge on skill development, or how much students actually learn and retain. In 2017, MIT researchers from the Center for Brains, Minds & Machines surveyed the scientific literature and concluded there is no evidence that anything significant and "unused" is remembered beyond two years. The "Universal Law of Forgetting," said the researchers, is that content knowledge that is not refreshed decays according to the Ebbinghaus curve.[23]

Hermann Ebbinghaus was a nineteenth-century German psychologist who pioneered the study of memory. In 1885, he published "On Memory," which revealed the "forgetting curve," where knowledge decays according to the formula $R = e^{-(t/s)}$, where R is retention, s is the relative strength of memory, and t is time. According to the MIT researchers, the upshot—consistently reproduced across hundreds of experiments—is that we lose 50 percent of unrefreshed content knowledge every two years.

In a related presentation at MIT, researcher Brian Subirana was critical about the structure of traditional higher education, hypothesizing that "what we learn in the classroom is irrelevant for students in the long run" unless they reuse it soon and often. Subirana acknowledged that nearly all the research on this topic concerns content knowledge and not skills. And there are obvious examples of unrefreshed retention beyond two years, such as facial recognition or motor skills like riding a bicycle. So the key question for higher education is whether critical thinking, problem solving, and the other core cognitive skills that college aims to inculcate are more like content knowledge, or more like riding a bike.[24]

In his presentation, Subirana and a colleague discussed an MIT paper from 2009: "What Do Seniors Remember from Freshman Physics." In the study, seniors are surprised with a request to retake a physics exam they took during their freshman year. Those who hadn't continued in physics or a physics-related field achieved at approximately half the level of 3.5 years earlier. Only those who went on to major in physics, mechanical engineering, and aeronautics/astronautics did as well or better.[25]

While a freshman physics exam is primarily about content knowledge, performance on such a test isn't unrelated to cognitive skill development. Subirana surmised that unused cognitive skills are not exempt from Ebbinghaus's curve. "Forgetting is unavoidable," he said. He and his colleagues speculate that "the brain may behave a bit like regular physical muscles and practice may increase their ability."

In a general sense, every graduate practices the cognitive and noncognitive muscles flexed in college, which improves problem solving and critical thinking abilities. Graduates enter the workforce and encounter problems that must be solved. But Subirana's work points toward much greater specificity: The closer the practice to the original skill "memory," the more likely the skill will be retained.

If our goal is to increase society's store of skills, we must mount a vigorous defense to the tyranny of Ebbinghaus's curve. The most effective defense is to link practice of skills in the workforce as closely as possible to the context in which they were learned. Unfortunately for higher education, the mountain (work) will not come to Muhammad (higher education). So Muhammad must go to the mountain. This means that if a student's first job is going to be in mobile UX/UI design, she'll be more likely to retain and deepen cognitive and noncognitive skills developed in formal postsecondary education if they were inculcated as part of a mobile UX/UI design program.

This is exactly the point of last-mile training and faster + cheaper alternatives. There's reason to believe student A's retention of cognitive and noncognitive skills following a last-mile training program plus two years' work experience as a mobile UX/UI designer may rival or exceed student B, who earns an unrelated bachelor's degree and then miraculously is hired and works for two years in the same job.

By introducing the concept of forgetting, I'm not trying to engage in educational nihilism. It should be instructive for determining how best to deploy the hundreds of billions of dollars that are currently flowing overwhelmingly to a single model of higher education. And it indicates that if we begin to diversify, we may lose much less than we fear.

●   ●   ●

But as students shift from traditional colleges to faster + cheaper options, there is a lot at risk. First are colleges and universities themselves and the communities they support. I'm particularly concerned about small and midsize nonurban institutions—schools far from major centers of employment. The troubles of rural colleges are relatively well known. You probably hadn't heard of Sweet Briar College before it closed its doors, but you may now know that the school is a rural Virginia women's college that faced years of declining enrollment and budget challenges. After announcing its closure, Sweet Briar was revived as a result of an intense alumnae campaign and continues to rely nearly exclusively on contributions to fund operations.

Moody's predicts that small institutions—with revenue below $200 million—will begin failing at three times historical levels and merging into other schools at twice the rate we've seen. The percentage of small institutions with revenue growth below the level of inflation now exceeds 50 percent—a five times increase in five years. In terms of market share, Moody's says sub-thousand-student institutions are losing share to schools with enrollment over 10,000. Simply put, small and midsize institutions have become relatively less attractive to students focused on employment.[26] And unfortunately, smaller institutions are more likely to be nonurban institutions.

Exploring this phenomenon at the state level—and beginning alphabetically, as I like to do—Alabama's four largest public universities are thriving. The University of Alabama, Auburn University, University of Alabama at Birmingham, and University of South Alabama have experienced enrollment growth over the past five years, with the majority of total growth at the largest institution, UA. At the same time, nine smaller schools in the state are seeing flat to declining enrollment.[27]

Because you shouldn't expect to see faster + cheaper alternatives arise anywhere other than large metropolitan areas, in a country that's already concerned about the divide between thriving cities and stagnating rural areas, enrollment shifts away from smaller rural colleges to urban faster + cheaper alternatives that will exacerbate America's urban-rural divide.

The second major risk is an educated citizenry. I've seen a few warning signs recently. Apparently NBA star Kyrie Irving believes the Earth is flat. The *Washington Post* quoted Irving as saying, "If you really think about it from a landscape of the way we travel, the way we move and the fact that—can you really think of us rotating around the sun, and all planets align, rotating in specific dates, being perpendicular with what's going on with these 'planets' and stuff like this?"[28] Then there's the 16 percent of Americans who think chocolate milk comes from brown cows.[29] While these examples are trivial, they do point to something my childhood hero Carl Sagan (astronomer, philosopher, PBS celebrity, bon vivant) predicted just before he passed away twenty or more years ago:

> I have a foreboding of an America in my children's or grandchildren's time—when the United States is a service and information economy . . . when awesome technological powers are in the hands of a very few, and no one representing the public interest can even grasp the issues; when the people have lost the ability to set their own agendas or knowledgeably question those in authority; when . . . our critical faculties in decline, unable to distinguish between what feels good and what's true, we slide, almost without noticing, back into superstition and darkness.[30]

Tennyson famously said, "Ring out the old, ring in the new . . . Ring out the false, ring in the true." So it's essential to make sure that as faster + cheaper alternatives proliferate, we're not simultaneously ringing in the false and ringing out the true. In other words, even if these new pathways to good jobs help millions of our economically disenfranchised and disgruntled brothers and sisters join the vibrant American economy, will we find we're all more susceptible to fake news because we're unable to critically engage with information we find on Facebook? Or because faster + cheaper alternatives may well develop deep skills, but not broad ones (and particularly not the broad knowledge typically required to be a good citizen), will anyone know who the heck Tennyson was? This is something that keeps me up at night.

Third is the loss of discovery, serendipity, and wonder. Floating through the first few years of college allows for a great deal of academic and personal discovery that many students take advantage of. But this four-year extension of childhood has become too expensive to remain the norm; it turns out there's a price at which discovery and serendipity don't make sense. What this means is that discovery will have to happen earlier, and in more discrete components: in high school and over summers.

It's not as though we're going to be cutting childhood short and sending twelve-year-olds off to work in the mines. But from high school on, it will become standard to think about skills and careers, particularly digital skills and careers. For young adults, discovery will also have to happen in medias res—on vacations, between gigs, contracts, and jobs, and even on the job through lifelong learning.

Finally, and sadly, will be the loss of fun—or all the dumb college stories I've subjected you to. Bootcamps and other faster + cheaper alternatives not only have less time for fun, they're not residential. You'll note that none of my college stories occur in class. They're all extracurricular (and mostly extra-extracurricular). They arise from interactions that can only occur when you put a group of like-minded college-age students together in a cloistered environment for an extended period of time. And as you can tell, they're what I remember and treasure most.

Of course, it's about more than antics and memories. College is about developing lifelong friendships and for many—myself included—partnerships. For all these reasons, as I've noted, this book is somewhat of an elegy, or maybe even a eulogy, for many colleges. But if it proves to be a eulogy, I'll tell you who should be indicted for the death: college and university leaders who allowed costs to get out of control in the last twenty-five years.

While these risks are sobering, I've always believed in triage when confronted with a complex problem. If you've seen a medical show on television, you know what I mean by triage: A patient comes in with a dozen medical problems, ER docs address the most life-threatening one first.

For higher education, faster + cheaper alternatives address the fact that the patient is bleeding out on the table. For me, lofty debates about the importance of education for discovery and well-rounded citizens ended with the advent of the $30,000 tuition bill. Once we've addressed the issue of economic security and stabilized the patient, we can worry about the rest. Treatments for these other problems can and will be found.

CHAPTER 10 • KEY POINTS

- Faster + cheaper alternatives to college have the potential to solve a range of critical social and economic problems.
- They're unlikely to lead to less skill development and economic growth.
- The emergence of faster + cheaper alternatives does put at risk the communities currently supported by colleges, discovery, fun, and an educated citizenry.
- However, given the society- and economy-threatening issues surrounding higher education, the logic of triage suggests addressing economic security first.

Colleges in a Faster + Cheaper World

PROFESSOR HATHAWAY: When you first started at Pacific Tech you were well on your way to becoming another Einstein, and then you know what happened?

CHRIS: I got a haircut?

—*Real Genius (1985)*

An experience in law school taught me it is possible to have too much of a good thing. I was living with my brother Aaron and friend Dave in a third-floor garret that ventilated to treetops via a gaping hole in the roof, providing ample access for squirrels. The downside was winter; it got cold in there. The upside was that the visiting squirrels brought Joe Sweeney from Animal Control into our lives. Joe would lecture us about the "bunny-rats," as he called them—transfixing us with his one working eye like a character from an Adam Sandler movie.

Not surprisingly, none of the girls we liked were fond of bunny-rats. Few were interested in as much as a visit until—on a break from my relationship with Yahlin—I met Wendy. Wendy was angelic. Beautiful, sweet, willing to visit and to tolerate overnight freezing temperatures and rustling sounds. A few weeks after I introduced Wendy to Aaron, he brought a girl home as well. She was also named Wendy, but to me, she was aggressively unpleasant and a long way from angelic and sweet. The Wendys were opposites and had no interest in becoming friends. As a result, there was tension, and I saw less of my brother.

A few weeks later, my Wendy ("Good Wendy") put our kitchen and oven to good use, baking an impressive cake for my birthday and warming up the place in the process. The cake was summarily devoured by my cold, hungry roommates, and a few days later she produced a batch of oatmeal raisin cookies. After that, Dave and Aaron let her hold the TV remote (their highest compliment).

Then Bad Wendy heard about Good Wendy's baking exploits. The next day, Bad Wendy whipped up a batch of double chocolate chip cookies. Which led to Good Wendy baking a pie, then Bad Wendy baking a cake. And so it went until one day Dave realized the passive-aggressive baking had caused him to gain ten pounds. It was truly too much of a good thing. So in the presence of the dueling dough-rolling Wendys, Dave disabled our tired oven and solemnly declared a baking moratorium.

● ● ●

The current state of college can be summed up in six words: too much of a good thing. American higher education has tilted way too far in the direction of what was initially intended to be a finishing school for the elite. America's nonselective colleges and universities have always been drawn by the siren song of trying to be the "Harvard" of wherever they happen to be located. And why not? Their leaders were educated at selective universities. They know what excellence looks and feels like and they try to emulate it, even from platforms that can never sustain it in terms of resources and in the level of talent and motivation of students.

Another reason is that they haven't seen a viable alternative model. Workforce development isn't an appealing option. It sounds vocational or blue collar—not what universities were set up to do. According to Anthony Carnevale, Director of Georgetown's Center on Education and the Workforce, the upshot is that when "we need . . . more skill in the work force, we turn . . . to colleges and say, 'You have a new mission.' Higher education . . . doesn't like to see itself that way."[1]

Over the next few years, the day of reckoning will come for many non-selective schools as students begin voting with their feet and choosing faster + cheaper alternatives over unaffordable four-year degree programs. To paraphrase my friend P. J. Pronger: colleges and universities won't change because they see the light, they'll change because they feel the heat. Non-selective colleges and universities that find themselves bleeding enrollment will have three options to compete for students.

Their first option is to become selective, meaning to significantly increase the number of students applying. Although a few schools have attained selectivity via marketing, sports, new facilities, or other tricks, given the employment imperative, the only sure path to selectivity is via better employment outcomes.

For many college leaders, the natural inclination will be to increase investment in career services. And while spending on career services can't be worse for students than spending on valet parking or lazy rivers, Andy Chan, a vice president at Wake Forest University, is correct in saying "career services must die." Better employment outcomes won't be the result of hiring more career services lifers and giving them a nicer, or even more centrally located office. It will require putting the university's fingers on the pulse of what employers are seeking, then engaging employers in novel ways. And that will require new and different programs that prioritize a good first job.

Rochester Institute of Technology's degree in software engineering is a good example. The program has an active employer advisory board that reviews course curriculum and current events in the field. It also requires students to complete three co-ops, meaning three terms working away from campus. The department's goal is to ensure students are employable for their first job, as well as their whole career. Another is the North Carolina Sales Institute, part of the Business School at the University of North Carolina, Greensboro. The Institute was created in 2015 "to address the demand for well-trained sales talent."[2] If students take the five sales courses offered by the Institute—professional selling, sales management, key account selling, sales internship, and effective selling—they've minored in sales. Companies recruiting from the Sales Institute include 3M, Carolina Material Handling, Mac Tools, Marriott, Martinsville Speedway, Pepsi Bottling, and

State Farm.[3] But there are too few examples of such programs because they require a major departure from traditional academic thinking.

• • •

The second option is for nonselective colleges to offer faster or cheaper degrees. Let's start with faster. I'm not talking about three-year degrees compressing 120 credits into three years. Saving a year doesn't seem blindingly fast compared with new faster + cheaper alternatives. I'm talking about building off-ramps into degree programs.

The idea of an off-ramp is simple. When requiring co-ops, like RIT's software engineering program, why not allow employers to retain top-performing students beyond the co-op term? Employers could keep students on part-time, while they return to complete their degrees. Or employers might decide to offer full-time jobs. Then colleges could provide on-ramps for students to return and complete their programs, and award credits for relevant work experience.

While off-ramps could become the first real university reflection of the priority students now place on employment, the problem is that they'd result in lost enrollment and revenue. Northeastern University offers the most comprehensive co-op program of any American institution. But the idea of off-ramps is anathema even to Northeastern. According to a Northeastern official, "Students are expected to come back to complete their degree. Some may continue to work part-time for employers as they complete. But we do not offer off-ramps."[4] Left unanswered was the question of whether an employer that made such an offer to a student would jeopardize its participation in Northeastern's co-op program.

If colleges are unlikely to shift to faster programs, how about cheaper ones? If nonselective schools want students to continue pursuing four years of postsecondary education before their first job, they'll need to radically reduce the cost to students and stop assuming students will be willing to take on tens of thousands of dollars in student loan debt. For nonselective schools, college as currently constructed simply costs too much.

Over the past few years, we've seen numerous examples of institutions resetting tuition levels. Birmingham Southern University is reducing tuition by 50 percent starting in fall 2018.[5] Sweet Briar, which failed and was resuscitated by alumnae, has offered a 40 percent reduction.[6] Concordia

University in Minnesota lowered tuition by 34 percent.[7] Drew University—one of New Jersey's most expensive schools—cut tuition by 20 percent.[8] The problem with all these examples is that while list price is lowered, there has been a commensurate cut in discount rates. Just as some real estate agents price houses below market to attract lots of bids, the idea is that by lowering list price, schools can attract more applications. Somehow, it's supposed to result in more students coming in the door for about the same net price. So it's not really cheaper.

In association with Strada Education, the Gallup organization has begun polling students on a range of higher education issues. Brandon Busteed of Gallup concluded that "universities should focus on *cutting* costs [and] *reducing* their physical footprint and overhead."[9] While I'm unable to cite a single example of cost reductions directed to reducing net tuition for students, there are two promising cheaper models out there.

The first is in Dallas where Michael Sorrell has worked a minor miracle at Paul Quinn College, one of the historically black colleges and universities. When Sorrell signed on in 2007, enrollment had declined to fewer than 500 students. A report that year by Boston Consulting Group predicted the school was unlikely to survive another eighteen months due to declining enrollment, low stakeholder morale, an almost nonexistent graduation rate, the absence of a significant donor base, a history of deficit spending, an audit with more than thirty findings of noncompliance, the lack of a quality academic experience, a fractured board of trustees, a poor public reputation, and serious accreditation issues.

"Unburdened by a legacy of success," as he likes to say, Sorrell invented what he calls the "New Urban College." The model starts with making degrees affordable for all students. Tuition was lowered from $24,000 to just over $14,000. Then Sorrell and his team assembled the pieces for how low-income students would be able to afford Paul Quinn:

1. Pell Grant of $5,800—84 percent of Paul Quinn students are Pell-eligible
2. Work credit of $5,000—all Paul Quinn residential students are required to work a minimum of ten hours per week for all fifteen weeks each semester. Freshmen and sophomores work on-campus jobs, but juniors and seniors are assigned work off campus, in many cases in their chosen field of study. Corporate partners pay $6,000 per student per year—$5,000 of which goes to the college and $1,000 to the student to help defray personal expenses.

3. Federal Supplemental Educational Opportunity Grant or other state or institutional scholarships—$1,200
4. Free books—faculty can only use open source instructional materials, eliminating the need for students to spend additional money on textbooks
5. Loans or personal contributions—$2,300

The result is an all-in bachelor's degree for less than $10,000 in student loan debt, which makes it a lot easier to pass the Rule of 10 test. Moreover, most students receive employment experience in their field of study. Sorrell is not done with affordability. Paul Quinn has implemented a summer bridge program for freshmen to capture a prior year of Pell for students and help them graduate early, thereby reducing debt even further. Paul Quinn now has waiting lists and Sorrell expects enrollment to reach the target of two thousand before long.

While Paul Quinn is the first of the urban "work colleges," others that are truly free for students—no tuition and student work covers living expenses—have been around for decades, including Berea College and College of the Ozarks. I recently had the privilege of meeting Jerry Davis, President of College of the Ozarks for nearly thirty years, and learned about a student who came to him with a problem: his father was in the penitentiary, his mother had died, and he couldn't afford to bury her. College of the Ozarks ended up paying for the burial. That's a level of affordability that could help nonselective colleges become very selective.

The second option is to go online and reflect the lower cost of online delivery with lower tuition. As it turns out, the only online degree models that are priced materially lower than on-ground programs are competency-based. In competency-based programs, students proceed at their own pace. This is less expensive for colleges because there aren't formal cohorts or instructors. Supported by instructors and advisors, students progress through course materials and take exams when they're ready.

Western Governors University (WGU) is the clear leader in inexpensive competency-based online degrees. Annual tuition is about $6,000, so students can go as fast as they like. Students with a need for speed can complete a degree in just over two years for about $15,000. About 83,000 students are currently enrolled in WGU, and six states—Indiana, Missouri, Nevada, Tennessee, Texas, and Washington—have invited WGU to create an in-state branch. New WGU President Scott Pulsipher has an unorthodox background for higher education: he was a successful executive at Amazon. He says WGU is different because it puts the "student at the center,"[10] which explains why WGU hasn't raised tuition in the last nine years. WGU is helping to redefine what it means to be a public university.

• • •

If few nonselective schools are positioned to offer faster or cheaper degree programs, could they offer faster + cheaper alternatives like bootcamps and college MVPs themselves? That's a third option for colleges that find themselves at a competitive disadvantage in a faster + cheaper era.

University of Virginia's College at Wise, a campus located in the state's southwest corner, near the Kentucky border, thinks it can. After a division of Frontier Communications decided to open a new customer care center that would create five hundred much-needed new jobs in Wise, UVa-Wise launched a free last-mile training bootcamp (paid for by the local workforce development board) to prepare local workers for these jobs. Frontier established the center to support Intuit's QuickBooks Online product. So the UVa-Wise bootcamp trains candidates in accounting fundamentals, communication, and customer service, before providing intensive technical training on the Quickbooks SaaS product. (The Frontier division has since been acquired by Sykes Enterprises and the customer care center is now known as Sykes-Wise Intuit.)

But for every UVa-Wise bootcamp, there are 100 university-based bootcamps that are intended to provide last-mile training to new graduates for an additional fee: top-up programs for new bachelor's degree–toting grads, not faster + cheaper alternatives. The Trilogy coding bootcamps that are popping up on campuses across the country are a good example. Universities—in particular, the continuing or extended education units of universities with mandates to produce incremental revenue—are delighted to host Trilogy bootcamps because Trilogy shares its revenue. For its part, Trilogy is delighted to have the imprimatur of the universities, even if it's through the less prestigious continuing education wing.

Then there's the University of Utah's new "degree plus" certificates: seven- or eight-week last-mile training courses. Utah urges new graduates to "take your history degree into the creative fields of web design or digital marketing. Or discover that the interests that led you to a degree in English may also be a great match for a career in operations or project

management."[11] All of which begs the question: why doesn't Utah incorporate these skills into degree programs to begin with?

To demonstrate that the bootcamp-on-campus may have already
jumped the shark, Duke is now offering a bootcamp in civic engagement
in American democracy. Only an elite university could take the bootcamp concept and divorce it from its raison d'être: employability. As Jake
Schwartz of General Assembly tweeted: "A part-time bootcamp at a university without job placement is just a continuing ed. course."[12]

● ● ●

I've intentionally avoided discussing community colleges. With a few excep-
tions, they don't offer bachelor's degrees, so I don't include them on the
matrix in the introduction. The degrees they do offer, associate's degrees,
are the least valued credentials in American higher education; aside from
select fields requiring associate's degrees for licensure, few employers care
if you have an associate's degree.

But it's now time to talk about community college. First, I love community college. My mother spent her career as a faculty member at Toronto's
George Brown College where she taught sociology and courses to nursing
students on dealing with death and dying, which led to many memorable
but grim conversations around the house. Second, they're extremely important. Depending on whether we count part-time students, community colleges enroll between 25 and 40 percent of all undergraduates.[13]

Although most students enroll in community colleges because they're
cheaper, they're often not faster, and the lower-income populations primarily served by community colleges means that students are working full time
at one or more jobs to feed and house themselves and their families as well
as studying. Of students who started at a community college in 2010, only 16
percent earned a bachelor's degree in six years.[14] Similarly, only 20 percent
of community college students earn an associate's degree in three years.[15]

A second major complication is transfer credits. A shocking new GAO
report has revealed that students who transfer lose 43 percent of credits
they've earned, which means even more time for life to get in the way.[16]
Recall this is exactly what happened to Simon Kim, who dropped out
before enrolling in AlwaysHired. I don't blame community colleges for
this, although they could achieve a great deal more by adding structure and

support to their existing programs.[17] What I do blame them for is failing to align their programs to jobs.

Community colleges originated as the first higher education institutions "in the community" when four-year colleges and universities were inaccessible to all but a small segment of the population. They were the first open-enrollment institutions and revolutionized accessibility in an era before a college degree became the sine qua non of the labor market. Conveniently, they also delivered vocational programs in the trades with which four-year institutions didn't wish to concern themselves.

So from the outset, community colleges had a split personality: the place to pull yourself up by the bootstraps and transfer, Horatio Alger–like, to a university, as well as being higher education's grease-stained freaky younger cousin. In recent years, community colleges have demonstrated the most success with vocational certificate programs that have a clear connection to good jobs; in areas like advanced manufacturing, community colleges are directly preparing students for good jobs.

Unfortunately, these programs remain the exception. The majority of community college students are enrolled in academic programs conceived of and led by academics who, by and large, would prefer to work at a selective college (and, like my mom, were probably educated there). Most community colleges have been firmly established on an academic foundation with presidents or chancellors, registrars and bursars, not to mention sociology departments.

But in an era where students care more about jobs than academic credentials, there's little reason for community colleges to continue to operate on an academic paradigm. Students don't want associate degrees or even certificates. They want good first jobs. So if community colleges want to become an attractive option in a faster + cheaper world, they'll need to reinvent themselves as placement colleges.

Placement colleges would be a hybrid of today's community colleges and the workforce investment boards responsible for placing unemployed workers in open jobs but which fail to provide meaningful training. Rather than starting by asking faculty what curriculum they might like to offer, placement colleges would start with employers and available jobs, then aim to provide the requisite (last-mile) training that students need to be considered for these jobs. Whether or not students would receive a recognizable academic credential for such training would be a secondary concern.

Pathways to good first jobs in growing sectors of the economy don't need to be shoehorned into credentials.

Academic College	Placement College
• Faculty-centric • Curriculum-centric • Little focus on assessment of competencies • Outcomes not measurable • Little to no focus on placement ("prepare for fifth job, not first job")	• Assessment of competencies • Employer-connected • Placement-centric • Education/training viewed as instrumental to placement, not as end in itself • Clear, measurable outcomes

Placement colleges would be in the business of taking students where they find them, equipping them with new competencies, and delivering them to jobs that (1) utilize their newly acquired skills, and (2) provide for upward career and economic mobility. This means no more "one-size-fits-all"; each student is different and requires a tailored pathway to a good job. Although employers wouldn't have traditional academic credentials with which to judge candidates, they would have e-portfolios, microcredentials, and other measures of real skills.

There is no likelihood that shifting thousands of community colleges to placement colleges will bust federal and state budgets. Placement colleges could require less government funding than the current model. First, pathways will be shorter than current degree- and credit-centric programs. Second, for higher-skill positions in high-demand areas, placement colleges could generate revenue from employers in the form of placement fees.

Sadly, given the academic leadership at most community colleges, placement colleges are probably a pipe dream. In the same way that many K–12 schools and school districts are hobbled by decisions made for the benefit of those who've opted to enter the education profession rather than students, so are community colleges, which have provided good careers to hundreds of thousands of terrific, well-meaning educators like my mom.

Ensuring that our extensive community college infrastructure is not wasted as the faster + cheaper revolution unfolds will require leadership at the state level. In Nevada, the State Assembly is pushing community colleges to move to an employer-specific training model. The vision, according to one community college president, is "a process where manufacturing employers can select from a menu of skills that they need and we can package those skills in a way that meets their training needs as concisely as possible."[18]

California has also made surprising progress; under the leadership of Van Ton-Quinlivan, the dynamic California Community Colleges' vice chancellor for workforce and economic development, local workforce boards now have a say in how additional state funding is being deployed.[19] The lesson is that without political leadership in the states, looking to community colleges to close the skills gap is tantamount to looking to the department of motor vehicles to invent self-driving cars—it won't happen, and community colleges will remain a bystander as students flock to more employer-connected faster + cheaper pathways.

● ● ●

On the other end of the spectrum, our most selective colleges and universities also have a lot of work to do as higher education gets faster + cheaper. As we see more bifurcation between selective and nonselective colleges and universities, top schools have an even greater responsibility to ensure they're admitting students with the most potential, not just the most wealth.

With the recent news that Harvard's new class of 2021 is 29 percent legacy, coupled with a report from Politico showing that the wealth of students' families is directly correlated to an institution's *US News* ranking (driving applications and selectivity), there is a risk that selective schools will become even more exclusive.[20] As Roger Schank has warned, faster + cheaper options may mean "that only rich people will go to college . . . Kids who want jobs will go to bootcamps."[21]

While the admissions process at selective schools considers a range of relevant factors, the pivotal criteria for the vast majority of applicants are the easiest to observe and quantify or rank: grades, test scores, extracurricular activities, and recommendations. All these factors reflect absolute achievement by eighteen-year-old applicants. And while absolute achievement says a great deal about a young applicant's talent and motivation, it may say as much if not more about the resources and support he or she has received.

As a result, admitted students are increasingly children from families with the resources to own houses in great school districts or afford private school. Here's the explanation Princeton's Dean of Admissions gave to the *Daily Princetonian* as to why Princeton admits between 30 and 40 percent of legacy applicants: "They have had the fortune of going to good schools. They have had opportunities that they've taken advantage of and are very strong applicants."[22] This "absolute achievement" definition risks driving even more inequality. While wealthy students are able to display great talent, many are born on third base and—because they're admitted to a good school—think they hit a triple.

A better metric for selective college admissions would be a "distance traveled" approach: achievement contextualized by the student's challenges and resources. A student who has traveled a greater distance—overcoming a lack of resources, family structure or support, and discrimination of any kind—is more likely to have the grit that is probably a better predictor of lifetime/career success (and certainly a better indicator of potential) than absolute achievement at the age of eighteen. A number of leading state universities have already begun to implement such an approach, at least informally. But few private universities have done so, and no school has done anything to popularize it.

What would a distance traveled approach to college admissions look like? It would require a concerted effort to evaluate student achievement relative to unique background and resources. Selective schools should consider establishing an "adversity index" for high schools to weight applicant test scores via a combination of factors like percentage free and reduced price lunch, diversity in terms of minorities and immigrants, local income level, unemployment rate, and crime rate. More than any other metric, test scores should be indexed; wealthy students utilize SAT tutors and take the test multiple times whereas most low-income students are untutored and take them once. In terms of grades, the admissions process should focus on class rank rather than absolute GPA.

In terms of essays and response questions, selective colleges and universities should ask both applicant and parent about family income, resources, and structure from a young age to try to get a sense of the distance. They should also ask if applicants are helping to take care of siblings or other family members (or if a sibling or other family member has played a major role in helping to take care of them). Questions should focus on how applicants have solved problems with the resources they've had. Finally, colleges must make clear that they recognize and reward paid work, no matter how manual or menial, and particularly if applicants have helped to support their families.

Reorienting admissions according to distance traveled also means deemphasizing the most egregious examples of absolute achievement culture. Schools should not reward flashy volunteer experiences or unpaid internships. Stop focusing solely on participation or leadership in extracurricular activities and ask students to reflect on their impact on the group and the impact of the activity on their own development. Legacies should not receive a leg up. The status of recommenders should be irrelevant. CEOs and custodians should have equal say; what should matter is the content of the recommendation. Stop rewarding students who have the resources to travel to campus. Whether students have visited campus before being admitted is irrelevant in a distance traveled world.

Finally, it would help level the playing field if the SAT and ACT were administered universally and free of charge to students.[23] Colleges should provide templates to all students for résumés, essays, and response questions: students who've traveled a greater distance probably haven't seen these done right, let alone practiced them.

While this would be a major shift for our top two hundred or so institutions, we should insist that they do the work. The stakes are too high. Our best schools must stop being part of the problem and take the lead in the development of a solution. Taking a distance traveled approach to admissions can help. American colleges and universities need to do much more to measure potential than simply looking at absolute achievement at the age of eighteen.

● ● ●

As faster + cheaper alternatives proliferate, and as enrollment flows away from nonselective colleges and universities to these new pathways to jobs, it's not all bad news for higher education. While colleges and universities will cede market share to alternatives preparing students for first jobs, there will be a concomitant increase in the demand for secondary and tertiary pathways: programs will be essential for young professionals already in their first or second job but who require additional cognitive and noncognitive skill development to move up to a managerial role, or move on to another role. These probably won't be master's programs, but rather specific pathways to turn entry-level tech workers into stronger critical thinkers, better problem solvers, effective communicators, and inspiring leaders.

I hope employers will insist on these secondary and tertiary pathways. I also hope higher education leaders start developing them now. The common goal should be not only to regain enrollment and revenue but also to address the Kyrie Irving–Carl Sagan problem: ensuring an educated, effective citizenry. It would be senseless to strengthen our economy in a way that puts our democracy at risk.

For some colleges and universities, developing secondary and tertiary pathways may mean changing the institution's mission to focus entirely post–first job, where students don't require the level of employer connectivity or placement assistance that they do for their first job. Fortunately, at many colleges and universities, the most innovative schools are graduate and professional programs that serve exactly this population.

I look forward to the many innovative and successful post–first job pathways that colleges and universities will produce. While nonselective colleges and universities may not succeed in becoming selective, or at offering faster + cheaper degree programs, or in developing faster + cheaper alternatives, secondary and tertiary pathways represent a viable fourth option.

● ● ●

When I was in college, one of the iconic experiences was visiting the Yankee Doodle—a greasy spoon at the corner of York and Elm Streets—and taking the Doodle Challenge. The Doodle Challenge involved eating as many burgers as quickly as possible in a single sitting. At the time, the record was nineteen burgers in two and a half hours. For my roommate Chris, twenty burgers became his white whale. Twenty burgers meant two things: immortality by way of his name on a plaque above the door and also not having to pay for twenty burgers. While Doodle burgers were small, both the buns and patty were soaked in butter before frying (the Doodle was renowned for its fried donut). Chris trained for months with loaves of bread. On the day, we all headed to the Doodle, supportive of our hero but also making side bets.

Chris was going strong at burger #8. At burger #10 he began to slow. And at burger #12, Chris coughed and a tiny speck of burger flew out of his mouth. We knew his quest was at an end. We paid the bill and enveloped Chris like a fallen prizefighter, hustling him out of the Doodle and back to our college. That was the last Chris saw of the Doodle for some time, but not the last he saw of those burgers.

The shift from degrees to faster + cheaper alternatives to college, followed by prescribed secondary and tertiary pathways, is something Chris would have supported that day at the Doodle. I'm not suggesting it would be a good idea to reduce our level of postsecondary education—in aggregate or per capita. That would be economic suicide and potentially calamitous for young people as they search for their second, third, or fourth job. What I am arguing for is a radical restaging of how we consume higher education. Young people shouldn't be forced to eat as much education as they can in one sitting in order to have a shot at a good first job. It's got to shift to what we need when we need it—hopefully before our full-employment economy takes a turn for the worse, which means underemployment of new grads will be joined by its evil twin: unemployment. Whether it's Doodle burgers, baked goods from the dueling Wendys, or postsecondary education, American higher education is currently too much of a good thing all at once.

Just because these emerging alternatives are faster doesn't mean we'll lose the fun. Successful faster + cheaper programs will scale and their many cohorts will need places to live; Revature, for example, already provides housing. So successful faster + cheaper alternatives will find themselves in the business of operating something like campuses. Smart ones will take advantage of the immersive environment, even if only for a short period of time, to develop and evaluate the soft skills that employers value. It wouldn't surprise me in the least if future faster + cheaper students not only land great first and second jobs with no debt (or tuition) but, after hours, they also find themselves at a local greasy spoon, trying to set a new (faster + cheaper) record of their own.

A decade from now, the fact that young people were encouraged to load up on debt just as they were starting their careers will seem bizarre and anachronistic—a practice that benefited providers of higher education more than the Millennials they aimed to serve. In hindsight, given all the uncertainty around technological change and the future of work, it will seem incredible that Millennials risked taking on all that debt at one time, at such a young age. The faster + cheaper future may prove to be less memorable. We'll have fewer heroic stories of Doodle burgers and fallen pizzas. But by breaking college up into pathways—by staging postsecondary education—more students will finish their meals and make it to work. And no one should go broke or get sick.

Directory of Faster+ Cheaper Alternatives to College

Name Locations, Program Length Website	Bachelor's required?	Preparing students for these jobs	Other admissions requirements
Program Type: Apprenticeship			
8th light *Chicago, Los Angeles, New York, London, 2–8 months* 8thlight.com/apprenticeship	No	Software development	Multiple tracks (Student, Resident, Journeyman) based on prior experience / educational requirements
Accenture Federal Services *Eastside Promise Zone, San Antonio, Varies* sanantonio.gov/East-Point/PromiseZone	No	IT, consulting, federal services	Students and adults in Eastside Promise Zone, San Antonio, TX
Aon *US (Chicago and Lincolnshire, IL) and UK, Varies, typically 2 years* aoncampus.com/apprenticeships	No	Insurance, technology, HR	
BLUE 1647 *St. Louis, 6–12 weeks* blue1647.com	No	IT	Focus on minorities, GED/high school diploma
BlueCross BlueShield *South Carolina, Varies* apprenticeshipcarolina.com	No	IT	Current employee or college graduate
BMW *Spartanburg, SC, Varies* bmwusfactory.com/education/commitment-to-education/?r=1503353866978#scholars-program	No	Manufacturing	Enrolled at participating technical college

Curriculum	Employer engagement	Student financing available	Statistics (placement statistics include percentage in jobs in field, starting salary)
Software development; mentorship	Apprenticeship is the largest path to employment at 8th light. Apprentices are software generalists who rotate regularly through client projects before joining general team as Software Consultants	N/A	
On-the-job training combined with technical education at participating educational partners	Public-private partnership with the City of San Antonio and Bexar County, Texas, providing up to 50 paid apprenticeships for students and adults from the Eastside Education and Training Center, Sam Houston High School, and St. Philips College	N/A	
Accreditation-focused technical skills (e.g. Actuarial); professional skills	Full-time employment combined with certification-focused training provided by Aon	N/A	
Information Technology (IT) and Science, Engineering, Art and Mathematics (STEAM) applications; focus on group activities, shared problem solving and mentorship	Paid apprenticeship with guaranteed employment after program completion	N/A	
On-the-job training and mentorship combined with certification-focused technical education	Paid apprenticeship serves as path to employment at BCBS	N/A	
Partnership with local technical colleges to provide associate's degree in tandem with on-the-job training	BMW provides paid apprenticeship including on-the-job training	N/A	

Name Locations, Program Length Website	Bachelor's required?	Preparing students for these jobs	Other admissions requirements
Cleveland Clinic—Sleep Technologist Program (ASTEP) *Cleveland, 2 weeks* my.clevelandclinic.org /departments/neurological /medical-professionals/astep	No	Sleep technologist	High school diploma, CPR certification
Cooperative Home Care Associates *Bronx, NY, Varies* chcany.org	No	Home care	Low-income and unemployed women in the Bronx
Craftsmanship Academy by RoleModel *Holly Springs, NC, 9–18 months* craftsmanshipacademy.com	No	Software development	
CVS Health *Arkansas, Wisconsin, Rhode Island, Michigan, Missouri, Texas, Varies* cvshealth.com	No	Retail pharmacy and management	
Eagle Technologies *Bridgman, MI, 4 years* eagletechnologies.com /apprenticeship-program	No	Manufacturing	

Curriculum	Employer engagement	Student financing available	Statistics (placement statistics include percentage in jobs in field, starting salary)
Certification-focused sleep technologist training	Students are eligible to apply for a Sleep Technology Position at Cleveland Clinic contingent on successful completion of the ASTEP I program and 6 months of patient care experience. If hired they are eligible to seek reimbursement of tuition.	No	
Home care technical and on-the-job training as a path to employment at CHCA	Home Care training as a path to employment at CHCA	N/A	
Three phases: skills immersion, apprenticeship, and residency. First phase focuses on technical skills, followed by a 3–6 month apprenticeship, followed by a 3–9 month residency at RoleModel with the expectation of full-time placement at RoleModel or referrals to another company	Includes 3–6 month apprenticeship, followed by a 3–9 month residency at RoleModel with the expectation of full-time placement at RoleModel or referrals to another company	No	100% hired into technical roles within 120 days
On-the-job training combined with technical education	Paid apprenticeship including on-the-job training with expected career path at CVS	N/A	Since 2005, placed more than 1,500 colleagues in Registered Apprenticeship career tracks in retail pharmacy and management
Technical manufacturing skills	Company-provided manufacturing content leading to certification and job placement in the company	N/A	

Name Locations, Program Length Website	Bachelor's required?	Preparing students for these jobs	Other admissions requirements
Fresh Tilled Soil *Massachusetts, Varies* freshtilledsoil.com/aux	No	UX/UI design	Some background in design and development
GE Healthcare Commercial Leadership Program (CLP) *US and Canada, 2 years* https://www.ge.com/careers /working-at-ge/commercial -leadership-program	Yes	Medical device sales/ other services	
IBM P-TECH *New York, Connecticut, Colorado, Illinois, Rhode Island, Maryland, 4–6 years (HS and associate's degree)* ptech.org	No	IT, software development, cybersecurity	
Kaiser Permanente *Colorado, Varies* arapahoe.edu/news-story/2016 /acc-mlt-program-partners-kaiser -permanente	No	Medical laboratory technician/medical technologist	
Lockheed Martin *Washington DC, 4 years (including high school)* lockheedmartin.com	No	IT	High school junior

Curriculum	Employer engagement	Student financing available	Statistics (placement statistics include percentage in jobs in field, starting salary)
UX/UI Design with specialization in UI design, front-end development, or strategy	Employer-paid apprenticeship including on-the-job training	N/A	
Medical device technical training; sales skills; final 8 months of program are in field / operating room with a mentor to provide ramp-up to full-time employment	Paid apprenticeship followed by 8 months of on-the-job training, with path to employment at GE	N/A	100% placement at GE Healthcare
On-the-job training in partnership with high schools and colleges leading to high school diploma and associate's degree	IBM has jointly developed curricula with the local community college, as well as 1-year and 2-year courses aligned with the company's hiring needs	N/A	
Arapahoe Community College's Medical Laboratory Technology (MLT) program and the Kaiser Permanente Laboratory Department have partnered to offer a paid on-the-job training and technical skills program	On-the-job training and technical skills program leading to 2-year commitment to full-time hire at Kaiser Permanente Colorado Laboratory	N/A	
3.5 years of on-the-job training combined with technical education culminating in Registered IT Specialist I certification, followed by 12–15 months in rotational work assignments	Paid apprenticeship and rotational work assignments serve as path to employment at Lockheed Martin	N/A	

Name Locations, Program Length Website	Bachelor's required?	Preparing students for these jobs	Other admissions requirements
MemoryBlue *Virginia, California, Texas, Varies* memoryblue.com	No	High tech inside sales and consulting	
Mercuria *Houston, TX, Varies* mercuria.com	No	IT, finance, commodities trading and logistics	
Mercy Hospital—Medical Laboratory Science *Ardmore, PA; Ada, OK, 1 year* mercy.net	No	Medical laboratory science	Senior year college student at one of 7 partner schools in Oklahoma and Texas
Mercy Hospital—Pathway to Employment *St. Louis and Crystal City, MO, 1 year* mercy.net	No	Hospital services	High school student with disabilities
NetGalaxy Studios *Charleston, SC, 2 years* netgalaxystudios.com/careers	No	Web development, software development	High school junior, senior, or graduating senior
Nextiva *Arizona, Varies* nextiva.com	No	IT	

Curriculum	Employer engagement	Student financing available	Statistics (placement statistics include percentage in jobs in field, starting salary)
Sales technical and soft skills combined with on-the-job training leading to full-time regular hire with MemoryBlue (outsourced inside sales staffer)	Apprenticeship including on-the-job training leading to full-time regular position	N/A	
On-the-job training combined with technical education delivered onsite at Houston trading hub, based on original Mercuria Swiss program	Paid apprenticeship serves as path to employment at Mercuria	N/A	
Classroom and lab rotation-based laboratory science	Mercy hired 100% of participants from first 2 years of program. Also offers scholarship program for students who commit to work for at least 2 years in a Mercy facility on graduation	Yes (scholarships based on commitment to work full time)	
Overview of health care job opportunities; on-the-job mentorship with goal of achieving 80%+ competency in core skills	Mercy provides apprenticeship training and assists students who achieve 80%+ competency in job placement at Mercy or other hospitals	N/A	
On-the-job training combined with traditional high school education and technical education at partner technical college Trident Tech	Paid apprenticeship serves as path to employment at netGALAXY	N/A	
On-the-job training and mentorship combined with technical education	Paid apprenticeship serves as path to employment at Nextiva	N/A	

Name Locations, Program Length Website	Bachelor's required?	Preparing students for these jobs	Other admissions requirements
Research Medical Center—StaRN *Kansas City, MO, 13-week apprenticeship followed by 2-year commitment to work at sponsor hospital* researchmedicalcenter.com/careers/education/starn-program.dot	Yes	Specialty nursing	Must be newly licensed RN
Resilient Coder *Boston, 8 weeks* resilientcoders.org	No	Web development	Low-income youth (ages 13–19) in Boston
Siemens *US (Charlotte; Fort Payne, AL; Atlanta; Sacramento) and UK, 3.5 years (part time during community college)* siemens.com	Yes	Manufacturing	
Techtonic Group *Boulder, CO, Varies* techtonicgroup.com/academy	No	Web development	Focus on women, minorities, and veterans
The Hartford *Hartfort, CT, and Tempe, AZ, Varies* thehartford.com/careers/claims-apprentice	No	Insurance (claims)	Enrolled at participating community college

Curriculum	Employer engagement	Student financing available	Statistics (placement statistics include percentage in jobs in field, starting salary)
Specialty nursing	Apprenticeship followed by 2-year employment at sponsor hospital	N/A	
Software technical skills; soft skills	At least once per bootcamp, students meet client and complete paid work on client website; Resilient Lab hosts 2 month paid technical fellowship for bootcamp graduates	N/A	
Technical manufacturing skills	Siemens-provided manufacturing content leading to certification and job placement in the company	N/A	
Technical skills; professional development skills such as creativity, critical thinking, conflict management, goal setting, and how to run a meeting effectively	Apprentices work as outsourced developers for local companies, with opportunity for employment at clients after graduating	N/A	
Partnership with local community colleges to provide associate's degree in tandem with on-the-job training; tuition reimbursement for bachelor's post-hire	Paid apprenticeship including on-the-job training	Yes (tuition reimbursement for bachelor's post-hire)	

Name Locations, Program Length Website	Bachelor's required?	Preparing students for these jobs	Other admissions requirements
TranZed Apprenticeship Services (TAS) *Mid-Atlantic area, Varies* tranzedapprenticeships.com	No	IT	
Trinity Health—Certified Nursing Assistant (CNA) *22 US states, N/A* trinityhealth.org/careers_professional	No	CNA	
Wells Fargo *Florida, Illinois, Massachusetts, Missouri, New York, California, Varies* myfuture.wf.com/veteran	No	Financial services (branch management, collections, financial crimes)	Military veterans
Zurich North America *Schaumburg, IL, Varies* zurichna.com/en/careers/apprenticeships	No	Insurance (underwriting and claims)	Enrolled at Harper College
Program Type: Apprenticeship Service Provider			
Apprentice.io *US and Europe (varies by participating companies), 3–6 months* apprentice.io	No	Software development	
Apprenticeship 2000 *Charlotte, NC, Varies* apprenticeship2000.com	No	Manufacturing	

Curriculum	Employer engagement	Student financing available	Statistics (placement statistics include percentage in jobs in field, starting salary)
Partnership with employers and 3aaa, a UK Apprenticeship Service Provider, to provide paid on-the-job training as well as 144+ hours of technical and soft skills professional training	Partnership with employers and 3aaa, a UK Apprenticeship Service Provider, to place and train candidates	N/A	
CNA basic requirements	Free training offered through hospital to improve CNA employee funnel; potential hiring for graduates	N/A	
On-the-job training combined with technical education	Paid apprenticeship including on-the-job training with expected career path at Wells Fargo	Yes (use GI Bill education benefits to receive a tax-free monthly payment, decreases as paid salary increases)	The average starting salary of apprentices is about $60K a year
On-the-job training; weekly classes at Harper College leading to associate's degree	Paid apprenticeship including on-the-job training	N/A	
Varies by employer	Apprentice.io is an apprenticeship service resource connecting students to employer-run apprenticeships. Engagement varies by employer	No	
On-the-job training and mentorship combined with technical education	Paid apprenticeships within NC and relevant high school curriculum run by local participating schools; path to long-term employment at partner employers	N/A	

Name Locations, Program Length Website	Bachelor's required?	Preparing students for these jobs	Other admissions requirements
Apprenticeship Carolina *South Carolina, Varies* apprenticeshipcarolina.com	No	Various technical fields including IT, advanced manufacturing, construction, energy, healthcare, tourism, transportation	
CareerWise Colorado *Colorado, Varies* careerwisecolorado.org	No	IT, business operations, finance, advanced manufacturing	Rising high school juniors and seniors
College of Engineering and Applied Science Active Learning Program, University of Colorado Boulder *Colorado, Varies* colorado.edu /activelearningprogram/	No	Skilled trades	Participation in UCB-related courses (Private pay) mandatory
Community Health Worker Apprenticeship Program *Bronx, NY, 6 months* nyachnyc.org	No	Community health	
Franklin *US, 1–6 years* franklinapprenticeships.com	Varies	Varies	Varies by employer
Greater Peoria Apprenticeship *Peoria, IL, Varies* gpapprentice.org	No	Software development, cybersecurity	
Guam Community College Apprenticeship Program *Guam, Varies* guamcc.edu/Runtime /apprenticeshpprogrequiremnts .aspx	No	Judiciary, law enforcement, others	

Curriculum	Employer engagement	Student financing available	Statistics (placement statistics include percentage in jobs in field, starting salary)
On-the-job training combined with technical education	Run by the SC Technical College System, partners with employers to run 870+ apprenticeship programs combining on-the-job training with technical education typically delivered by the technical college	N/A	
On-the-job training combined with technical education	Employer-managed apprenticeship with CareerWise assistance	N/A	
Apprenticeship run by employer, related educational curriculum run by UCB	UCB partners with local employers to offer apprenticeships to students of skilled trades	N/A	
Classroom learning combined with on-the-job training in Bronx Lebanon Hospital and LaGuardia Community College	Paid apprenticeship serves as path to employment at Bronx Lebanon or other hospitals	N/A	
Technical and soft skills tailored to employer	Employer-managed apprenticeship program combining on-the-job training with paid work, with Franklin consulting assistance	N/A	
On-the-job training combined with certification-focused technical education in Secure Software Development	Run by the Greater Peoria Economic Development Council, partners with employers to run apprenticeship programs combining on-the-job training with technical education delivered at GP site	N/A	
On-the-job training combined with technical education delivered by community college	Guam Community College partners with employers to run apprenticeship programs combining on-the-job training with technical education delivered at college	N/A	

Name Locations, Program Length Website	Bachelor's required?	Preparing students for these jobs	Other admissions requirements
Lakeshore Technical College *Wisconsin, Varies* gotoltc.edu/academics/apprenticeship/	No	Skilled trades (carpentry, plumbing, construction, machinery, etc.)	Participation in LTC-related courses (private pay) mandatory
Lansing Community College Apprenticeship Program *Missouri, Varies* lcc.edu/cit/itapprenticeship	No	IT	
LaunchCode *St. Louis, Kansas City, Miami, Rhode Island, Seattle, Portland, 14 weeks full time, 16 weeks part time* launchcode.org	No	IT, web development, mobile development, data science, business, technical writing	Coding puzzles, interview
MinedMinds *Pittsburgh and Waynesburg, PA; Clendenin and Beckley, WV, 32+ weeks* minedminds.org	No	Software development	Focused on coal miners
OpenTech LA *Los Angeles, Varies* opentech.la	No	Web development, software development, IT	Application through OpenTech
Per Scholas *New York City, Atlanta, Cincinnati, Columbus, Dallas, Washington DC, 14–18 weeks or longer for part-time courses* perscholas.org	No	IT	10th grade reading and math, basic professional skills, interview-based problem-solving assessment
Sales Bootcamp *San Francisco, New York City, 13 weeks (1 week online followed by 12-week in-person fellowship)* salesbootcamp.com	No	Tech sales	

Curriculum	Employer engagement	Student financing available	Statistics (placement statistics include percentage in jobs in field, starting salary)
Apprenticeship run by employer, related educational curriculum run by LTC	LTC partners with local employers to offer apprenticeships to students of skilled trades	Yes (Title IV)	
On-the-job training combined with technical education delivered by community college	Lansing Community College partners with employers to run apprenticeship programs combining on-the-job training with technical education delivered at college	N/A	
Web development	Pairs people aiming to work in technology with top-level employers through paid apprenticeships and job placement	No	More than four out of five apprentices convert to permanent employment at their company in a median of 12 weeks, with average 2x prior salary
16-week software development curriculum followed by 16-week apprenticeship	Coordination with outside institutions (colleges, employers) to place students	No	80% job placement rate
On-the-job training and mentorship combined with technical education	OpenTech coordinates between employers, training programs, and career counselors to support candidates on their path to gain skills and attain and complete on-the-job apprenticeships	N/A	
IT technical skills; professional skills	Employers advise in developing trainings that directly align to workforce needs and to open jobs. In some cases, Per Scholas partners with companies to develop trainings tailored directly to that company	N/A	80% of graduates land jobs, and graduate annual incomes increase by 429% on average
Sales training followed by 12-week fellowship at local tech company	12-week fellowship at local tech company	N/A	Guaranteed hiring at ~$85,000

Name Locations, Program Length Website	Bachelor's required?	Preparing students for these jobs	Other admissions requirements
TechHire *US, Varies* techhire.org	No	IT	Varies by employer
Year Up *Boston and 15 other sites nationally, 1 year (6 months of classes, 6 months of internship)* yearup.org	No	IT, digital marketing, financial operations, sales	
Youthforce NOLA *New Orleans, Varies* educatenow.net/youthforce-nola	No	Health science, digital media, skilled crafts	New Orleans public school senior
Program Type: Bootcamp—No Fee			
Able-Disabled Advocacy— Pathways2Paychecks *San Diego, 18 months* able2work.org/programs /apprenticeships	No	IT	Disabled student or adult with High School Diploma/GED
Ada Developers Academy *Seattle, 27 weeks* adadevelopersacademy.org	No	Web development, software development	Video, résumé, logic puzzle, women-only program
BankWork$ *Pasadena, Chicago, Denver, Houston, Phoenix, Portland, San Francisco, Seattle, 8 weeks* bankworks.org	No	Financial services	Written and spoken English fluency, high school diploma equivalent
Black Men Code *Atlanta, Varies* blackmencode.org	No	Software development	Focus on black men in high school or undergraduate programs

Curriculum	Employer engagement	Student financing available	Statistics (placement statistics include percentage in jobs in field, starting salary)
Varies—TechHire connects underskilled job seekers to partner IT training programs and potential employers	Varies by training provider	N/A	
Technical skills; professional skills	6-month internship placement as part of program; 1,300 employer partners	N/A	Internship-to-hire rate was 42% for the January and July 2016 cohorts, and 90% of participants were employed or continuing their education within four months of graduation
Career pathway programs hosted by partner schools; on-the-job training at employers	Employer-managed internship program with Youthforce support	N/A	
6-month IT curriculum linked to industry credentials followed by paid on-the-job training	Organization finds employers for 12-month apprenticeships	N/A	
JavaScript; job search skills; professional skills; leadership and inclusion	Program includes internship placement	No	
Financial services skills; soft skills	Local bank sponsor for each program; members of partner banks are encouraged to visit classrooms and participate in class lessons. Job fair at end of program with partner banks.	N/A	75% job placement rate
Team-first, project-based learning in Python and other languages	Nonprofit works with institutions including several HBCU's to offer free tech training to college students in any discipline	N/A	75% job placement rate

Name Locations, Program Length Website	Bachelor's required?	Preparing students for these jobs	Other admissions requirements
Cultivating Coders *New Mexico, 8 weeks* cultivatecoders.com	No	Web development, mobile development	
Data Science for Social Good *Chicago, 3 months* dssg.uchicago.edu	No	Data science	Application process
Digital Citizen *Miami, 8 weeks* ecotechvisions.com	No	Web development, digital marketing	
Hack the Hood *Northern California, 6 weeks* hackthehood.org	No	Web development	Low-income minority youth in California
Hidden Genius Project *Oakland, CA, 18 months (during high school)* hiddengeniusproject.org	No	Software development, entrepreneurship	Black male youth in high school in Oakland
Hospitality Training Academy *Los Angeles, Varies* lahta.org	No	Hospitality	Hospitality workers in LA

Curriculum	Employer engagement	Student financing available	Statistics (placement statistics include percentage in jobs in field, starting salary)
Full stack development	Travelling bootcamp that trains coders wherever employers or other sponsors request a new bootcamp	N/A	
Data mining, machine learning, big data, and other data science projects with social impact	Data science projects in partnership with nonprofits and government agencies	No	
Programming, Agile methodology, SEO, web marketing, and social media	Students work with local businesses to help them develop their web presences, hosted in a sustainable business coworking, innovation & manufacturing space	N/A	
Development; soft skills (time management, interpersonal skills); career development	Participants create websites for local businesses	N/A	
Software development, entrepreneurship; business skills and principles; personal identity and community awareness	Mentorship, hiring partner network	N/A	
Hospitality training and upskilling programs; career development; professional skills	Partners with educational institutions, community organizations, and employers to provide formal training to facilitate entry and advancement along the extensive career ladders within the hospitality and food service industries	N/A	

Name Locations, Program Length Website	Bachelor's required?	Preparing students for these jobs	Other admissions requirements
Insight *Silicon Valley, New York City, 7 weeks* insightdatascience.com	Yes	Data science, software development	Generally a doctoral degree in physics, astrophysics, mathematics & statistics, neuroscience & bioinformatics, or engineering & computer science, competitive application
JobCorps *US and Puerto Rico, 8–24 months* jobcorps.gov	No	Manufacturing, repair, construction, finance, health care, hospitality, IT, public service, renewable resources, retail, transportation	Low-income young adults ages 16–24
Microsoft Research Data Science Summer School *New York City, 8 weeks* ds3.research.microsoft.com	No	Data science	Enrolled in undergraduate program
Opportunity Junction *San Francisco Bay Area, 12 weeks* opportunityjunction.org	No	Administrative roles	Evaluation prior to entry for motivation, basic reading and writing
Samaschool *Online or at partner location, Varies* samaschool.org	No	"Gig economy" platforms (Taskrabbit, Care.com, Handy.com, etc.)	
Techtonica *San Francisco, 6 months* techtonica.org	No	Software development	Women and nonbinary people in the Bay Area

Curriculum	Employer engagement	Student financing available	Statistics (placement statistics include percentage in jobs in field, starting salary)
Postdoctoral training fellowship building data science-solutions in self directed collaborative environment	Mentorship from current data sciences/600+ Insight alumni; interviews with top companies at end of program	N/A	
Technical training; career development	Varies by track—some apprenticeship programs, internships, and shadowing opportunities available in addition to hiring network and career services	N/A	Nearly 82% of Job Corps graduates in the last five years were placed in education programs, the military, or careers
Project-based introduction to data science for upper-level undergraduates	The summer school is taught by leading scientists at Microsoft Research, and is held at the new Microsoft Research office in the heart of New York City.	N/A	
Computer skills; soft skills (conflict management, workplace behavior)	Interview connections	N/A	90% placement within 6 months
Digital and professional soft skills, immersive, hands-on application of the 21st-century skills necessary to identify and secure work through gig marketplaces, and to leverage this type of work to achieve career goals	Works with US job-focused community organizations to provide "gig economy" training to increase graduate employability	N/A	
Software development	Corporate hiring partners provide mentors, sponsor students, and participate in diversity training	N/A	N/A—first cohort in 2017

Name Locations, Program Length Website	Bachelor's required?	Preparing students for these jobs	Other admissions requirements
The Stride Center *Oakland, CA, 6 months, optional 2-month advanced certification* stridecenter.org	No	IT	Basic literacy and motivation
TXT (Teens Exploring Technology) *Los Angeles, 15 weeks* exploringtech.org	No	Software development	Low-income/ underserved male teens in LA
Program Type: Bootcamp—Tuition-Pay			
2020Shift / The Yard *New York City, 7 weeks part time* 2020shift.com	No	Data science, UX/ UI design, product management, digital marketing, sales	
30 weeks *New York City, 30 weeks* 30weeks.com	No	Product management, entrepreneurship	At least 1 year of work experience
4Geeks Academy *Miami, Caracas, Varies, part time* 4geeksacademy.co	No	Web development, mobile development, digital marketing	
Academy X *San Francisco, Los Angeles, Sacramento, San Diego, Online, Varies* academyx.com	No	Web development	
AcadGild *Online, Varies* acadgild.com	No	Web development, mobile development, data science, digital marketing	

Curriculum	Employer engagement	Student financing available	Statistics (placement statistics include percentage in jobs in field, starting salary)
IT technical skills; soft skills (general professional skills)	None	N/A	Graduates of the program earn an average entry wage of between $19 and $20 per hour and achieve, on average, a 30% wage increase in the first 18 months after graduation
Software development; mentorship; career development	Visits and mentoring from technology employers	N/A	
Technical skills; general professional and soft skills; diversity-focused professional skills	2020Shift has built relationships with contemporary companies to attract, recruit, and place diverse students and increase workforce diversity and inclusion. The organization also offers employer-facing diversity trainings, which encourage retention.	No	
Lean start-up methodology; product management; entrepreneurship	Collaboration between Hyper Island, Parsons, SVA, Cooper Union, Pratt, and Google, including mentorship, coworking, and opportunities to pitch to investors	No	
Project-based full stack web development, mobile development, and digital marketing	Hiring partners; lifelong job placement services and support	Yes (payment plans, partner loan programs)	
Web development	None	Yes (discounts, prepay credit)	
Varies by course (self-paced and instructor-led courses)	None	No	

Name Locations, Program Length Website	Bachelor's required?	Preparing students for these jobs	Other admissions requirements
Acclaim Education *Silicon Valley, 8 weeks* acclaimeducation.com	No	Mobile development	
Altcademy *Hong Kong, Online, Varies* altcademy.com	No	Data science	
AlwaysHired *San Francisco, 1–3 weeks* alwayshired.com	No	Tech sales	
American Graphics Institute *Boston, Philadelphia, New York City, Online, Varies* agitraining.com	No	Web development, UX/UI design	
App Academy *San Francisco, New York City, 12 weeks* appacademy.io	No	Web development	
Array School of Technology and Design *Cheyenne, WY, 24 weeks* arrayschool.com	No	Web development	
ATI *Greenville, SC, 2-week introductory or 8-month full training program* atischool.org	Yes	Medical device sales/other services	Bachelor's preferred, associate's degree and experience in related health field permissible
Atlantis Coding *Miami, 12 weeks* atlantiscoding.com	No	Web development	
Austin Coding Academy *Austin, 10 weeks or 9 month* austincodingacademy.com	No	Web development, software development	
Awesome Inc U *Lexington, KY, 12 weeks* awesomeincu.com	No	Web development, software development	

Curriculum	Employer engagement	Student financing available	Statistics (placement statistics include percentage in jobs in field, starting salary)
Mobile development	Career services	No	
Data science self-study, guided coding challenges, and tutorial labs	Mentorship from industry professionals	No	
Tech industry background; sales skills; soft skills	AlwaysHired contracts with employer partners for student placement	No	90% placement at 100+ companies, with average of $84K starting salary
UX/UI Design and rapid prototyping for mobile devices and touch screens	None	No	
Web development in multiple languages with focus on Ruby; soft skills	None	No	$105K average starting salary in San Francisco
Web development	Career services, hiring network	Yes (partner loan programs)	
Didactic preparation interspersed with clinical practice and hands-on skills laboratories	Hiring partner network	Yes (partner loan programs)	99% job placement rate
Theoretical and practical front-end and/or back-end development	None	Yes (partner loan programs, scholarships)	
Full stack development	None	Yes (scholarships)	
Full stack development	Curriculum developed in coordination with companies in the region; employer hiring partners	Yes (scholarships)	100% hired in field

Name Locations, Program Length Website	Bachelor's required?	Preparing students for these jobs	Other admissions requirements
Beach Coders Academy *Los Angeles, 4 weeks* beachcoders.com	No	Web development, UX/UI design	
Beginex *New York City, 8 weeks* beginex.com	No	UX/UI design	
Berkeley Boot Camps *Berkeley and San Francisco, 12 weeks full time, 24 weeks part time* bootcamp.berkeley.edu	No	Data science	Bachelor's recommended
Betamore Academy *Baltimore, MD, 12 weeks* betamore.com	No	Web development	Varies, often some technical skill required
Big Nerd Ranch *Georgia, Northern California, 1 week* bignerdranch.com	No	Mobile development, UX/UI design	
Big Sky Code Academy *Bozeman, Missoula, Billings, Helena, 3 months full time, 5 months part time* bigskycodeacademy.org	No	Web development, data science	
BitBootCamp *New York City, Boston, Washington DC, Cleveland, 4 weeks* bitbootcamp.com	No	Data science	
Bitmaker Labs *Toronto, 9 weeks full time, 12 weeks part time* bitmaker.co	No	Web development, data science, UX/UI design, digital marketing, product management	Prep work course
Bloc *Online, 6–24 months* bloc.io	No	Web development, software development, UX/UI design	

Curriculum	Employer engagement	Student financing available	Statistics (placement statistics include percentage in jobs in field, starting salary)
Front end web development; UX/UI design; career development	Partner affiliations with non-profit job placement agencies and tech recruiting companies, career services	Yes (partner loan programs)	90% hired full time within 90 days
Design skills; team building; client management skills	Mentorships	No	
Full stack development; career development	Employer hiring partners	Yes (scholarships)	
Front end and web development; digital marketing/analytics	Once students graduate, they will have access to the Betamore Works program, a personalized career concierge service. If students take a job with one of the Betamore Works Partners, they'll get 80% of tuition back.	80% tuition refund if job taken with hiring partner	
Mobile development; UX/UI design skills	Career services	Yes (scholarships)	
Full stack JavaScript focused development	After passing final exam, candidates are offered employment with Digital Impact LLC, a Montana development shop and digital agency	Yes (payment plans, scholarships)	
Data science technical skills	Employer hiring partners	Yes (partner loan programs)	
Full stack development and/or other technical courses	Curriculum developed in coordination with tech companies	Yes (partner loan programs)	90% placement in technology jobs
Web, software, and/or design curriculum	None	Yes (partner loan programs, scholarships)	

Name Locations, Program Length Website	Bachelor's required?	Preparing students for these jobs	Other admissions requirements
Blur State *Fayetteville, AK, 12–15 weeks* blurstate.com	No	Web development, mobile development, UX/UI design	
BoiseCodeWorks *Boise, 12 weeks* boisecodeworks.com	No	Web development, UX/UI design	
Bottega *Lehi, UT; Scottsdale, AZ, 12 weeks* bottega.tech	No	Web development	
Bov Academy *Online, 6–9 months* bovacademy.com	No	Web development, data science, cybersecurity, AI, digital arts	
BrainStation *Toronto, Vancouver, New York City, San Jose, Online, 10 weeks full time, varies part time* brainstation.io	No	Web development, UX/UI design, product management, digital marketing	
CareerFoundry *Online, 6 months* careerfoundry.com	No	Web development, mobile development, UX/UI design	
Cincy Code IT *Cincinnati, 3 months* maxtrain.com/career	No	IT, web development	
Claim Academy *St. Louis, 3 months* claimacademystl.com	No	Web development	Technical challenge, technical interview
Code Career Academy *Atlanta, 16 weeks* codecareeracademy.com	No	Web development	
Code Chicago *Chicago, 12 weeks* codechicago.com	No	Web development	

Curriculum	Employer engagement	Student financing available	Statistics (placement statistics include percentage in jobs in field, starting salary)
Full stack development; mobile app development; UX/UI design; Microsoft. NET	Career services	No	
Web development	Employer hiring partners	Yes (scholarships)	
Full stack development	Career services	Yes (partner loan programs, scholarships)	Graduates see an average increase in earning potential of $20K+ per year
Curriculum focused on "Career Path" trajectories to drive employability	Career services	Yes (payment plans)	
Combined online and in-person project-based learning in web development/ design	Tours with employer partners, networking	No	
Mentor-driven web development, iOS development, and/ or UX/UI design	Students are paired with mentors currently employed in relevant fields to provide feedback, career advice, and networking for potential job placement	No	95% placement in 6 months
Software/IT skills	Job placement coaching, mentoring, networking, hiring network	No	98% job placement rate
Web development	Employer hiring partners	Yes (partner loan programs, scholarships)	95% job placement rate, average salary $58,000
Project-based agile full stack web and mobile development	None	Yes (partner loan programs)	
Mobile development; web development; design thinking	Career services, networking events	No	

Name Locations, Program Length Website	Bachelor's required?	Preparing students for these jobs	Other admissions requirements
Code Fellows *Seattle, Portland, 1 day–9 weeks* codefellows.org	No	Web development, mobile development, software development, software architecture, technical writing, product management, consulting	Phone interview, entrance test
Code Platoon *Chicago, 14 weeks* codeplatoon.org	No	Web development	Service in armed forces
CodeCore Bootcamp *Vancouver, 12 weeks* codecore.ca	No	Web development	
CodeCraft School *Boulder, CO, 12 weeks full time, 24 weeks part time* codecraftschool.com	No	Web development, UX/UI design	Pre-program learning
CodeMasters Academy *Orange County, 14 weeks* codemastersacademy.com	No	Web development	Basic computer and critical thinking skills
CodeNinja *Milwaukee, Mexico City, Maui, Koh Lanta, Online, 4–12 weeks* code-ninja.co	No	Web development, mobile development, software development, UX/UI design	
Coder Camps *Seattle, Phoenix, Online, 12 weeks* codercamps.com	No	Web development, software development	
Coder Foundry *Charlotte and Triad, NC; New York City, 3–18 weeks* coderfoundry.com	No	Web development	
Codesmith *Los Angeles, New York City, Oxford University, 12 weeks* codesmith.io	No	Web development, software development	Technical communication, problem solving, JavaScript and programming knowledge, non-technical communication and engineering best practices

Curriculum	Employer engagement	Student financing available	Statistics (placement statistics include percentage in jobs in field, starting salary)
Full stack development	Employer hiring partners	Yes (partner loan programs, scholarships)	80% job placement rate
Job support and internship placement; web development	Employer hiring partners	Yes (partner loan programs, scholarships)	
Ruby-focused web development	Mentoring, networking, a "hiring day" open house for employer partners, curriculum refined with input from hiring partners	Yes (scholarships)	
Web development	Career services	Yes (partner loan programs, scholarships)	
Project-based agile development	Career services	Yes (partner loan programs)	Average salary is $76,000
Full stack development	None	Yes (partner loan programs)	
Full stack development	Company hiring partners	Yes (partner loan programs, scholarships)	
Web development	Professional job placement services and in-house recruiters, hiring partners	Yes (partner loan programs, scholarships)	
Advanced programming learning through "project of significance" that must be released into production; JavaScript focus	Career services	Yes (partner loan programs, scholarships)	95% job placement rate

Name Locations, Program Length Website	Bachelor's required?	Preparing students for these jobs	Other admissions requirements
Codeup *San Antonio, 16 weeks* codeup.com	No	Web development, software development	
Codify Academy *San Francisco, Online, 16 weeks* codifyacademy.com	No	Web development	
Coding Dojo *Berkeley, Chicago, Dallas, Los Angeles, Orange County, Seattle, Silicon Valley, Washington DC, Online, 14 weeks* codingdojo.com	No	Web development, mobile development	
Coding Temple *Chicago, Washington DC, 10 weeks* codingtemple.com	No	Web development	
Covalence *Birmingham, Chattanooga, 10 weeks* covalence.io	No	Web development	Coding assessment
Data Application Lab *Los Angeles, Silicon Valley, Online, 19 weeks* dataapplab.com	Yes	Web development, data science	
Data Science Dojo *Seattle, New York City, Austin, Chicago, Las Vegas, Silicon Valley, Washington DC, Toronto, Amsterdam, Barcelona, Dubai, Paris, Singapore, 5 days* datasciencedojo.com	No	Data science	Knowledge of at least one programming/ scripting language or computing environment
DaVinci Coders *Denver, 12–13 weeks training, 8 weeks practical application* davincicoders.com	No	Web development	Computer literacy, job interview

Curriculum	Employer engagement	Student financing available	Statistics (placement statistics include percentage in jobs in field, starting salary)
Full stack development	Career services, 73 employer partners	Yes (refund with employment, partner loan programs, scholarships)	100% of graduates receive offers, 7 average weeks to hire
HTML, CSS, JavaScript	Career services, employer hiring partners	Yes (payment plans, partner loan programs)	
Ruby on Rails, LAMP, MEAN, Python, .NET Core and Swift/iOS	None	Yes (partner loan programs, scholarships)	
Full stack development; job search skills	Career services	Yes (partner loan programs, scholarships)	95% job placement rate
Web development	None	Yes (payment plans, scholarships)	
Project-based data science and development	Employer hiring partners, alumni network	No	
Data science; professional skills	Networking opportunities with fellow attendees	No	
Theoretical and practical development; team working	Career development training, demo day	Yes (H1B application, partner loan programs)	

Name Locations, Program Length Website	Bachelor's required?	Preparing students for these jobs	Other admissions requirements
DecodeMTL *Montreal, 8 weeks* decodemtl.com	No	Web development	
Deep Dive Coders *Albuquerque, 10 weeks* deepdivecoding.com	No	Web development	
Delta V Code School *Cedar Rapids, 4–10 weeks* deltavcodeschool.com	No	Web development	
DESIGNATION *Chicago, Online, 24 weeks* designation.io	No	UX/UI design	Basic programming knowledge
Dev League *Honolulu, 16, 30, 34, 40 weeks* devleague.com	No	Web development, software development, data science, cybersecurity	
devCodeCamp *Milwaukee, 12 weeks* devcodecamp.com	No	Web development	Pre-course aptitude quiz
Developer Bootcamp *Chelmsford, Houston, Dallas, Chicago, Irvine, San Jose, Online, 6–10 weeks* developer-bootcamp.com	No	Web development	
DevMountain *Phoenix, Dallas, Provo, Salt Lake City, 12–16 weeks* devmountain.com	No	Web development, mobile development, QA, UX/UI design	
DevPoint Labs *Salt Lake City, 11 weeks* devpointlabs.com	No	Web development, UX/UI design	
DeVry Bootcamp *Denver, Chicago, Online, 24 weeks part time* manufacturing.devry.edu	No	Web development, advanced manufacturing	Varies, often some technical skill required

Curriculum	Employer engagement	Student financing available	Statistics (placement statistics include percentage in jobs in field, starting salary)
Full stack JavaScript; project management	Demo day with employer hiring partners at end of bootcamp, career services	Yes (partner loan programs)	
Web development	Professional development and coaching	Yes (partner loan programs, GI Bill, scholarships)	$45K average starting salary
Web development; job search skills	None	Yes (scholar-ships)	
Design essentials; portfolio development	Career services, employer hiring partners	Yes (partner loan programs)	94% got new design job with salary increase of 62%
Full stack development; certification-focused technical courses	Career services, employer hiring partners	Yes (partner loan programs, scholarships)	
Web development; job search skills	Demo day with potential employers, career services, employer hiring partners	Yes (partner loan programs)	91% job placement rate
Web development	None	Yes (payment plans, scholarships)	
Web/Mobile/UX/UI design; job search skills	DevMountain career network introduces students to employers	Yes (payment plans)	
Web development	Networking events	Yes (partner loan programs, scholarships)	
Full stack JavaScript coding; IoT/advanced manufacturing	None	No	

Name Locations, Program Length Website	Bachelor's required?	Preparing students for these jobs	Other admissions requirements
DigitalCrafts *Atlanta, Houston, 16 weeks full time, 24 weeks part time* digitalcrafts.com	No	Web development, software development, UX/UI design	
Divergence Academy *Addison, TX, 12 weeks* divergenceacademy.com	Yes	Data science	Background in quantitative discipline, working knowledge of programming language, usually 0–15+ years industry experience
Epicodus *Portland, Seattle, 27 weeks* epicodus.com	No	Web development, mobile development, UX/UI design	Phone interview, some experience in coding for full-time program
Evolve Security Academy *Chicago, 17 weeks* evolveacademy.io	No	Cybersecurity	IT or development experience, scripting experience
Flatiron School *New York City, 12–15 weeks* flatironschool.com	No	Software development	
Fullstack Academy *New York City, Chicago, Online, 13 weeks* fullstackacademy.com	No	Web development, software development	Online assessment, phone interview
Gainesville Dev Academy *Gainesville, FL, 8 weeks full time, 12 weeks part time* gainsvilledevacademy.com	No	Web development, mobile development, software development	
Galvanize *Austin, Boulder, Denver, New York City, Phoenix, San Francisco, Seattle, 12–24 weeks* galvanize.com	No	Web development, data science	High school diploma or equivalent

Curriculum	Employer engagement	Student financing available	Statistics (placement statistics include percentage in jobs in field, starting salary)
Web development; soft skills	None	Yes (partner loan programs, scholarships)	
Python, statistical modeling, and Unix/Linux command line	Career services	Yes (partner loan programs)	
Intro to programming; JavaScript; on-the-job training	Five-week internship with local business, demo day with potential employers, career services	Yes (partner loan programs)	65% in field employment
Theoretical and practical cybersecurity curriculum	During the course, students gain real work experience through the live security assessment work they perform on not-for-profit companies. Evolve Security Academy also prepares students to find a job with interview preparation and a job placement process.	Yes (payment plans, partner loan programs)	92% hiring rate with an average 60% salary increase
Software development; job search skills	Interview connections	Yes (partner loan programs)	98% placement within 120 days; $40K–$90K starting salary
Web development with JavaScript focus; software development; job search skills	Employer hiring partners	Yes (scholarships)	86% in field employment
Web and mobile development	Employer hiring partners, 2 guaranteed job interviews	Yes (partner loan programs)	
Web development; data science; soft skills	Galvanize campuses facilitate student mentorship and networking through coworking and community programming between students, entrepreneurs, and leading tech companies	Yes (partner loan programs)	91% placement within 6 months, average starting salary of $76,838

Name Locations, Program Length Website	Bachelor's required?	Preparing students for these jobs	Other admissions requirements
General Assembly *Los Angeles, New York City, San Francisco, Washington DC, Atlanta, Singapore, Melbourne, Denver, Chicago, Boston, Austin, Seattle, Hong Kong, Sydney, London, Online, 10–13 weeks full time, 1 week accelerated courses* generalassemb.ly	No	Web development, mobile development, data science, product management, business, digital marketing	
Grace Hopper Academy *New York City, 17 weeks* gracehopper.com	No	Software development	Programming fundamental proficiency, women only
Grand Circus *Detroit, Grand Rapids, 10 weeks* grandcircus.co	No	Web development, mobile development, digital marketing	
GrowthX Academy *San Francisco, Online, 12 weeks* gxacademy.com	No	UX/UI design, digital marketing, tech sales, business development	
GTT Academy *US, Canada, Europe, South Africa, India, 16–24 weeks* gttacademy.com	No	Web development, mobile development, data science, digital marketing	
Hack Reactor *San Francisco, New York City, Los Angeles, Austin, Online, 12 weeks* hackreactor.com	No	Web development, software development	Some coding background required
Hackbright Academy *San Francisco, San Jose, 12 weeks* hackbrightacademy.com	No	Software development	Women only. Includes coding challenge, interview
HackerYou *Toronto, 6–9 weeks* hackeryou.com	No	Web development	HTML and CSS assessment test, interview

Curriculum	Employer engagement	Student financing available	Statistics (placement statistics include percentage in jobs in field, starting salary)
Technical web and mobile development; product management; data science; business; marketing	General Assembly offers corporate training to Fortune 1000 companies, helping build relationships with 2,500 employers to increase student hiring opportunities	Yes (partner loan programs)	
Web development; job search skills; career development	Career services, career/ networking events, employer hiring partners	Payment deferred until hiring (not income-share based)	100% employed in field positions within 180 days; refund of security deposit if not hired in 1 year
Full stack development; job search skills	60+ corporate partners review curriculum and provide feedback, and are committed to hiring graduates	Yes (partner loan programs, scholarships)	
Technical skills; personal and professional branding; job search skills; other professional skills	Students work with companies to identify, build, and execute go-to market strategies; GrowthX is part of coworking tech community at Galvanize	Yes (partner loan programs, scholarships)	
Full stack development	None	No	
Web development/ software development	Internal career development / placement services	Yes (partner loan programs)	98% placement rate in mid- to senior-level positions, average graduate salary of $104K
Computer science; modern web development	Hiring partners, mentorships, career day	Yes (tuition refund with employment, payment plans)	71% job placement rate
Introductory and advanced web development	Hiring partners	No	

Name Locations, Program Length Website	Bachelor's required?	Preparing students for these jobs	Other admissions requirements
Helio Training *Salt Lake City, 13 weeks full time, 16 weeks part time* hellotraining.com	No	Web development	
Horizons Academy *Boston, 12-week summer program or 2-year fellowship* joinhorizons.com	No	Web development, mobile development	Enrolled in college
Hunter Business School *Levittown and Medford, NY, 30 weeks* hunterbusinessschool.edu	No	Web development, software development	Program assessment test
i2 Labs Academy *Miami, 12 or 20 weeks* i2labs.co	No	Web development, cybersecurity	
Interview Kickstart *Sunnyvale, 8 weeks part time* interviewkickstart.com	No	Software development— technical interviews	At least one coding language, data structure experience
Ironhack *Miami, Madrid, Barcelona, Paris, Mexico City, 8–9 weeks full time, 24 weeks part time* ironhack.com	No	Web development, UX/ UI design	
ITHAKAI *Online, 12 weeks* ithakai.com	No	UX/UI design	
Ivy Data Science *New York City, Boston, Washington DC, San Francisco, 8–12 weeks* ivydatascience.com	No	Data science, AI	Programming background, background in physical science or business experience

Curriculum	Employer engagement	Student financing available	Statistics (placement statistics include percentage in jobs in field, starting salary)
Project-based full stack JavaScript development; job search skills	Hiring partners	Yes (partner loan programs, scholarships)	
Immersive software development courses that provide the software skills of an engineer and the perspective of an entrepreneur	Mentorship network with top tech companies	No	
Full stack development	180-hour externship with local business	Yes (partner loan programs, scholarships, federal loans, GI Bill)	
Full stack development	Coworking space with tech companies	Yes (partner loan programs)	
Technical interview preparation; job search skills	None	No	
Web development and UX/UI design	Extensive network of hiring partners	Yes (scholar-ships)	94% job placement rate
Project-based curriculum with one-on-one coaching; job search skills	Career services	Yes (payment plans)	
Cloud computing; databases; SQL/NoSQL; Spark; Hadoop; Flnk; Julia and Python; machine learning	None	Yes (partner loan programs, scholarships)	

Name Locations, Program Length Website	Bachelor's required?	Preparing students for these jobs	Other admissions requirements
JRS Coding School *Charleston, SC, 12 weeks* jackrussellsoftware.com	No	Web development	Pre-admissions challenge, Skype video
K2 Data Science *Online, 3–12 months* k2datascience.com	Yes	Data science	
Launch Academy *Boston, Philadelphia, Washington DC, Online, 10 weeks* launchacademy.com	No	Web development	Washington, DC, women-only program
LEARN Academy *San Diego, 3 months* learnacademy.org	No	Web development	
LearningFuze *Orange County, Irvine, 12 weeks* learningfuze.com	No	Web development	
Level *Seattle, Charlotte, Boston, San Jose, Toronto, 8–20 weeks* leveledu.com	Yes	Data science	Phone interview, technical aptitude test
Lighthouse Labs *Toronto, Vancouver, Victoria, BC, 8 weeks* lighthouselabs.ca	No	Web development, mobile development	Prep course
Lumenbrite *Austin, Houston, Phoenix, San Antonio, Atlanta, Dallas, Denver, Honolulu, Los Angeles, San Diego, San Francisco, Washington DC, Online, 12–30 hours* lumenbrite.com	No	Software development/ consulting for digital media/digital marketing	

Curriculum	Employer engagement	Student financing available	Statistics (placement statistics include percentage in jobs in field, starting salary)
Full stack JavaScript; agile methodology; soft skills	Events with area hiring managers	No	
Flipped classroom with offline learning and weekly video call discussion; one-on-one mentorship; job search skills; technical interview skills	Career services	No	
Web development; career development	Employer hiring partner network; employer-sponsored for some job placements	Yes (scholarships, payment plans, employer pay with job placement)	93% of full stack web graduates find jobs in the field
Full stack JavaScript, full stack Ruby	4-week internship with local tech company, Career services	Yes (partner loan programs, scholarships)	
Full stack and back end development	Career services, employer hiring partners	Yes (partner loan programs)	
Data analysis; professional skills	Each student is paired with an industry-leading employer partner on a 1:1 capstone project	Yes (scholarships)	
Full stack web/iOS development	Demo day with potential employers, career services, employer hiring partners	Yes (partner loan programs)	96% job placement rate
Software skills training and consulting for digital media and marketing	None	No	

Name Locations, Program Length Website	Bachelor's required?	Preparing students for these jobs	Other admissions requirements
Market Campus *Online, Varies* learn.marketcampus.com	No	Digital marketing	
Medical Sales College *Denver, Tampa, Austin, Los Angeles, Detroit, Online, 6–10 weeks* medicalsalescollege.com	No	Medical device sales/ other services	
Metis *New York City, San Francisco, Chicago, Seattle, Washington, Online, 12 weeks* thisismetis.com	No	Data science	Programming experience, statistics experience, technical assessment and data science project challenge, interview
Montana Code School *Bozeman, Missoula, 12 weeks* montanacodeschool.com	No	Web development	
Nashville Software School *Nashville, 6 months* nashvillesoftwareschool.com	No	Software development	
NYC Data Science Academy *New York City, Online, 12 weeks* nycdatascience.com	Yes	Web development	Master's degree or PhD in Science, Technology, Engineering, or Math (STEM), online written application, virtual/in-person interview
Omaha Code School *Omaha, 12 weeks* omahacodeschool.com	No	Web development	
Open Cloud Academy *San Antonio, 9 weeks* opencloudacademy.rackspace.com	No	Cybersecurity	
OpenClassrooms *Online, 12 months* openclassrooms.com	No	Web development, mobile development, UX/UI design, product management	
Operation Spark *New Orleans, 5+ weeks* operationspark.org	No	Software development	

Curriculum	Employer engagement	Student financing available	Statistics (placement statistics include percentage in jobs in field, starting salary)
Comprehensive digital marketing content	None	No	
Industry background; sales skills; other soft skills	Hiring partner network, including employer portal for candidate review; career development resources	Yes (partner loan programs)	94.8% job placement rate (88% for online courses)
Interactive project-centered Data Science curriculum; career development	Employer hiring partners, Career services	Yes (partner loan programs, scholarships)	
Web development	Employer hiring partners	Yes (scholar-ships)	
Software development	Employer hiring partners	Yes (partner loan programs, scholarships)	90% job placement rate
Data science; career development; job search skills	Company site visits, hiring partners, career services	Yes (partner loan programs, scholarships)	
Web development	Employer hiring partners, career services	Yes (scholar-ships)	90% job placement rate / 15% promotion rate
Linux SysAdmin and Network Operation	None	No	
Degree- and certification-focused curriculum	Employer feedback on curriculum, employer hiring partners	No	
Software development	Dev shop works on client projects for local startups	Yes (partner loan programs, scholarships)	

Name Locations, Program Length Website	Bachelor's required?	Preparing students for these jobs	Other admissions requirements
Orange County Code School *Orange County, 12 weeks* orangecountycodeschool.com	No	Web development	
Origin Code Academy *San Diego, 12 weeks* origincodeacademy.com	No	Software development	
PDX Code Guild *Portland, 12 weeks* pdxcodeguild.com	No	Web development, data science	
PrepMD *Braintree, MA, 6 months* prepmd.com	Yes	Medical device sales/other services	Bachelor's or relevant work experience required
Prime Digital Academy *Minneapolis, 18–20 weeks* primeacademy.io	No	Web development, UX/UI design	
Principal Analytics Prep *New York City, 12 weeks* principalanalyticsprep.com	Yes	Data science	Basic programming, past experience with data analysis, 2–5 years work experience
Product School *San Francisco, New York City, Silicon Valley, Los Angeles, 8 weeks* productschool.com	No	Product management	
Q College *Victoria, BC, 12 weeks* qcollege.ca	No	Web development, digital marketing	Basic Computer Skills Assessment
RED Academy *Toronto, Vancouver, London, 12–24 weeks* redacademy.com	No	Web development, mobile development, UX/UI design, digital marketing	Interview, program-specific assignment/test
Redwood Code Academy *Irvine, Orange County, 12 weeks* redwoodcodeacademy.com	No	Web development	

Curriculum	Employer engagement	Student financing available	Statistics (placement statistics include percentage in jobs in field, starting salary)
Full stack JavaScript	Employer hiring partners	No	100% placement rate in 4 months, $65K average salary
Web development; career development	Tailored to technologies employers are using in Southern California, career services	Yes (partner loan programs)	
Agile Python-focused development	None	Yes (scholar-ships)	
Medical device knowledge; sales skills; other soft skills	PrepMD contracts with major employers for placement, and also offers temporary positions in Medical Device Services until students are permanently placed	Yes (partner loan programs)	90%+ placement with salary range of $65K–$85K
Full stack engineering and UX/UI design	Curriculum developed with tech employers, guest speakers, mentors, career day, career services	No	
Multiple programming languages; career development	Located in Harvard Business School Startup Studio with coworking and career counseling	Yes (partner loan programs)	
Product management; career development	Network of local hiring partners	Yes (partner loan programs)	
Web development; digital marketing	Instructors currently work in the industry	Yes (payment plans, employer grants)	
Full stack design; UX design; UI design; career development	Work on client projects with local employers	No	
Full stack software development for web applications, mobile and desktop applications, and cloud services	Employer hiring partners	Yes (scholar-ships)	

Name Locations, Program Length Website	Bachelor's required?	Preparing students for these jobs	Other admissions requirements
Rithm School *San Francisco, 18 weeks* rithmschool.com	No	Web development	Interview, program-specific assignment/test
RMOTR *Online, 4 weeks* rmotr.com	No	Web development	Basic programming or more required for each course
Rutgers Bootcamps *Somerset, Jersey City, 12 weeks full time, 24 weeks part time* bootcamp.rutgers.edu	No	Web development, data science	Phone interview, problem-solving coding test, final interview
Sabio *Orange County, Los Angeles, Seattle, 12 weeks* sabio.la	No	Web development, mobile development, software development	Focused on Latinos and other underserved minorities
Sales 2 Job Academy *Online, 5 weeks* sales2jobacademy.com	No	Sales	
San Antonio Coding Academy *San Antonio, 10 weeks or 9 months* sanantoniocodingacademy.com	No	Web development	
Science to Data Science *London, Online, 5 weeks* s2ds.org	Yes	Data science	Academic profile (PhD, MSc)
SD Code Bootcamp *Sioux Falls, SD, 8 weeks* sdcodebootcamp.com	No	Web development	

Curriculum	Employer engagement	Student financing available	Statistics (placement statistics include percentage in jobs in field, starting salary)
Web development	Work on client projects with venture-backed companies, 4 weeks of tech interview prep	Yes (partner loan programs, scholarships)	6 month job placement guarantee or tuition reimbursed
Python and Django coding	None	Yes (scholarships)	
Full stack development; career development	Employer hiring partners	Yes (scholarships for Rutgers alumni)	
Technical skills focus on .NET/C# and train across the full-stack in Mobile, Front End, Back End, Source Control, Database and Development platforms; soft skills include Agile/Scrum and technical project management	None	Yes (partner loan programs, state and federal grants)	80–93% placement with median salary of $63K–$70K
Sales, technical, and soft skills, including Microsoft Certification	Hiring network and placement services	Yes (partner loan programs, partnership with state agency for some grants)	Placement within 8 weeks
Web development	None	Yes (scholarships)	
Real-world projects focused on helping academics learn practical Data Science applications	Sponsor companies bring in data science programs for students to work on	Yes (scholarships)	75% placement in three months
Web development; professional skills	Networking with potential employers	Yes (scholarships from sponsors)	

Name Locations, Program Length Website	Bachelor's required?	Preparing students for these jobs	Other admissions requirements
SecureSet Academy *Denver, 20 weeks* secureset.com	No	Cybersecurity	Basic working knowledge in networking and/or programming
Shillington School *New York City, London, Manchester, Sydney, Melbourne, Brisbane, 3 months full time, 9 months part time* shillingtoneducation.com	No	UX/UI design	
Skill Distillery *Denver, 16 weeks* skilldistillery.com	No	Web development	Online assessment, logic assessment
Skillcrush *Online, 12 weeks* skillcrush.com	No	Web development, UX/UI design	
Smart Factory *Minneapolis, Varies* smartfactory.com	No	Web development, software development, UX/UI design	
SMU Coding Boot Camp *Dallas, 24 weeks* codingbootcamp.smu.edu	No	Web development	Pre-course tutorials
Software Guild *Akron, OH; Louisville, KY; Minneapolis, MN; Online, 12–24 weeks* thesoftwareguild.com	No	Software development, data science, QA	Interview, aptitude admissions test
Springboard *Online, 1–6 months* springboard.com	Yes	Data dcience, UX/UI design	Basic programming or more required for each course
Starter League *Chicago, 10–11 weeks* starterleague.com	No	Web development, UX/UI design, QA	

Curriculum	Employer engagement	Student financing available	Statistics (placement statistics include percentage in jobs in field, starting salary)
Information security	Multiple hiring partners and industry partners committed to placing graduates and building a cybersecurity community	Yes (partner loan programs, government grants)	Most gradates placed in 3 months
Design theory and software including Adobe and Sketch	None	Yes (scholar-ships)	
HTML, CSS, JavaScript, Java, SQL, and Spring; soft skills	Career services, work with job placement firms	Yes (partner loan programs, scholarships)	92% job placement rate, $70K starting salary
Web design/ development; career development	None	No	
Mobile UI design; mobile development; web production; Ruby on Rails; Android development	Coworking with designers, engineers, and entrepreneurs	No	
Web development; career development; job search skills	Career services, employer hiring partners	Yes (scholar-ships)	
Full-stack .NET/C# or Java, and mobile for Android	Career services, employer hiring partners	Yes (partner loan programs, scholarships)	88% job placement rate
Python, SQL, Spark, and big datasets; career development; soft skills	Mentorship from industry experts	No	
Web development	Joined Full stack Academy; access to FA hiring network	Yes (partner loan programs)	

Name Locations, Program Length Website	Bachelor's required?	Preparing students for these jobs	Other admissions requirements
Startup Ignition *Provo, UT, 13 weeks "after hours"* startupignition.com	No	Entrepreneurship	
Startup Institute *Boston, New York City, 1–8 weeks* startupinstitute.com	No	Web development, UX/UI design, digital marketing, sales, account management	
Sun Training Center *Miami, 10 weeks full time, 24 weeks part time* suntrainingcenters.com	No	Web development, cybersecurity	Basic working knowledge in networking and/or programming
Tech Elevator *Cleveland, Columbus, Cincinnati, 14 weeks* techelevator.com	No	Software development	
Tech Talent South *Asheville, Atlanta, Charlotte, Raleigh, New Orleans, Jacksonville, Dallas, Phoenix, Wilmington, Columbus, San Antonio, 8 weeks* techtalentsouth.com	No	Web development	
Tech901 *Memphis, 2–4 months* tech901.org	No	Web development, cybersecurity	
TechPoint Sales Bootcamp *Indianapolis, 6 weeks* techpoint.org/sales-bootcamp	No	Tech sales	
The Dev Masters *Irvine, Los Angeles, 12 weeks* thedevmasters.com	No	Data science, AI	
The Institute for Statistics Education *Online, 4 weeks* statistics.com	No	Data science	

Curriculum	Employer engagement	Student financing available	Statistics (placement statistics include percentage in jobs in field, starting salary)
Validation, scaling, finance, lean start-up methodology, and other entrepreneurship skills	None	No	
Web development/design, digital marketing; sales skills; account management skills	Curriculum designed in coordination with corporate partners, demo days, hiring partners	Yes (partner loan programs and scholarships)	92% within 100 days, 76% within 60 days
Web development; cybersecurity	None	No	
Web development; career development	Career services, employer hiring partners	Yes (partner loan programs, scholarships)	90% job placement rate
Web development and programming	None	Yes (scholarships, partner loan programs, payment plans)	
IT; web development; information security	None	No	
Training and working hands-on with several local tech companies	After graduation, students are available for hire to TechPoint clients and partners in Indianapolis	No	100% placement of first cohort
Project-based learning; job search skills	None	Yes (partner loan programs, scholarships)	
Programming for data science	None	No	

Name Locations, Program Length Website	Bachelor's required?	Preparing students for these jobs	Other admissions requirements
The Tech Academy *Online, 15–20 weeks* learncodinganywhere.com	No	Software development	
Thinkful *Online, 6 months* thinkful.com	No	Web development, data science	
ThoughtKite *Toronto, 12 weeks part time* thoughtkite.com	No	Mobile development, UX/UI design, product management	
tradecraft *San Francisco, 12 weeks* tradecraft.com	No	Software development, product management, UX/UI design, sales, business development, business	
Turing *Denver, 7 months* turing.io	No	Engineering	Résumé, video response, writing sample, logical challenge, interview
TurnToTech *New York City, 16 weeks* turntotech.io	No	Mobile development, software development, cybersecurity	
UnCollege *San Francisco, 10-week professional development program followed by 12-week internship* uncollege.org	No	All (pre-college gap year program including student-selected internships)	High school diploma or equivalent
Upscale Academy *Los Angeles, Online, 14 weeks* upscaleacademy.com	No	Web development, mobile development	
USC Viterbi Data Analytics Boot Camp *Los Angeles, 24 weeks* databootcamp.viterbi.usc.edu	No	Data science	2 years experience in business, management, finance, statistics, or a related field

Curriculum	Employer engagement	Student financing available	Statistics (placement statistics include percentage in jobs in field, starting salary)
Web development; career development	None	Yes (scholarships)	95% job placement rate, with average graduate salary of $60K
Web development; career development	None	Yes (payment plans)	79% placement in 180 days with median salary of $57K
iOS product development, product management, and lean product growth; community building; career development	Active member of the start-up community in Toronto through meetups, conferences, hackathons, and workshops	No	
Start-up focused technical skills, soft skills, and career development	Career services, employer hiring partners	Yes (partner loan programs)	
Back-end engineering; front-end engineering	Career services, employer hiring partners	Yes (partner loan programs, scholarships)	80% placement with $75K average salary
Technical skills; career development	Career services	Yes (scholarships)	
Professional, personal, and other soft skills; career development	Employers attend networking and mentoring workshops	No	
Portfolio-focused development; MeteorJS; career development	Career services	No	
Technical skills; career development	Career services, employer hiring partners	Yes (scholarships)	

Name Locations, Program Length Website	Bachelor's required?	Preparing students for these jobs	Other admissions requirements
V School *Provo, Salt Lake City, 12 weeks* vschoool.io	No	Web development	
Vital Accelerator *Online, Varies* vitalaccelerator.com	No	Software development, cybersecurity, business	
We Can Code IT *Cleveland, Columbus, 3–5 months* wecancodeit.org	No	Web development	
Wyncode *Miami, 10 weeks full time, 12 weeks part time* wyncode.co	No	Web development	
Zip Code Wilmington *Wilmington, 12 weeks* zipcodewilmington.com	No	Web development, software development	Application process
Program Type: Income Share			
Academy Pittsburgh *Pittsburgh, 12 weeks* academypgh.com	No	Web development	
Byte Academy *New York City, Singapore, Bangalore, Online, 14–24 weeks* byteacademy.co	No	Web development, mobile development, data science, cybersecurity	
C4Q *Queens, NY, 10 months* c4q.nyc	No	Web development, software development	18+, salary <$45K
Holberton School *San Francisco, 2 years* holbertonschool.com	No	Software development	

Curriculum	Employer engagement	Student financing available	Statistics (placement statistics include percentage in jobs in field, starting salary)
Web development; soft skills; career development	Career services, employer hiring partners	Yes (partner loan programs, scholarships)	100% placement into tech jobs
Software development; cybersecurity; business intelligence and networks	Employer-sponsored skill training	N/A	
Web development	Career fairs, career services, employer hiring partners	Yes (partner loan programs, scholarships)	
Ruby-focused web development; professional skills; business leadership skills	Hiring partner network and career development resources	Yes (partner loan programs, scholarships)	86% employment rate within 120 days and average salary of $46,216
JavaScript; Java; job search skills	12+ hiring partners pay for most of student tuition post-placement, curriculum based on projects for Fortune 500 companies	Yes (scholarships, payment plans, employer reimbursement)	93% in 3 months, 96% in 6 months
Front-end development	Cohort builds a real-world application for local nonprofit partner	Yes (ISAs, partner loan programs, scholarships)	
Web development	Curriculum developed in coordination with tech companies	Yes (ISAs, payment plans, partner loan programs)	
Web development; soft skills	Curriculum developed and taught by employees at leading tech companies and start-ups	Yes (ISAs)	
Web development	6 month internship included in program, mentorship from industry professionals	Yes (ISAs)	

Name Locations, Program Length Website	Bachelor's required?	Preparing students for these jobs	Other admissions requirements
Lambda School *Online (live), 6 months* lambdaschool.com	No	Web development	
Learners Guild *Oakland, CA, 10 months* learnersguild.org	No	Web development, software development	21+, basic English proficiency, advanced beginner programming
Make School *San Francisco, Oakland, Los Angeles, Chicago, New York City, Atlanta, Washington DC, Tokyo, Osaka, Hong Kong, Beijing, Online, 2 years (includes 6-month tech internship) product school, 8-week iOS/VR development* makeschool.com	No	Product management, mobile development, software development	Some coding background required
New York Code + Design Academy *New York City, Atlanta, Austin, Philadelphia, Raleigh, Salt Lake City, Washington DC, Amsterdam, 12–24 weeks* nycda.com	No	Web development, UX/UI design	
PowderHouse Studios *Somerville, MA, 18 months* powderhouse.org	Yes	Teacher, principal, K–12 administrator, education policy expert	
Watson University *Boulder, CO, 15 weeks or 2-year degree track in partnership with a university* watsonuniversity.org	No	Entrepreneurship	Student innovators and entrepreneurs ages 18–23

Curriculum	Employer engagement	Student financing available	Statistics (placement statistics include percentage in jobs in field, starting salary)
JavaScript-focused development	None	Yes (ISAs)	
Web development; software development; some job search skills	None	Yes (ISAs)	
Computer science theory covered by traditional universities paired with the practical experience of building and shipping products; soft skills such as ethics, storytelling, and interpersonal communication	Corporate partners for 6-month internship and job placement, including large corporations such as Lyft, LinkedIn, Dailymotion, and Girls Who Code	Yes (scholarships, ISAs)	
Web development; career development	Career services	Yes (scholarships, partner loan programs, ISAs)	
Technical and professional skill training based on both MBA (executive and managerial program) and MFA (applied, performance program) methodologies	Robust employer engagement. Curriculum development, mentoring students, and connecting with future employers	Yes (ISAs)	
Venture-focused hard skills; soft skills; community-building and mentorship	Funders engage in 1-week program and award funding to strongest proposals; demo day at end of program	Yes (ISAs, crowdfunding, work study, scholarships)	

Name Locations, Program Length Website	Bachelor's required?	Preparing students for these jobs	Other admissions requirements
Program Type: Online Education Provider			
180 Skills *Online, Varies* 180skills.com	No	Manufacturing	
CareAcademy *Online, Varies* careacademy.com	No	Home care	
DataCamp *Online, Varies* datacamp.com	No	Data science	
DesignLab *Online, 4 weeks per course* trydesignlab.com	No	UX/UI design	
Knod *Online, Varies* knod.net	No	Digital marketing, digital accounting, entrepreneurship	Pre-admission tests assess competency/ certification and design learning path accordingly
R.A.I. Medical Sales Career Training *Online, Varies* raimedicalsalescareertraining .com	No	Medical sales	
Yellowbrick *Online, Varies* yellowbrick.co	No	Fashion, sports, beauty	Application process

Curriculum	Employer engagement	Student financing available	Statistics (placement statistics include percentage in jobs in field, starting salary)
Manufacturing technical skills; some soft skills	Each course's content verified by corporate partner	No	90% job placement rate
Home care training; soft skills	CareAcademy is hired by home care agencies to provide à la carte or tailored online onboarding and training for care workers	N/A	
Data science (R, Python, SQL)	None	No	
Mentor-led UX/UI Design curriculum in stackable 4-week courses	Students are paired with mentors currently employed in UX/UI Design to provide design feedback, career advice, and networking for potential job placement	No	95% placement for UX Academy course students
Business management and finance-related degrees and certifications through online college	After completing employability requirements, students participate in project-based learning through paid online projects for Knod partners	No	
Online, self-paced modules on Medical Sales industry background and sales skills	Employer partners; job board for all enrolled students	No	
Online, self-paced certificate programs that provide industry background and soft skills needed to enter a career path aligned to a student's passions	Curriculum developed and taught in partnership with leading brand-name employers and higher education institutions	Yes (scholar-ships)	

Name Locations, Program Length Website	Bachelor's required?	Preparing students for these jobs	Other admissions requirements
Program Type: Staffing/Placement Provider			
Avenica *Atlanta, Chicago, Dallas, Minneapolis, Philadelphia, Phoenix, St. Louis, Candidates placed with employers for 4-month trial period* avenica.com	Yes	IT, banking, non-profit, logistics, insurance, financial services, others	Candidates interviewed for transferable competencies and soft skills to determine fit for employers
Code2040 *San Francisco, Varies* code2040.org	No	Web development	African American or Latino student or professional in Computer Science
Cook Systems Bootcamp *Memphis, Phoenix, Dallas, Jacksonville, 8 weeks* cooksys.com/fasttrack	No	Web development	18+
The Data Incubator *New York City, Washington DC, San Francisco, Seattle, Boston, Online, 8 weeks* thedataincubator.com	Yes	Data science	Master's degree or PhD
Knack *Online, Varies* knack.it	No	Varies	
Revature *US, 12 weeks* revature.com	Yes	IT, web development, software development	
Skillful *Online, Varies* skillful.com	No	Varies	High school diploma or equivalent and/or some college experience

Curriculum	Employer engagement	Student financing available	Statistics (placement statistics include percentage in jobs in field, starting salary)
N/A (students interviewed to identify interests, skills, and fit for job opportunities)	Job requirements and Avenica evaluation criteria selected in partnership with Avenica clients; candidates complete 4-month trial period working directly for future employers	N/A	85–90% of placed candidates convert to full-time
Soft skills for minorities in computer science	Employers of interns participate in diversity training	N/A	Students receive return offers from their internship placement at twice the industry rate
Java/.Net/ Mainframe development	Program run by Cook Systems, outsourced development company, with potential hire at end of program	N/A	85% hired and placed on client projects
Technical and business skills focused on training PhDs to enter industry	Bootcamp offered free to students and paid for by employers; hiring network of 250+ hiring and training partners	N/A	
Job-specific skills training via an online video game to adult job seekers	Paid relationships with employers and educational institutions for placement of candidates based on performance	N/A	
Software development; soft skills	Graduates employed full-time by Revature and placed on software engineering projects for Revature client companies across US. Curriculum developed and refined based on technology needs of Revature clients.	N/A	100% of program graduates hired by Revature
Online and offline tools to connect middle-skill job seekers to employers, educators, and community coaches	Employer hiring network; student and employer facing tools (e.g., skills-based job posting templates, interview questions) to connect middle-skill job seekers to employers, educators, and community coaches	N/A	

Name Locations, Program Length Website	Bachelor's required?	Preparing students for these jobs	Other admissions requirements
Strive Talent *San Francisco, Los Angeles, Chicago, N/A* strivetalent.com	No	Sales and customer service/success	Candidates complete a multidomain composite assessment consisting of a cognitive & non-cognitive assessment, structured interview, and work sample test (work sample varies by placement)

Curriculum	Employer engagement	Student financing available	Statistics (placement statistics include percentage in jobs in field, starting salary)
1:1 coaching	For premium enterprise clients, Strive qualitatively and quantitatively analyzes the company's open role to identify the traits/competencies that are necessary to succeed and then creates a pre-intro and post-intro evaluation process.	N/A	~50% of Strive-approved candidates receive employment offers; average starting salary is ~$50K (~25% increase over previous employment)

GLOSSARY

Anticredential: increasing tendency of college dropouts to flaunt that they've dropped out as if that is in itself a credential; byproduct of student frustrations around affordability and employability.

Applicant tracking systems (ATS): keyword matching software most employers use to screen and filter résumés.

Apprenticeships: faster + cheaper alternative to college where employer hires student on day one and relevant training is provided; most U.S. apprenticeships remain in industrial and building trades.

Apprenticeship service provider: apprenticeship-coordinating intermediary standing between employer, student, and government; engine of future growth of new collar apprenticeships.

Bootcamp: intensive last-mile program most common in coding and software development, now emerging across many industries; primarily tuition-pay.

Career services: the college or university department that's supposed to help college students get jobs.

Cognitive skills: critical thinking, problem solving, numerical reasoning, locating information, analytical skills.

College MVP: faster + cheaper alternative to college that starts with last-mile but adds curriculum to build requisite cognitive and noncognitive skills per employer expectations at minimum time and cost; primarily income share funded.

College premium: higher income of college graduates (relative to noncollege graduates).

Competency data: data indicative of a candidate's competencies, sourced from e-portfolios, microcredentials, microassessments, simulations, or perhaps academic transcripts.

Competency profile: candidate profile consisting of competency data.

Competency marketplace: online marketplace matching candidates and employers based on competencies.

Credential gap: the gap between the degree requirements of job postings and the levels of educational attainment of people currently employed in those positions; a measure of degree inflation.

Degree inflation: tendency of employers unable to find talent matching job descriptions to require higher-level degrees than people currently employed in those positions.

Distance traveled: a new model for selective university admissions based on the distance traveled by the student given his or her challenges and resources.

Dystopian counterfactual: what if the college premium results from self-selection rather than value added by college?

Employment imperative: the overriding objective of students enrolling in college is now a good first job in a growing sector of the economy; this is the single biggest change in higher education in the past decade.

Entry-level jobs: jobs with no experience requirement accessible to new college graduates.

e-portfolio: digital archive of work product giving rise to relevant competency data.

Experience inflation: tendency of employers unable to find talent matching job descriptions to require specific experience for jobs that could or should be entry-level.

Generation Z: generation born starting in 2000, now reaching college age.

Hiring friction: the cost of hiring + the risk of a bad hire that leads employers to be extra cautious about hiring; staffing companies reduce hiring friction and help close the skills gap by providing select and trained talent on an evaluation-to-hire basis (bearing most of the cost and risk).

Income share agreements (ISAs): contract between school and graduate to pay a defined percentage of income for a defined period of time; new method for financing postsecondary education with guardrails like time cap, dollar cap, and income floor.

Income share programs: faster + cheaper alternatives funded through income share agreements; typically college MVPs.

Last-mile: the final leg of a connection; in telecom, the connection to each home; in education, technical training and placement.

Last-mile program: a program that delivers technical training and placement; a faster + cheaper alternative to college.

Massive open online courses (MOOCs): free self-paced online courses, open to anyone.

Microassessments: short online assessments on distinct competencies.

Microcredentials: credentials at the level of the competency; badges.

Middle-skills jobs: jobs that require some postsecondary education, but not necessarily a college degree; new collar jobs are digital middle-skills jobs.

Millennials: born between 1980 and 2000; the victims of college's deteriorating affordability and employability.

Minimum viable product (MVP): the simplest, smallest product that provides enough value for consumers to adopt and actually pay for it.

New collar jobs: entry-level jobs that require some level of specialized technology training but not four years of cognitive and noncognitive skill development from a college degree.

Nonselective college: a school that admits 50 percent or more of applicants.

Off-ramps: real work experience incorporated into college curriculum where students would be permitted to remain with an employer before graduating; would require on-ramps back into degree programs.

One-and-done: increasing tendency of elite college basketball players to attend college for only one year before turning professional.

Outsourced apprenticeship: a new American model of apprenticeships in which apprentices are recruited, trained, and employed by service providers to enterprises; service providers expressly provide entry-level talent to clients in addition to services.

Peak credential: the point at which credentials (i.e., college degrees) were most valuable in the labor market; we are past "peak credential."

People analytics: technologies adopted by employers that allow tracking of employee performance based on competencies (or factors predictive of competencies) with feedback loop to job descriptions and hiring.

Pittsburgh Airport test: test used by McKinsey & Company in hiring process—is the candidate someone you could bear being stuck with for eight hours in the Pittsburgh Airport?

Placement colleges: concept for future of community colleges that would be a hybrid of community colleges and workforce investment boards.

Related technical instruction (RTI): classroom training provided during an apprenticeship program—whether by employers, colleges, unions, or apprenticeship service providers—that aims to improve the skills of apprentices in order to qualify them for permanent, full-time positions.

Rule of 10: college affordability test developed by the Lumina Foundation—students should pay no more for college than the savings their families have generated through 10 percent of discretionary income for the past ten years, plus the earnings from working ten hours a week while in school.

SaaS: software-as-a-service; cloud-based software with functionality purchased as required; platforms now used by most companies and organizations to manage a wide range of business functions; metaphor for how higher education will be consumed in the future.

Secondary and tertiary pathways: programs for young professionals already in their first or second job, but who require additional cognitive and noncognitive skill development to move up to a managerial role, or move on to another role.

Selective college: a school that admits fewer than 50 percent of applicants.

Skills gap: the gap between (perceived) employer needs and talent currently produced by colleges and universities; manifested most prominently by 6 million unfilled jobs.

Soft or noncognitive skills: wide range of skills not categorized as cognitive or technical, such as teamwork, communication, organization, creativity, adaptability, and punctuality.

Staffing company: business that specializes in locating and screening talent demanded by employers and either providing personnel to employer-clients in return for a placement fee, or hiring and staffing out to employer-clients for a period of time.

Technical skills: digital skills ranging from knowledge of software or SaaS platform to coding.

Top-up programs: last-mile programs directed at underemployed college graduates; coding bootcamps began life as top-up programs.

Underemployment: college graduates working in jobs that don't require college degrees.

Wage scarring: graduating during a recession leading to lower starting wages that tend to persist for decades.

NOTES

Introduction

1. Clayton Christensen, *The Innovator's Dilemma: The Revolutionary Book That Will Change the Way You Do Business* (New York: HarperBusiness, 2008), xviii.
2. Ibid, xx.
3. Ibid, xix.
4. Paul Fain, "Mixed Views on Higher Ed," *Inside Higher Education,* May 11, 2017, https://www.insidehighered.com/news/2017/05/11/americans-see-value-higher-education-survey-finds-are-unhappy-current-system
5. Doug Lederman, "Duncan on Ratings and Debt," *Inside Higher Education,* July 3, 2014, https://www.insidehighered.com/news/2014/07/03/arne-duncan-talks-about-ratings-and-student-debt-expansive-interview
6. Jordan Weissman, "America's Awful College Dropout Rates in Four Charts," *Slate,* November 19, 2014, http://www.slate.com/blogs/moneybox/2014/11/19/u_s_college_dropouts_rates_explained_in_4_charts.html
7. Camilla Turner, "Private School Pupils 'Forced to Take Degrees' Because Other Options Are Seen as 'Disgrace,'" *The Telegraph,* August, 15, 2017, http://www.telegraph.co.uk/education/2017/08/15/private-school-pupils-forced-take-degrees-options-seen-disgrace/
8. Anthony P. Carnevale, Tanya I. Garcia, and Artem Gulish, "Career Pathways: Five Ways to Connect College and Careers," *Georgetown University Center on Education and the Workforce,* July 11, 2017, https://cew.georgetown.edu/cew-reports/careerpathways/
9. Lisa Scherzer, "The College Earnings Premium is Near Record Highs," *Yahoo Finance,* August 10, 2016, https://finance.yahoo.com/news/college-earnings-premium-near-record-000000150.html
10. Paul Basken, "Trump Will Push Apprenticeships Using Accreditation and Student Aid," *Chronicle of Higher Education,* June 7, 2017, http://www.chronicle.com/article/Trump-Will-Push/240288

Chapter 1—The Ol' College Try

1. "Yale College Programs of Study: Fall and Spring Terms 2016–2017," *Bulletin of Yale University* 112, no. 9 (2016): 21, http://catalog.yale.edu/pdf/2016-17 -ycps.pdf

2. Ibid, 21–22.

3. Ibid, 20.

4. Ibid, 23.

5. Lewis Thayne, "Small Bites Can't Substitute for a College Degree," *Hechinger Report*, May 3, 2017, http://hechingerreport.org/opinion-small-bites -cant-substitute-college-degree

6. John R. Thelin, *A History of American Higher Education* (Baltimore, MD: Johns Hopkins University Press, 2004), 20.

7. Ibid, 31.

8. Ibid, 20.

9. Bureau of Labor Statistics, "Unemployment Rate 2.5 Percent For College Grads, 7.7 Percent For High School Dropouts," January 2017, *TED: The Economics Daily*, February 7, 2017, https://www.bls.gov/opub/ted/2017/unemployment -rate-2-point-5-percent-for-college-grads-7-point-7-percent-for-high-school -dropouts-january-2017.htm

10. Lisa Scherzer, "The College Earnings Premium Is Near Record Highs," *Yahoo Finance*, August 10, 2016, https://finance.yahoo.com/news/college-earnings -premium-near-record-000000150.html

11. "Completing College: A National View of Student Attainment Rates—Fall 2009 Cohort," *National Student Clearinghouse Research Center*, November 16, 2016, https://nscresearchcenter.org/signaturereport10/#Executive Summary

12. Laura Horn and Paul Skomsvold, *Community College Student Outcomes: 1994–2009* (Washington, DC: US Department of Education, Institute of Education Sciences, and National Center for Education Statistics, November 2011), Tables 1-A, 5-A, and 7-A, http://nces.ed.gov/pubs2012/2012253.pdf

13. Allianz Tuition Insurance, Executive Summary: 2017 College Confidence Index, https://www.allianztuitioninsurance.com/resources/research /executive-summary-2017-cci

14. Douglas Belkin, "Many Colleges Fail to Improve Critical-Thinking Skills," *Wall Street Journal*, June 5, 2017, https://www.wsj.com/articles/exclusive -test-data-many-colleges-fail-to-improve-critical-thinking-skills-1496686662

15. Peter W. Wood, "How To Stop Complaining and Fix America's Higher Education Crisis," *The Federalist*, May 15, 2017, https://thefederalist.com/2017/05/15 /stop-complaining-start-fixing-americas-higher-education-crisis

16. Scott Jaschik, "Well-Prepared in Their Own Eyes," *Inside Higher Education*, January 20, 2015, https://www.insidehighered.com/news/2015/01/20 /study-finds-big-gaps-between-student-and-employer-perceptions

17. David Glenn, "New Book Lays Failure to Learn on Colleges' Doorsteps," *Chronicle of Higher Education*, January 18, 2011, http://www.chronicle.com /article/New-Book-Lays-Failure-to-Learn/125983

18. Megan Oprea, "College Students Spend Far More Time Playing Than Studying," *The Federalist,* September 11, 2016, http://thefederalist.com/2016/09/11/study-college-students-spend-far-time-playing-studying
19. Craig Brandon, *The Five-Year Party* (Dallas, TX: BenBella Books, 2010), 21.
20. Ibid, 48–49.
21. Ibid, 49–51.
22. Ibid, 3.
23. Melanie Phillips, "Labour Undermined the Point of Universities," *Times of London,* July 10, 2017, https://www.thetimes.co.uk/article/labour-undermined-the-point-of-universities-f23js8cvr
24. Brandon, *The Five-Year Party,* 30.
25. Eric Kelderman, "On Administrative Spending, Which Colleges Get the Most Bang for the Buck?" *Chronicle of Higher Education,* July 25, 2017, http://www.chronicle.com/article/On-Administrative-Spending/240728
26. Jon Marcus, "Bureaucratic Costs at Some Colleges Are Twice What's Spent on Instruction," *Hechinger Report,* July 25, 2017, https://hechingerreport.org/bureaucratic-costs-colleges-twice-whats-spent-instruction
27. Erik Brady, Steve Berkowitz, and Christopher Schnaars, "College Athletics Finance Report: Non-Power 5 Schools Face Huge Money Pressure," *USA Today,* May 26, 2015, http://www.usatoday.com/story/sports/college/2015/05/26/ncaa-athletic-finances-revenue-expense-division-i/27971457
28. Rochelle Sharpe, "Those Hidden College Fees," *New York Times,* November 3, 2016, http://www.nytimes.com/2016/11/06/education/edlife/those-hidden-college-fees.html
29. Courtney Rubin, "Making a Splash on Campus," *New York Times,* September 19, 2014, http://www.nytimes.com/2014/09/21/fashion/college-recreation-now-includes-pool-parties-and-river-rides.html
30. Brandon, *The Five-Year Party,* 25.
31. Ibid, 24–25.
32. Dave Figlio and Morton O. Shapiro, "Are Great Teachers Poor Scholars," *Brookings Institute,* January 26, 2017, https://www.brookings.edu/research/are-great-teachers-poor-scholars
33. Kim Phillips-Fein, "In 'Campus Confidential,' a Professor Laments that Teaching Is Not the Priority of Teachers," *New York Times,* August 22, 2017, https://www.nytimes.com/2017/08/22/books/review/campus-confidential-jacques-berlinerblau.html
34. Danielle Douglas-Gabriel, "Tuition at Public Colleges Has Soared in the Past Decade, but Student Fees Have Risen Faster," *Washington Post,* June 22, 2016, https://www.washingtonpost.com/news/grade-point/wp/2016/06/22/tuition-at-public-colleges-has-soared-in-the-last-decade-but-student-fees-have-risen-faster
35. Ron Lieber, "Does God Want You to Spend $300,000 for College?" *New York Times,* June 23, 2017, https://www.nytimes.com/2017/06/23/your-money/notre-dame-tuition-father-jenkins-golden-dome-.html

36. Alexandra Johnson, "Porn Star Tells Students They're Being Screwed—By Higher Ed Costs," *The College Fix*, September 10, 2014, https://www.the collegefix.com/post/19213

37. Miriam Weeks, "'Duke Porn Star': I Lost My Financial Aid," *Time*, June 16, 2014, http://time.com/2873280/duke-porn-star-belle-knox-college-cost

38. Remarks by President Trump at Signing of an Executive Order on Apprenticeship and Workforce of Tomorrow Initiatives, *The White House Office of the Press Secretary*, June 15, 2017, https://www.whitehouse.gov/the -press-office/2017/06/15/remarks-president-trump-signing-executive -order-apprenticeship-and; and 2015, http://www.theonion.com/article /online-university-allows-students-amass-crippling--50805

39. "Tuition and Fees and Room and Board over Time, 1976–77 to 2016–17, Selected Years," *The College Board*, September 18, 2017, https://trends .collegeboard.org/college-pricing/figures-tables/tuition-and-fees-and-room -and-board-over-time-1976-77_2016-17-selected-years

40. Ben Myers, "How Colleges Give Students a Flawed Sense of Living Costs," *Chronicle of Higher Education*, July 10, 2017, http://www.chronicle.com /interactives/cost-of-living?cid=trend_au&elq

41. "A Look at the Shocking Student Loan Debt Statistics for 2017," *Student Loan Hero*, September 13, 2017, https://studentloanhero.com /student-loan-debt-statistics

42. Naema Ahmed, "Average US household has 828% more student debt than in 1999," *Axios*, July 21, 2017, https://www.axios.com/american-household -debt-2458678450.html; and Michael Corkery and Stacy Cowley, "Household Debt Makes a Comeback in the US," *New York Times*, May 17, 2017, https:// www.nytimes.com/2017/05/17/business/dealbook/household-debt-united -states.html

43. Abigail Hess, "Here's How Much the Average American in Their 30s Has in Student Debt," *CNBC.com*, June 23, 2017, http://www.cnbc.com/2017/06/23/heres -how-much-the-average-american-in-their-30s-has-in-student-debt.html

44. Rana Foroohar, "The US College Debt Bubble Is Becoming Dangerous," *Financial Times*, April 9, 2017, https://www.ft.com/content/a272ee4c -1b83-11e7-bcac-6d03d067f81f; and Daniel Pianko, "The Looming Student Loan Subprime Catastrophe—And How To Fix It," *FoxNews.com*, July 17, 2017, http://www.foxnews.com/opinion/2017/07/17/looming-student-loan -subprime-catastrophe-and-how-to-fix-it.html

45. Josh Mitchell, "More Than 40% of Student Borrowers Aren't Making Payments," *Wall Street Journal*, April 7, 2016, https://www.wsj.com/articles /more-than-40-of-student-borrowers-arent-making-payments-1459971348; and Josh Mitchell, "Nearly 5 Million Americans in Default on Student Loans," *Wall Street Journal*, December 13, 2017, https://www.wsj.com/articles /nearly-5-million-americans-in-default-on-student-loans-1513192375

46. Kim Dancy and Ben Barrett, "Fewer Borrowers Are Repaying Their Loans Than Previously Thought," *New America Foundation*, January 13, 2017,

https://www.newamerica.org/education-policy/edcentral/fewer-borrowers
-are-repaying-their-loans-previously-thought

47. Ben Barrett, "There's Plenty of Risk to Go Around," *New America Founda-tion*, September 14, 2016, https://www.newamerica.org/education-policy
/edcentral/theres-plenty-risk-go-around/?platform=hootsuite

48. David Scobey, "The Other Student Debt Crisis," *Inside Higher Education*, December 4, 2017, https://www.insidehighered.com/views/2017/12/04
/other-student-debt-crisis-one-you-havent-heard-opinion

49. Annie McClanahan, "Stop Calling Millennials the Facebook Generation.
They're The Student Loan Generation," *Forward*, August 8, 2017, http://forward
.com/opinion/379348/stop-calling-millennials-the-facebook-generation
-theyre-the-student-loan-ge/

50. Jake New, "Not Worth It?" *Inside Higher Education*, September 29, 2015, https://www.insidehighered.com/news/2015/09/29/half-college-graduates
-say-college-worth-cost-survey-finds

51. Raji Chakrabarti, Andrew Haughwout, Donghoon Lee, Joelle Scally, and Wilbert van der Klaauw, "Press Briefing on Household Debt, with Focus on Student Debt," *Federal Reserve Bank of New York*, April 3, 2017, https://
www.newyorkfed.org/medialibrary/media/press/PressBriefing-Household
-Student-Debt-April32017.pdf#page=29

52. "Student Debt Has 17% Saying They Should Have Said No to College," *ConsumerCredit.com*, October 30, 2014, http://www.consumercredit.com
/about-us/media-mentions/student-debt-has-17-saying-they-should-have
-said-no-to-college; and Brian Headd, "Student Debt Among Young Entrepre-neurs," *SBA Small Business Facts*, November, 2014, https://www.sba.gov/sites
/default/files/Student%20Debt%20Among%20Young%20Entrepreneurs%20
Nov%202014.pdf

53. Lin Grensing-Pophal, "How America's Student Debt Crisis Affects the Coun-try's Largest Corporations," *SoFi*, March 27, 2017, https://www.sofi.com/blog
/how-americas-student-debt-crisis-affects-the-countrys-largest-corporations

54. "Student Debt Has 17% Saying They Should Have Said No to College," *ConsumerCredit.com*, October 30, 2014, http://www.consumercredit
.com/about-us/media-mentions/student-debt-has-17-saying-they-should
-have-said-no-to-college

55. Simon Zhen, "How Far Would You Go to Get Rid of Your Student Debt?" *MyBankTracker.com*, March 9, 2017, http://www.mybanktracker.com/news
/how-far-would-you-go-get-rid-your-student-debt-infographic

56. "Kaplan Test Prep and MONEY Survey: Many Parents and High School Counselors Question the Value-for-Cost of College," *Kaplan*, December 7, 2015, http://press.kaptest.com/press-releases/kaplan-test
-prep-and-money-survey-many-parents-and-high-school-counselors
-question-the-value-for-cost-of-college

57. "More Young Adults Live with Parents than Partners, a First," *Associated Press*, May 24, 2016, http://www.latimes.com/business/la-fi-millennials-live
-at-home-20160524-snap-story.html

58. Zachary Bleemer, Meta Brown, Donghoon Lee, Katherine Strair, and Wilbert van der Klaauw, "Echoes of Rising Tuition in Students' Borrowing, Educational Attainment, and Homeownership in Post-Recession America," Federal Reserve Bank of New York Staff Reports, Staff Report No. 820 July 2017, https://www.newyorkfed.org/medialibrary/media/research/staff_reports/sr820.pdf?la=en

59. "The Changing Economics and Demographics of Young Adulthood from 1975 to 2016," *US Census Bureau*, April 19, 2017, https://www.census.gov/newsroom/press-releases/2017/cb17-tps36-young-adulthood.html?cid=17TPS36

60. Ibid.

61. Robert W. Fairlie, Arnobio Morelix, E. J. Reedy, and Joshua Russell, "2015 Kauffman Index of Startup Activity," *Kauffman Institute*.

62. Brian Headd, "Student Debt Among Young Entrepreneurs," *SBA Small Business Facts*, November 2014, https://www.sba.gov/sites/default/files/Student%20Debt%20Among%20Young%20Entrepreneurs%20Nov%202014.pdf

63. Ibid.

64. Ibid.

65. Mike Brown, "70% of Millennials Believe US Student Loan Debt Poses Bigger Threat to US Than North Korea," *Lendedu,* June 19, 2017, https://lendedu.com/news/millennials-believe-u-s-student-loan-debt-bigger-threat-than-north-korea

66. Rick Seltzer, "Discounting Keeps Climbing," *Inside Higher Education,* May 15, 2017, https://www.insidehighered.com/news/2017/05/15/private-colleges-and-universities-increase-tuition-discounting-again-2016-17

67. Jeff Selingo, "Incomes Aren't the Only Thing Not Keeping Pace with Rising Tuition. Neither Are Scholarships," *Washington Post,* September 16, 2016, https://www.washingtonpost.com/news/grade-point/wp/2016/09/16/incomes-arent-the-only-thing-not-keeping-pace-with-rising-tuition-neither-are-scholarships

68. Rick Seltzer, "Discounting Keeps Climbing," *Inside Higher Education,* May 15, 2017, https://www.insidehighered.com/news/2017/05/15/private-colleges-and-universities-increase-tuition-discounting-again-2016-17

69. Rochelle Sharpe, "Why Upperclassmen Lose Financial Aid," *New York Times,* April 6, 2016, http://www.nytimes.com/2016/04/10/education/edlife/why-upperclassmen-pay-more-they-may-get-less.html

70. Kevin Eagan, Ellen Bara Stolzenberg, Abigail K. Bates, Melissa C. Aragon, Maria Ramirez Suchard, and Cecilia Rios-Aguilar, "The American Freshman: National Norms Fall 2015," *Cooperative Institutional Research Program at the Higher Education Research Institute at UCLA,* https://www.heri.ucla.edu/monographs/TheAmericanFreshman2015.pdf

71. Douglas Belkin and Andrea Fuller, "Former Students of College in Chicago Earn Less than High-School Dropouts," *Wall Street Journal,* April 21, 2016, http://www.wsj.com/article_email/former-students-of-college-in-chicago-earn-less-than-high-school-dropouts-1461288553

72. Sheldon Gardner, "Flagler College VP Resigns After Investigation," *St. Augustine Record,* http://staugustine.com/news/local-news/2014-02-17/flagler-college-vp-resigns-after-investigation#.Vx1-ZPkrLX5

73. "Completing College: A National View of Student Attainment Rates Fall 2009 Cohort," *National Student Clearinghouse Research Center,* November 2015, https://nscresearchcenter.org/wp-content/uploads/SignatureReport10.pdf; and Drew Hasselback, "The Cost to Get Adult Kids Out of the House? We'll Pay $24,000, Finds Bank Poll," *National Post,* July 27, 2017, http://www.nationalpost.com/cost+adult+kids+house+says+bank+poll/13922264/story.html

74. Doug Lederman, "Duncan on Ratings and Debt," *Inside Higher Education,* July 3, 2014, https://www.insidehighered.com/news/2014/07/03/arne-duncan-talks-about-ratings-and-student-debt-expansive-interview

75. Molly Corbett Broad, "Educating the Public on the Value of a College Degree," *Chronicle of Higher Education,* May 7, 2017, http://www.chronicle.com/article/Educating-the-Public-on-the/240005?cid=wcontentlist; and Susan Dynarski, "Why Students with the Smallest Debts Have the Larger Problem," *New York Times,* August 31, 2015, http://www.nytimes.com/2015/09/01/upshot/why-students-with-smallest-debts-need-the-greatest-help.html

76. Selingo, "Incomes Aren't the Only Thing Not Keeping Pace with Rising Tuition. Neither Are Scholarships."

77. "Indications of Higher Education Equity in the United States," The Pell Institute (2016): 59. http://www.pellinstitute.org/downloads/publications-Indicators_of_Higher_Education_Equity_in_the_US_2016_Historical_Trend_Report.pdf

78. "The Upshot, Some Colleges Have More Students from the Top 1 Percent than the Bottom 60. Find Yours," *New York Times,* January 18, 2017, https://www.nytimes.com/interactive/2017/01/18/upshot/some-colleges-have-more-students-from-the-top-1-percent-than-the-bottom-60.html

79. Lee Gardner, "Public Colleges Backslide on Access, Report Says," *Chronicle of Higher Education,* October 26, 2017, http://www.chronicle.com/article/Public-Colleges-Backslide-on/241557

80. Frank Bruni, "Class, Cost and College," *New York Times,* April 18, 2014, http://www.nytimes.com/2014/05/18/opinion/sunday/breuni-class-cost-and-college.html

81. Terry Hartle, "Where Have All the Low-Income Students Gone?" *Higher Education Today (American Council on Education),* November 25, 2015, http://www.higheredtoday.org/2015/11/25/where-have-all-the-low-income-students-gone

82. Jennifer Glynn, "Opening Doors: How Selective Colleges and Universities Are Expanding Access for High-Achieving, Low-Income Students," *Jack Kent Cooke Foundation,* August 2017, https://outreach.jkcf.org/opening-doors

83. Meredith Kolodner, "Why Are Low Income Students Not Showing Up to College, Even Though They Have Been Accepted," *Hechinger Report,* August 14, 2015, http://hechingerreport.org/why-are-low-income-students-not-showing-up-to-college-even-though-they-have-been-accepted

84. David Brooks, "How We Are Ruining America," *New York Times,* July 11, 2017, https://www.nytimes.com/2017/07/11/opinion/how-we-are-ruining -america.html

85. "Educational Attainment in the United States: 2016," US Census Bureau, June 24, 2017, https://www.census.gov/data/tables/2016/demo/education -attainment/cps-detailed-tables.html

86. Brooke Metz, "Is College Worth It? Goldman Sachs Says Not So Much," *USA Today,* December 10, 2015, http://college.usatoday.com/2015/12/10 /is-college-worth-it-goldman-sachs-says-not-so-much

87. Doug Lederman, "The Culling of Higher Ed Begins," *Inside Higher Education,* July 18, 2017, https://www.insidehighered.com/news/2017/07/18 /number-colleges-and-universities-drops-sharply-amid-economic-turmoil

88. "Trends in Higher Education: Total Student Aid and Nonfederal Loans in 2016 Dollars over Time," College Board, https://trends.collegeboard.org /student-aid/figures-tables/total-student-aid-and-nonfederal-loans-2016 -dollars-over-time

89. Maureen Groppe, "Purdue President Mitch Daniels Says Universities Should Pay Part of Student Loan Defaults," *Indianapolis Star,* June 21, 2017, http://www.indystar.com/story/news/2017/06/21/daniels-says-universities -should-pay-part-student-loan-defaults/412850001

90. Kate Bachelder, "How to Save American Colleges," *Wall Street Journal,* April 24, 2015, https://www.wsj.com/articles/how-to-save-american-colleges -1429913861

Chapter 2—The Employment Imperative

1. Rachel Fishman, "College Decisions Survey: Deciding to Go to College," *New America Foundation,* May 28, 2015, https://www.newamerica.org/education -policy/edcentral/collegedecisions; and Kevin Eagan, Ellen Bara Stolzenberg, Abigail K. Bates, Melissa C. Aragon, Maria Ramirez Suchard, and Cecilia Rios-Aguilar, "The American Freshman: National Norms Fall 2015," *Cooperative Institutional Research Program at the Higher Education Research Institute at UCLA,* https://www.heri.ucla.edu/monographs/TheAmerican Freshman2015.pdf

2. David Glenn, "New Book Lays Failure to Learn on Colleges' Doorstep," *Chronicle of Higher Education,* January 18, 2011, http://www.chronicle.com/article /New-Book-Lays-Failure-to-Learn/125983

3. "Early Millennials: The Sophomore Class of 2002 a Decade Later," National Center for Education Statistics, June 29, 2017, https://nces.ed.gov/pubsearch /pubsinfo.asp?pubid=2017437

4. Abigail Carlton, "New Survey Research: Key Findings on the State of Entry-Level Employment in the US," *Rockefeller Foundation*, March 21, 2017, https://www.rockefellerfoundation.org/blog/key-findings-on-the -state-of-entry-level-employment-in-the-us

5. "Accenture Strategy 2016 U.S. College Graduate Employment Study, Class of 2016: Passionate, Prepared and Committed," *Accenture,* 2016, https://www .accenture.com/t20160512T073844__w__/us-en/_acnmedia/PDF-18 /Accenture-Strategy-2016-Grad-Research-Comparison-Infographic-v2.pdf

6. Robert LaBombard, "'I Don't Know What to Do with My Major' and Other Reasons College Grads Can't Find Good Jobs," *CNBC.com,* December 15, 2016, http://www.cnbc.com/2016/12/15/why-college-grads-cant-find-jobs -commentary.html

7. Craig Brandon, *The Five-Year Party* (Dallas, TX: BenBella Books), 76.

8. Jaison Abel and Richard Deitz, "Underemployment in the Early Careers of College Graduates Following the Great Recession," *Federal Reserve Bank of New York,* figure 2, http://www.nber.org/chapters/c13697.pdf

9. Jeff Selingo, "Two-Thirds of College Grads Struggle to Launch Their Careers," *Harvard Business Review,* May 31, 2016, https://hbr.org/2016/05 /two-thirds-of-college-grads-struggle-to-launch-their-careers

10. Danielle Kam, "10 Reasons Why You Shouldn't Freak Out if You're Graduating Without a Job," *Cosmopolitan,* April 26, 2017, http://www.cosmopolitan .com/college/a9256859/graduating-without-a-job-dont-panic

11. Austin Weinstein, "US College Grads See Slim-to-Nothing Wage Gains Since Recession," *Bloomberg Markets,* March 29, 2017, https://www.bloomberg.com /news/articles/2017-03-30/u-s-college-grads-see-slim-to-nothing-wage-gains -since-recession

12. "Millennials Earn 20% Less Than Boomers Did at Same Stage of Life," *USA Today,* January 13, 2017, https://www.usatoday.com/story/money/2017/01/13 /millennials-falling-behind-boomer-parents/96530338

13. Josh Mitchell, "More than 40% of Student Borrowers Aren't Making Payments," *Wall Street Journal,* April 7, 2016, https://www.wsj.com/articles /more-than-40-of-student-borrowers-arent-making-payments-1459971348

14. Jaison Abel and Richard Deitz, "College May Not Pay Off for Everyone," *Liberty Street Economics (Federal Reserve Bank of New York),* September 4, 2014, http://libertystreeteconomics.newyorkfed.org/2014/09/college-may-not-pay -off-for-everyone.html

15. "Left Behind," *The Economist,* September 10, 2011, http://www.economist .com/node/21528614

16. Patricia Cohen, "Bump in US Incomes Doesn't Erase 50 Years of Pain," *New York Times,* September 16, 2017, https://www.nytimes.com/2017/09/16/business /economy/bump-in-us-incomes-doesnt-erase-50-years-of-pain.html

17. Ben Steverman, "Why Aren't American Teenagers Working Anymore?" *Bloomberg,* June 5, 2017, https://www.bloomberg.com/news/articles/2017-06-05 /why-aren-t-american-teenagers-working-anymore

18. Ibid.

19. Jeff Selingo, "A Lazy Summer for Teenagers: Why Aren't More of Them Working?" *Washington Post,* June 9, 2017, https://www.washingtonpost.com/news /grade-point/wp/2017/06/09/a-lazy-summer-for-teenagers-why-arent-more -of-them-working

20. Ibid.
21. Neil Howe, "The Unhappy Rise of the Millennial Intern," *Forbes,* April 22, 2014, https://www.forbes.com/sites/realspin/2014/04/22/the-unhappy-rise-of-the-millennial-intern/#19d778911328
22. "The Rise of Corporate Inequality," *Harvard Business Review,* March 23, 2017, https://hbr.org/ideacast/2017/03/the-rise-of-corporate-inequality.html
23. Irving Wladawsky-Berger, "American Workers Evaluate the State of Jobs in the Digital Economy," *Wall Street Journal,* April 7, 2017, https://blogs.wsj.com/cio/2017/04/07/american-workers-evaluate-the-state-of-jobs-in-the-digital-economy
24. Roger Schank, "College Is Over," *LinkedIn,* January 3, 2017, https://www.linkedin.com/pulse/college-over-roger-schank
25. "Criteria for Accreditation," *Higher Learning Commission*, http://policy.hlcommission.org/Policies/criteria-for-accreditation.html
26. Shannon Najmabadi, "How to Revamp a Curriculum Quickly—but Not Too Quickly," *Chronicle of Higher Education,* May 21, 2017, http://www.chronicle.com/article/How-to-Revamp-a-Curriculum/240130
27. Kimberly Cassidy and Gina Siesing, "Solving the Work Force's Skills Gap," *Inside Higher Education,* November 9, 2017, https://www.insidehighered.com/views/2017/11/09/colleges-should-teach-technology-across-curriculum-essay
28. Allie Grasgreen, "Career Services Must Die," *Inside Higher Education,* May 15, 2013, https://www.insidehighered.com/news/2013/05/15/career-services-it-now-exists-must-die-new-report-argues
29. Jon Marcus, "As Graduates Obsess about Jobs, Colleges Cut Spending on Career Services," *Hechinger Report,* May 11, 2017, http://hechingerreport.org/graduates-obsess-jobs-colleges-cut-spending-career-services
30. "The NACE First-Destination Survey: Class of 2015," *National Association of Colleges and Employers,* http://www.naceweb.org/job-market/graduate-outcomes/first-destination/class-of-2015
31. Marcus, "As Graduates Obsess about Jobs."
32. Ibid.
33. Dan Wisniewski, "Forget the Law—Here's Why You Should Really Pay Your Interns," *HRMorning.com*, October 2, 2013, http://www.hrmorning.com/heres-why-you-should-pay-interns/
34. Katie Lobosco, "Rhode Island Governor Wants to Make Tuition Free, Too," *CNN Money,* January 16, 2017, http://money.cnn.com/2017/01/16/pf/college/rhode-island-free-tuition
35. Danielle Douglas-Gabriel, "Families Are Paying More Out of Pocket for College as Tuition Increases Surpass Grant Aid," *Washington Post,* October 25, 2017, https://www.washingtonpost.com/news/grade-point/wp/2017/10/25/families-are-paying-more-out-of-pocket-for-college-as-tuition-increases-surpass-grant-aid
36. Jessi Hempel, "Inside Peter Thiel's Genius Factory," *Wired,* December 7, 2016, https://backchannel.com/inside-peter-thiels-genius-factory-7bf38303c7be#.ywrvl5nq8

37. Kaitlyn Alanis, "4.0 K-State Student Drops Out, Says College Is a Scam," *Kansas State Collegian,* December 19, 2016, http://www.kstatecollegian .com/2016/12/19/4-0-k-state-student-drops-out-says-college-is-a-scam

38. Jon Marcus, "Universities and Colleges Struggle to Stem Big Drops in Enrollment," *Hechinger Report,* June 29, 2017, http://hechingerreport.org /universities-colleges-struggle-stem-big-drops-enrollment

39. Scott Jaschik, "The 2017 Survey of Admissions Directors: Pressure All Around," *Inside Higher Education,* September 13, 2017, https://www.insidehighered .com/news/survey/2017-survey-admissions-directors-pressure-all-around

40. Irving Wladawsky-Berger, "American Workers Evaluate the State of Jobs in the Digital Economy," *Wall Street Journal,* April 7, 2017, https://blogs .wsj.com/cio/2017/04/07/american-workers-evaluate-the-state-of-jobs -in-the-digital-economy

41. Marcus, "Universities and Colleges Struggle to Stem Big Drops in Enrollment."

42. Jaschik, "The 2017 Survey of Admissions Directors: Pressure All Around."

43. Jack Healy, "Out of High School, Into Real Life," *New York Times,* June 23, 2017, https://www.nytimes.com/2017/06/23/us/out-of-high-school-into-real -life.html

44. Matt Taibbi, "The Great College Loan Swindle," *Rolling Stone,* November 3, 2017, http://www.rollingstone.com/politics/features/taibbi-the-great -college-loan-swindle-w510880

45. Josh Mitchell and Douglas Belkin, "Americans Losing Faith in College Degrees, Poll Finds," *Wall Street Journal,* September 7, 2017, https://www.wsj.com /articles/americans-losing-faith-in-college-degrees-poll-finds-1504776601

46. Katy Steinmetz, "Move Over, Millennials: How Generation Z Is Disrupting Work as We Know It," *Time,* December 20, 2017, http://time.com/5066641 /generation-z-disruption

Chapter 3—Hiring and Jobs

1. Joni Holderman, "The Impact of Applicant Tracking Systems on Job Search," *Career Planning and Adult Development Journal,* 30/2 (Summer 2014).

2. Allan Ripp, "How Not to Get a Job," *New York Times,* July 7, 2017, https://www .nytimes.com/2017/07/07/opinion/how-not-to-get-a-job.html

3. Ibid.

4. Holderman, "The Impact of Applicant Tracking Systems on Job Search."

5. Ibid.

6. "'I Would Be Absolutely Perfect for This,' Report 1,400 People Looking At Same Job Posting," *The Onion,* June 27, 2013, http://www.theonion.com /article/i-would-be-absolutely-perfect-report-1400-people-l-53667

7. "Baseline Skills, The Human Factor: The Hard Time Employers Have Finding Soft Skills," *Burning Glass,* http://burning-glass.com/wp-content/uploads /Human_Factor_Baseline_Skills_FINAL.pdf

8. Julian Lewis Watkins, *The 100 Greatest Advertisements 1852–1958: Who Wrote Them and What They Did* (Mineola, NY: Dover, 1949), 1.

9. Pratibha Nanduri, "Talent Shortage Is Killing Innovation," *HR Technologist,* August 1, 2017, https://www.hrtechnologist.com/news/candidate-search -and-sourcing/talent-shortage-is-killing-innovation

10. "2016–2017 Talent Shortage Survey," *Manpower Group,* http://www.man powergroup.com/talent-shortage-2016

11. "Chances Are Your Next Job Will Require Salesforce Skills," *Medium,* February 8, 2017, https://medium.com/trailhead/chances-are-your-next -job-will-require-salesforce-skills-290f4da05e8c

12. "Crunched by the Numbers: The Digital Skills Gap in the Workforce," *Burning Glass,* http://burning-glass.com/research/digital-skills-gap

13. Robert B. Cohen, "Highly Stratified Occupations and the Digital Economy," working paper posted to *SlideShare,* June 15, 2017, https://www.slideshare.net /bcohen777/highly-stratified-occupations-and-the-digital-economy-061517

14. "Crunched by the Numbers: The Digital Skills Gap in the Workforce," *Burning Glass.*

15. Matt Sigelman, "Return to the Pyramid: How Tech Giants Are Using a 1980's Philosophy to Reinvent Their Workforce," panel discussion at CWS Conference in Dallas, TX, September 12, 2017.

16. Matt Sigelman, "Skills, Not Jobs: New Opportunities for Higher Education," presentation at SXSW.edu in Austin, TX, March 9, 2017.

17. Marco della Cava and Eli Blumenthal, "Here's What You Need to Land America's Best Jobs," *USA Today,* May 30, 2017, https://www.usatoday.com/story/tech /news/2017/05/30/heres-what-you-need-land-americas-best-jobs/101730006

18. Maya Pope-Chappell, "Here Are the Skills That Hiring Managers at the 50 LinkedIn Top Companies Want," *LinkedIn Pulse,* May 18, 2017, https://www.linkedin.com/pulse/here-skills-hiring-managers-50 -linkedin-top-companies-pope-chappell

19. Ibid.

20. Alison DeNisco, "Half of the 15 Highest Paying Jobs for Recent Grads Are in Tech," *TechRepublic,* May 11, 2017, http://www.techrepublic.com/article /half-of-the-15-highest-paying-jobs-for-recent-grads-are-in-tech

21. "Assessing the IT Skills Gap," *CompTIA,* May 2017, https://www.comptia.org /resources/assessing-the-it-skills-gap

22. Maya Beasley, "Are Today's Students Prepared to Enter the Tech Industry," *Center for American Progress,* June 23, 2017, https://www.americanprogress.org/issues /race/news/2017/06/23/434758/todays-students-prepared-enter-tech-industry

23. Eun-Young Jeong and Kwanwoo Jun, "What's a College Degree Worth? Not Much for Young South Koreans," *Wall Street Journal,* July 18, 2017, https:// www.wsj.com/articles/whats-a-college-degree-worth-not-much-for-young -south-koreans-1500370206

24. Jeff Selingo, "The Rise of the Double Major," *Chronicle of Higher Education,* October 11, 2017, http://www.chronicle.com/blogs/next/2012/10/11 /the-worrying-rise-of-double-majors

25. "The State of American Jobs," *Pew Research Center,* October 6, 2016, http:// www.pewsocialtrends.org/2016/10/06/the-state-of-american-jobs

26. Guy Berger, "Soft Skills Are Increasingly Crucial to Getting Your Dream Job," *LinkedIn Pulse,* August 30, 2016, https://www.linkedin.com/pulse/soft-skills -increasingly-crucial-getting-your-dream-guy-berger-ph-d-?published=t

27. Kate Davidson, "Employers Find 'Soft Skills' Like Critical Thinking in Short Supply," *Wall Street Journal,* August 30, 2016, https://www.wsj.com/articles /employers-find-soft-skills-like-critical-thinking-in-short-supply-1472549400

28. Emilie Rusch, "Finding Workers in Colorado with the Right Soft Skills an Increasing Challenge for Employers," *Denver Post,* September 4, 2016, http:// www.denverpost.com/2016/09/04/colorado-workers-soft-skills-limited

29. Alessandra Malito, "Why a College Degree Could Be One of the Worst Ways to Find a New Employee," *Marketwatch*, March 25, 2017, http://www.market watch.com/story/how-to-fix-the-big-disconnect-between-entry-level-job -candidates-and-employers-2017-03-21

30. Andrew McIlvaine, "Screening's Sorry State," *Human Resource Executive Online,* August 23, 2017, http://www.hreonline.com/HRE/view/story .jhtml?id=534362900

31. Rob Kaplan, "America Has to Close the Workforce Skills Gap," *Bloomberg View,* April 12, 2017, https://www.bloomberg.com/view/articles/2017-04-12 /america-has-to-close-the-workforce-skills-gap

32: Peter Capelli, *Why Good People Can't Get Jobs: The Skills Gap and What Companies Can Do About It* (Philadelphia: Wharton Digital Press, 2012), 10.

33. "41 Percent of Employers Are Hiring College-Educated Workers for Positions That Had Been Primarily Held by Those with High School Degrees, Finds CareerBuilder Survey," *Career Builder,* March 16, 2017, http://press .careerbuilder.com/2017-03-16-41-Percent-of-Employers-Are-Hiring-College -Educated-Workers-for-Positions-That-Had-Been-Primarily-Held-by-Those -with-High-School-Degrees-Finds-CareerBuilder-Survey

34. "Moving the Goalposts: How Demand for a Bachelor's Degree is Reshaping the Workforce," *Burning Glass,* http://burning-glass.com/wp-content/uploads /Moving_the_Goalposts.pdf

35. Matthew Sigelman, "Half of Supervisors Now Need a College Degree: Are You Getting Better Service?" *Burning Glass,* August 30, 2016, http://burning-glass .com/half-of-supervisors-now-need-a-college-degree-are-you-getting-better -service

36. Dan Restuccia, "Help Me Out Here: Does a Help Desk Job Require a College Degree?" *Burning Glass,* March 7, 2016, http://burning-glass.com /help-me-out-here-does-a-help-desk-job-require-a-college-degree

37. Richard Vedder and Justin Strehle, "The Diminishing Returns of a College Degree," *Wall Street Journal,* June 4, 2017, https://www.wsj.com/articles /the-diminishing-returns-of-a-college-degree-1496605241

38. Matthew Bidwell, "Unpacking Human Capital: Exploring the Role of Experience and Education in Shaping Access to Jobs," working paper.

39. Ibid.

40. "EY Transforms Its Recruitment Selection Process for Graduates, Undergraduates and School Leavers," *Ernst & Young,* August 3, 2015, http://www.ey.com

/uk/en/newsroom/news-releases/15-08-03---ey-transforms-its-recruitment
-selection-process-for-graduates-undergraduates-and-school-leavers

41. Rosemary Bennett, "Ban on CVs Boosts State-School Recruits," *Times of London,* February 2, 2017, http://www.thetimes.co.uk/edition/news /ban-on-cvs-boosts-state-school-recruits-98v0hmhhq

42. Sean Coughlan, "Penguin Scraps Degree Requirement," *BBC News,* January 18, 2016, http://www.bbc.com/news/education-35343680

43. Chris Matyszczyk, "Google: GPAs Are Worthless," *CNET,* June 20, 2013, https://www.cnet.com/news/google-gpas-are-worthless

44. Max Nisen, "Why Google Doesn't Care About Hiring Top College Graduates," *Quartz,* February 24, 2014, https://qz.com/180247/why-google-doesnt -care-about-hiring-top-college-graduates

45. Jennifer Alsever, "How AI Is Changing Your Job Hunt," *Fortune,* May 18, 2017, http://fortune.com/2017/05/19/ai-changing-jobs-hiring-recruiting

46. Cale Guthrie-Weissman, "Why More Tech Companies Are Hiring People Without Degrees," *Fast Company,* April 3, 2017, https://www.fast company.com/3069259/why-more-tech-companies-are-hiring-people -without-degrees; and Kai Ryssdal, Bridget Bodnar, and Emily Henderson, "You Don't Need to Be a College Grad to Work in Tech," *Marketplace,* August 1, 2017, https://www.marketplace.org/2017/08/01/tech /you-dont-need-be-college-grad-work-tech

47. Steve Lohr, "A New Kind of Tech Job Emphasizes Skills, Not a College Degree," *New York Times,* June 28, 2017, https://www.nytimes.com/2017/06/28 /technology/tech-jobs-skills-college-degree.html

48. Brandon, *The Five-Year Party,* 11.

49. "What America Needs to Know About Higher Education Redesign," *Gallup and Lumina Foundation,* February 25, 2014, http://www.gallup.com /services/176759/america-needs-know-higher-education-redesign.aspx

50. Hart Research Associates, "Falling Short? College Learning and Career Success," *Association of American Colleges & Universities,* January 20, 2015, https:// www.aacu.org/leap/public-opinion-research/2015-survey-falling-short

51. "What America Needs to Know About Higher Education Redesign."

Chapter 4—The Last Mile

1. Marco della Cava and Eli Blumenthal, "Here's What You Need to Land America's Best Jobs," *USA Today,* May 30, 2017, https://www.usatoday.com/story/tech /news/2017/05/30/heres-what-you-need-land-americas-best-jobs/101730006

2. MissionU post on Instagram, July 30, 2017, https://www.instagram.com/p /BXMpUokgAfD/

3. Email from Liz Simon, General Counsel and VP External Affairs, General Assembly, July 25, 2017.

4. Prashant Gopal and Matthew Townsend, "Want a $1 Million Paycheck? Skip College and Go Work in a Lumberyard," *Bloomberg Businessweek,* June 27, 2017, https://www.bloomberg.com/news/articles/2017-06-27/want -a-1-million-paycheck-skip-college-and-go-work-in-a-lumberyard

5. Jon Marcus, "Universities and Colleges Struggle to Stem Big Drops in Enrollment," *Hechinger Report,* June 29, 2017, http://hechingerreport.org /universities-colleges-struggle-stem-big-drops-enrollment

Chapter 5—Welcome to Bootcamp

1. Giovanni Bruno, "Galvanize CEO Deters Explains the Coding Web-Development-Based School on CNBC," *CNBC*, August 23, 2016, https://www.the street.com/story/13682635/1/galvanize-ceo-deters-explains-the-coding-web -development-based-school-on-cnbc.html
2. "Led by Co-founder/CEO Jake Schwartz, General Assembly Reimagines Learning for the 21st Century," *Free Enterprise*, October 9, 2014, https://www .freeenterprise.com/led-co-founder-ceo-jake-schwartz-general-assembly -hits-its-stride-teaching-21st-century
3. Liz Eggleston, "2017 Coding Bootcamp Market Size Study," *Course Report,* July 19, 2017, https://www.coursereport.com/reports/2017-coding -bootcamp-market-size-research
4. "About," *General Assembly,* August 1, 2017, https://generalassemb.ly/about
5. "Galvanize Outcomes: Where Our Graduates Work," *Galvanize*, September 5, 2017, https://www.galvanize.com/phoenix/web-development#outcomes
6. Steve Lohr, "Where Non-Techies Can Get with the Programming," *New York Times,* April 4, 2017, https://www.nytimes.com/2017/04/04/education/edlife /where-non-techies-computer-programming-coding.html
7. Sri Ravipati, "Report: 92 Percent of Coding Bootcamp Students Graduate On Time," *Campus Technology,* April 10, 2017, https://campustechnology .com/articles/2017/04/10/report-92-percent-of-coding-bootcamp-students -graduate-ontime.aspx
8. Rachel Koning Beals, "Beyond Bootcamp: Is Immersive Learning a Must for Coding?" *MarketWatch,* July 12, 2017, http://www.marketwatch.com/story /beyond-bootcamp-is-immersive-learning-a-must-for-coding-2017-07-10
9. "What Do Employers Really Think about Coding Bootcamps," *Indeed Blog,* May 2, 2017, http://blog.indeed.com/2017/05/02/what-employers -think-about-coding-bootcamp
10. Michelle Rafter, "Is Coding Bootcamp Right for You?" *Computerworld,* May 25, 2017, http://www.computerworld.com/article/3191988/it-skills-training /is-a-coding-boot-camp-right-for-you.html
11. Alison DeNisco, "Report: 80% of Companies Have Hired a Coding Bootcamp Graduate, All Said They Would Do It Again," *TechRepublic*, May 2, 2017, http://www.techrepublic.com/article/report-80-of-companies-have-hired-a -coding-bootcamp-graduate-all-said-they-would-do-it-again
12. Ryan Burke, "From the White House to Coding Bootcamp," *Medium*, March 23, 2017, https://medium.com/@ryanburke_97647/from-the-white -house-to-coding-bootcamp-5e973674add9
13. Ryan Burke, "If You Want to Go Quickly, Go Alone. If You Want to Go Far, Go Together," *Medium*, January 4, 2018, https://medium.com/@ryan

burke_97647/if-you-want-to-go-quickly-go-alone-if-you-want-to-go-far-go
-together-4b78b605cebc

14. Jeff Kauflin, "The 20 Most Popular Jobs for College Graduates," *Forbes*, May 23, 2017, https://www.forbes.com/sites/jeffkauflin/2017/05/23 /the-20-most-popular-jobs-for-college-graduates/#56f1142e71b4

15. Ryan Craig, "Providing Students with Pathways to High-Value Careers," *Change: The Magazine of Higher Learning* 48, no. 5 (2016): 62.

16. Liz Eggleston, "2017 Coding Bootcamp Market Size Study," *Course Report*, July 19, 2017, https://www.coursereport.com/reports/2017-coding -bootcamp-market-size-research

17. Jillian Berman, "Amid For-Profit College Crackdown, Feds Give For-Profit Schools Access to Funds," *MarketWatch*, August 16, 2016, http:// www.marketwatch.com/story/will-providing-aid-to-for-profit-programs -lead-to-exploitation-of-federal-funds-2016-08-16; and Lindsay McKenzie, "Military Victory for Alternative Providers," *Inside Higher Education*, August 24, 2017, https://www.insidehighered.com/news/2017/08/24 /new-gi-bill-includes-75-million-noncollege-provider-program-veterans

Chapter 6—The College MVP

1. Liz Eggleston, "2016 Course Report Alumni Outcomes & Demographics Study," *Course Report*, September 14, 2016, https://www.coursereport.com /reports/2016-coding-bootcamp-job-placement-demographics-report

2. Jason Delisle, "Student and Parent Perspectives on Higher Education Financing," *American Enterprise Institute*, January 26, 2017, http://www.aei.org/publication /student-and-parent-perspectives-on-higher-education-financing-2/

3. "A New Kind of Education," Holberton School, https://www.holbertonschool .com/education

4. Ibid.

5. Katie Benner, "Holberton, a Two-Year School, Emphasizes Diversity," *New York Times*, June 7, 2017, https://www.nytimes.com/2017/06/07/education /holberton-a-two-year-tech-school-emphasizes-diversity.html

6. "Prepare to Be Hired," *Mission U*, https://www.missionu.com/program

7. Megan Gambino, "This One-Year Alternative to College Promises to Land Students a Well-Paying Job, Debt-Free," *Smithsonian*, April 3, 2017, http:// www.smithsonianmag.com/innovation/this-one-year-alternative-college -promises-land-students-well-paying-job-debt-free-180962742

8. Leigh Buchanan, "This Startup Is Pitching a 1-Year Alternative to College for Zero Money Down," *Inc.*, August 7, 2017, https://www.inc.com/leigh -buchanan/missionu.html

9. Ibid.

10. Ryan Craig, "The Rise of Vocational 2.0 Jobs Will Revolutionize Higher Education," *Forbes*, May 18, 2017, https://www.forbes.com/sites/ryancraig/2017/05/18 /the-rise-of-vocational-2-0-jobs-will-revolutionize-higher-education

11. "Employment Projections," *Bureau of Labor Statistics*, November 9, 2016, https://www.bls.gov/emp/ep_data_occupational_data.htm

12. Clive Thompson, "The Next Big Blue Collar Job Is Coding," *Wired*, February 8, 2017, https://www.wired.com/2017/02/programming-is-the-new-blue-collar-job

13. Robert B. Cohen, "Highly Stratified Occupations and the Digital Economy," working paper posted to *SlideShare*, June 15, 2017, https://www.slideshare.net/bcohen777/highly-stratified-occupations-and-the-digital-economy-061517

14. "What Is New Collar?" *IBM*, http://www-03.ibm.com/employment/us/new_collar.shtml

15. Burning Glass, "Will Your Next Job Require Salesforce Skills?" February 10, 2017, http://burning-glass.com/will-next-job-require-salesforce-skills

16. "Fidelity Launches New Program for Employers to Help Workers Pay Off Student Debt," *Fidelity*, September 14, 2017, https://www.fidelity.com/about-fidelity/employer-services/fidelity-launches-new-program-employers-to-help-pay-off-student-debt

17. Email from Scott Bittle, Director of Communications, Burning Glass, July 31, 2017.

18. Steve Lohr, "Hot Spot for Tech Outsourcing: The United States," *New York Times*, July 30, 2017, https://www.nytimes.com/2017/07/30/technology/hot-spot-for-tech-outsourcing-the-united-states.html

19. Richard Price, "Innovators Worth Watching: MissionU," *Christensen Institute*, July 11, 2017, https://www.christenseninstitute.org/blog/innovators-worth-watching-missionu

Chapter 7—Get to Work

1. Debbie Reed, Albert Yung-Hsu Liu, Rebecca Kleinman, Annalisa Mastri, Davin Reed, Samina Sattar, and Jessica Ziegler, "An Effectiveness Assessment and Cost-Benefit Analysis of Registered Apprenticeship in 10 States," *Mathematica Policy Research*, July 25, 2012, https://wdr.doleta.gov/research/fulltext_documents/etaop_2012_10.pdf

2. "ApprenticeshipUSA Toolkit," Department of Labor, August 13, 2017, https://www.dol.gov/apprenticeship/toolkit/toolkitfaq.htm

3. Douglas Belkin and Eric Morath, "Apprenticeships Aren't Just for Welders Anymore," *Wall Street Journal*, June 14, 2017, https://www.wsj.com/articles/apprenticeships-arent-just-for-welders-anymore-1497437397

4. Stephen Exley, "Euan Blair: 'Apprenticeships Should Be for Smart Kids Too,'" *Tes*, January 6, 2017, https://www.tes.com/news/further-education/breaking-news/euan-blair-apprenticeships-should-be-smart-kids-too

5. Ibid.

6. Thad Moore, "South Carolina's Apprenticeship Initiative Cracks Growth Milestone as New US Labor Secretary Advocates for On-the-Job Training," *The Post and Courier*, May 18, 2017, http://www.postandcourier.com/business/south-carolina-s-apprenticeship-initiative-cracks-growth-milestone-as-new/article_72157c86-3c05-11e7-9514-7bb6c3409ac9.html

7. Steve Lohr, "A New Kind of Tech Job Emphasizes Skills, Not a College Degree," *New York Times,* June 28, 2017, https://www.nytimes.com/2017/06/28 /technology/tech-jobs-skills-college-degree.html

8. "For Siemens and Other Companies, Apprentice Programs Seen as Alternative to College," *NBC Nightly News with Lester Holt* (May 27, 2017; NBC), TV, http://www.nbcnews.com/nightly-news/video/for-siemens -and-other-companies-apprentice-programs-954953795785

9. Elizabeth Redden, "Importing Apprenticeships," *Inside Higher Education,* August 8, 2017, https://www.insidehighered.com/news/2017/08/08 /interest-grows-us-germanswiss-model-apprenticeships

10. Lisa Bertagnoli, "Not Just for Trades: Aon Wants Other White-Collar Firms to Adopt Its Apprenticeship Program," *Crain's Chicago Business,* September 18, 2017, http://www.chicagobusiness.com/article/20170918/NE WS01/170919906/not-just-for-trades-aon-wants-other-white-collar-firms-to -adopt-its-apprenticeship-program

11. Katherine Mangan, "The Making of a Modern-Day Apprentice," *Chronicle of Higher Education,* June 28, 2017, http://www.chronicle.com/article /The-Making-of-a-Modern-Day/240466

12. Alexia Elejalde-Ruiz, "Apprenticeship Programs Increasingly Put Workers On Track for Jobs in Finance," *Chicago Tribune,* April 24, 2017, http:// www.chicagotribune.com/business/ct-aon-finance-apprenticeship-0425-biz -20170424-story.html

13. Kathy Gurchiek, "Employers 'Unlocking the Potential' of Apprenticeship for White-Collar Jobs," *Society for Human Resource Management,* June 1, 2017, https://www.shrm.org/resourcesandtools/hr-topics/organizational -and-employee-development/pages/employers-unlocking-the-potential-of -apprenticeship-for-white-collar-jobs.aspx

14. Scott Carlson, "Why Colleges Need to Embrace the Apprenticeship," *Chronicle of Higher Education,* June 4, 2017, http://www.chronicle.com/article /Why-Colleges-Need-to-Embrace/240248

15. Belkin and Morath, "Apprenticeships Aren't Just for Welders Anymore."

16. Jena McGregor, "Apprenticeships, Long Common in Blue-Collar Industries, Are Coming to White-Collar Office Work," *Washington Post,* October 20, 2017, https://www.washingtonpost.com/news/on-leadership/wp/2017/10/20/app renticeships-long-common-in-blue-collar-industries-are-coming-to-white -collar-office-work

17. "CVS Health Celebrates First Annual National Apprenticeship Week," *CVS Health,* November 2, 2015, https://cvshealth.com/newsroom/press-releases /cvs-health-celebrates-first-annual-national-apprenticeship-week

18. Jena McGregor, "Apprenticeships, Long Common in Blue-Collar Industries, Are Coming to White-Collar Office Work," *Washington Post,* October 20, 2017, https://www.washingtonpost.com/news/on-leadership/wp/2017/10/20 /apprenticeships-long-common-in-blue-collar-industries-are-coming-to -white-collar-office-work

19. Ibid.
20. Kathryn Moody, "How Do You Create 5M Apprenticeships? 3 Practical Considerations," *HR Dive*, November 15, 2017, https://www.hrdive.com/news/how-do-you-create-5m-apprenticeships-3-practical-considerations/510983
21. Cynthia Poole and Steven Berchem, "How Much Runway Remains?" *American Staffing Association*, 2016, https://americanstaffing.net/posts/2016/11/02/how-much-runway-remains
22. Lauren Weber, "The End of Employees," *Wall Street Journal*, February 2017, https://www.wsj.com/articles/the-end-of-employees-1486050443
23. Ibid.
24. Bernard Marr, "Robots Come to Job Search: AI-Powered Head Hunters Disrupt Recruitment Industry," *Forbes*, November 27, 2017, https://www.forbes.com/sites/bernardmarr/2017/11/27/robots-come-to-job-search-ai-powered-head-hunters-disrupt-recruitment-industry
25. Lisa Frye, "The Cost of a Bad Hire Can Be Astronomical," *SHRM*, May 9, 2017, https://www.shrm.org/resourcesandtools/hr-topics/employee-relations/pages/cost-of-bad-hires.aspx

Chapter 8—Online Bootcamps (an Oxymoron) and Competency Marketplaces

1. Jacques Steinberg and Edward Wyatt, "Boola, Boola, e-Commerce Comes to the Quad," *New York Times*, February 13, 2000, http://www.nytimes.com/2000/02/13/weekinreview/the-nation-boola-boola-e-commerce-comes-to-the-quad.html
2. Caroline Hoxby, "The Returns to Online Postsecondary Education," working paper posted to the *National Bureau of Economic Research*, http://www.nber.org/chapters/c13709
3. Blaise Zerega, "Udacity: Reno Pilot Shows the Future of Tech Job Training," *VentureBeat*, June 14, 2017, https://venturebeat.com/2017/06/14/udacity-reno-pilot-shows-the-future-of-tech-job-training
4. Blaise Zerega, "Tech Jobs Needed: How to Bridge 'Skills' and 'Opportunity Gaps' in the Heartland," *VentureBeat*, June 17, 2017, https://venturebeat.com/2017/06/17/tech-jobs-needed-how-to-bridge-skills-and-opportunity-gaps-in-the-heartland
5. Steve LeVine, "In Bet Against College, WeWork Acquires a Coding Bootcamp," *Axios*, October 23, 2017, https://www.axios.com/in-a-bet-against-college-wework-acquires-a-coding-bootcamp-2500013575.html
6. "AWS Looks to Plug Skills Gap with Machine Learning 'Boot Camp,'" *Computer Business Review*, November 23, 2017, https://www.cbronline.com/emerging-technology/aws-looks-plug-skills-gap-machine-learning-boot-camp
7. "Entrepreneurship 101: Who Is Your Customer?" Massachusetts Institute of Technology, edX, August 21, 2017, https://www.edx.org/course/entrepreneurship-101-who-customer-mitx-bootcamp1-1

8. Jay Greene, "Microsoft to Acquire LinkedIn for $26.2 Billion," *Wall Street Journal*, June 14, 2016, https://www.wsj.com/articles/microsoft-to-acquire-linkedin-in-deal-valued-at-26-2-billion-1465821523

9. Frank Schmidt and John Hunter, "The Validity and Utility of Selection Methods in Personnel Psychology: Practical and Theoretical Implications of 85 Years of Research Findings," *Psychological Bulletin* 124, no. 2 (1998).

10. Lizzie Widdicombe, "The Programmer's Price," *The New Yorker*, November 24, 2014, http://www.newyorker.com/magazine/2014/11/24/programmers-price

11. Amie Tsang, "Want to Work for Jaguar Land Rover? Start Playing Phone Games," *New York Times*, June 19, 2017, https://www.nytimes.com/2017/06/19/business/jaguar-land-rover-app-puzzles.html

12. Ryan Craig, "The Hiring Game," *TechCrunch*, October 16, 2016, https://techcrunch.com/2016/10/16/the-hiring-game

Chapter 9—The Road I Didn't Take

1. "A Benchmark for Making College Affordable: The Rule of 10," *Lumina Foundation*, 2015, https://www.luminafoundation.org/files/resources/affordability-benchmark-1.pdf

2. Ibid.

3. Jeff Selingo, "Trump Administration Is Taking Aim at Affirmative Action in College Admissions. Why It Won't Fix What's Broken," *Washington Post*, August 2, 2017, https://www.washingtonpost.com/news/grade-point/wp/2017/08/02/trump-administration-is-taking-aim-at-affirmative-action-in-college-admissions-why-it-wont-fix-whats-broken-with-the-application-process

4. Jillian Berman, "Why So Many Small Private Colleges Are in Danger of Closing," *MarketWatch*, June 13, 2017, http://www.marketwatch.com/story/why-so-many-small-private-colleges-are-in-danger-of-closing-2017-06-13

5. Richard Vedder and Justin Strehle, "The Diminishing Returns of a College Degree," *Wall Street Journal*, June 4, 2017, https://www.wsj.com/articles/the-diminishing-returns-of-a-college-degree-1496605241

6. "Mass. Becomes 1st State To Have Half Its Labor Force Hold Bachelor's Degrees," *WBUR News*, August 23, 2017, http://www.wbur.org/news/2017/08/23/state-labor-force-bachelors-degrees

7. Jillian Berman, "Families in the Northeast Spend 70% More on College Because They Value Social Status," *MarketWatch*, July 17, 2017, http://www.marketwatch.com/story/families-in-the-northeast-spend-70-more-on-college-because-they-want-the-right-sticker-on-their-car-window-2017-07-17

8. Vedder and Strehle, "The Diminishing Returns of a College Degree."

9. Jeff Selingo, "Business Is the Most Popular College Major, but That Doesn't Mean It's a Good Choice," *Washington Post*, January 28, 2017, https://www.washingtonpost.com/news/grade-point/wp/2017/01/28/business-is-the-most-popular-college-major-but-that-doesnt-mean-its-a-good-choice

10. Jaschik, "The 2017 Survey of Admissions Directors: Pressure All Around."

11. Andrew Kreighbaum, "'Law Mart,'" *Inside Higher Education,* August 22, 2017, https://www.insidehighered.com/news/2017/08/22/anthropologist -examines-how-profits-wrought-change-among-law-schools
12. Ibid.
13. Jordan Malter, "Is Olive Garden Food That Bad? We Tried It," *CNN Money,* http://money.cnn.com/video/news/2014/09/30/olive-garden-food-taste-test -starboard.cnnmoney/index.html
14. Jonathan Barnett, "Shopping for Gucci on Canal Street: Reflections on Status Consumption, Intellectual Property and the Incentive Thesis," *Virginia Law Review,* April 23, 2005, http://papers.ssrn.com/sol3/papers .cfm?abstract_id=704721
15. Anna Fazackerley, "Academic Civil War as Elite Universities Lobby for Others to Drop Their Fees," *The Guardian,* October 17, 2017, https://www.theguardian .com/education/2017/oct/17/elite-universities-lobby-other-drop-fees-stu- dents
16. Max Nisen, "Why Google Doesn't Care About Hiring Top College Gradu- ates," *Quartz,* February 24, 2014, https://qz.com/180247/why-google-doesnt -care-about-hiring-top-college-graduates
17. Charles Duhigg, "Amex, Challenged by Chase, Is Losing the Snob War," *New York Times,* April 14, 2017, https://www.nytimes.com/2017/04/14/business /american-express-chase-sapphire-reserve.html
18. Ibid.
19. Ibid.
20. Ibid.
21. Ibid.
22. Ibid.
23. Mike McPhate, "Malia Obama's 'Gap Year' Is Part of a Growing and Expensive Trend," *New York Times,* May 3, 2016, https://www.nytimes.com/2016/05/03 /us/malia-obamas-gap-year-is-part-of-a-growing-and-expensive-trend.html
24. Matthew Bal, "How My Gap Year Taught Me That I Matter," *USA Today,* June 27, 2017, http://college.usatoday.com/2017/06/27/voices-how -my-gap-year-taught-me-that-i-matter
25. Guy Berger, "Will This Year's College Grads Job-Hop More Than Previous Grads?" *LinkedIn Official Blog,* April 12, 2016, https://blog.linkedin.com/2016/04/12 /will-this-year_s-college-grads-job-hop-more-than-previous-grads
26. Paul Glastris, "Let's Waste College on the Old," *New York Times,* October 31, 2017, https://www.nytimes.com/2017/10/31/opinion/adult-learners-college .html

Chapter 10—The Importance of Being Faster + Cheaper

1. J. D. Vance, *Hillbilly Elegy* (New York: Harper, 2016), 244.
2. Peter Brodnitz and Jill Normington, "House Majority PAC White Work- ing Class Voter Project," *Expedition Strategies,* July 2017, http://static.politico .com/f2/08/7cab64cb4a0a91a46b57a9a7784a/house-majority-pac-poll.27.pdf

3. Paul Fain, "Deep Partisan Divide on Higher Education," *Inside Higher Education,* July 11, 2017, https://www.insidehighered.com/news/2017/07/11/dramatic-shift-most-republicans-now-say-colleges-have-negative-impact
4. Vance, *Hillbilly Elegy,* 214.
5. Scott Jaschik, "Losing the White Working Class, Too," *Inside Higher Education,* July 31, 2017, https://www.insidehighered.com/news/2017/07/31/new-data-point-white-working-class-skepticism-value-college
6. Conversation with Harry Holzer, American Enterprise Institute, May 25, 2017.
7. Benjamin Wermund, "How *US News* College Rankings Promote Economic Inequality on Campus," *Politico,* September 10, 2017, https://www.politico.com/interactives/2017/top-college-rankings-list-2017-us-news-investigation
8. *Morning Joe* (May 9, 2017; MSNBC), TV.
9. Sarah Leonard, "Why Are So Many Young Voters Falling for Old Socialists?" *New York Times,* June 16, 2017, https://www.nytimes.com/2017/06/16/opinion/sunday/sanders-corbyn-socialsts.html
10. Ibid.
11. Eillie Anzilotti, "The End of Capitalism Is Already Starting—If You Know Where to Look," *Fast Company,* September 18, 2017, https://www.fastcompany.com/40467032/the-end-of-capitalism-is-already-starting-if-you-know-where-to-look
12. William Galston and Claire Hendrickson, "The Educational Rift in the 2016 Election," *Brookings,* November 18, 2016, https://www.brookings.edu/blog/fixgov/2016/11/18/educational-rift-in-2016-election
13. Edward-Isaac Dovere, "Teflon Don Confounds Democrats," *Politico,* September 13, 2017, http://www.politico.com/story/2017/09/13/teflon-trump-democrats-messaging-242607
14. Ibid.
15. Remarks by President Trump in Roundtable Discussion on Vocational Training with US and German Business Leaders, *The White House Office of the Press Secretary,* March 17, 2017, https://www.whitehouse.gov/briefings-statements/remarks-president-trump-roundtable-discussion-vocational-training-u-s-german-business-leaders/
16. Rep. Virginia Foxx, "Apprenticeships, Technical Education Offer a Path to a Successful Workforce—'College-Only' Is a Myth," *FoxNews.com,* June 21, 2017, http://www.foxnews.com/opinion/2017/06/21/apprenticeships-technical-education-offer-path-to-successful-workforce-college-only-is-myth.html
17. "A Tale of Two Cities," *The Economist,* February 20, 2016, https://www.economist.com/news/britain/21693223-britains-great-european-divide-really-about-education-and-class-tale-two-cities
18. Andy Westwood, "Forward Together in the Next Major Wave of Technical Education Policy," *WonkHE,* May 22, 2017, http://wonkhe.com/blogs/sweeping-manifesto-pledges-on-technical-education-will-need-all-corners-of-education-to-implement
19. Sandra Davie, "Is a Degree Really All-Important," *Singapore Straits-Times,* May 18, 2013, http://www.straitstimes.com/singapore/is-a-degree-really-all-important

20. "South Korea Is Losing Faith in an Elitist Education System," *The Economist,* July 22, 2017, https://www.economist.com/news/asia/21725267-courts-and-president-sympathise-south-korea-losing-faith-elitist-education-system?fsrc=scn/tw/te/rfd/pe

21. Elizabeth Redden, "Importing Apprenticeships," *Inside Higher Education,* August 8, 2017, https://www.insidehighered.com/news/2017/08/08/interest-grows-us-germanswiss-model-apprenticeships

22. Ofer Malamud, "Breadth versus Depth: The Timing of Specialization in Higher Education," *LABOUR* 24, no. 4 (2010), http://home.uchicago.edu/malamud/Timing_LABOUR_article.pdf

23. Brian Subirana, Aikaterini Bagiati, and Sanjay Sarma, "On the Forgetting of College Academics: At 'Ebbinghaus Speed'?" Center for Brains, Minds + Machines, Massachusetts Institute of Technology, June 20, 2017, http://cbmm.mit.edu/sites/default/files/publications/CBMM%20Memo%20068-On%20Forgetting%20-%20June%2018th%202017%20v2.pdf

24. "On the Forgetting of College Academics and the Role of Learning Engineering in Building Expertise," YouTube video, 48:38, posted by Center for Brains, Minds and Machines (CBMM), February 10, 2017, https://www.youtube.com/watch?v=DdMlI6R1MJ0

25. Ibid.

26. "Moody's: Small but Notable Rise Expected in Closures, Mergers for Smaller US Colleges," *Moody's Investor Service,* September 25, 2015, https://www.moodys.com/research/Moodys-Small-but-notable-rise-expected-in-closures-mergers-for--PR_335314

27. Seth Boster, "State Universities Strive to Attract Students as Some Campuses Shrink, Others Boom," *The Anniston Star,* October 10, 2015, http://www.annistonstar.com/news/state-universities-strive-to-attract-students-as-some-campuses-shrink/article_d0eb0bb8-6fc9-11e5-a074-8fb357cd23bf.html

28. Matt Bonesteel, "Kyrie Irving's Flat-Earth Beliefs Now the Bane of Middle-School Teachers," *Washington Post,* July 28, 2017, https://www.washingtonpost.com/news/early-lead/wp/2017/07/28/kyrie-irvings-flat-earth-beliefs-now-the-bane-of-middle-school-teachers

29. "Study Finds Surprising Number of Americans Think Chocolate Milk Comes from Brown Cows," *NBC4i.com,* June 15, 2017, http://nbc4i.com/2017/06/15/study-finds-surprising-number-of-americans-think-chocolate-milk-comes-from-brown-cows

30. Carl Sagan, *The Demon-Haunted World* (New York: Random House, 1995), 40.

Afterword: Colleges in a Faster + Cheaper World

1. Ryan Craig, "Amateur Hour," *Inside Higher Education,* November 20, 2015, https://www.insidehighered.com/views/2015/11/20/are-colleges-losing-ground-entities-focused-more-sharply-workforce-skills-essay

2. North Carolina Sales Institute home page, September 12, 2017, http://bryan.uncg.edu/ncsi.

3. Ibid.
4. Call with Maria K. Stein, Associate Vice President, Cooperative Education and Career Development, Northeastern University, June 7, 2017.
5. Erin Edgemon, "Birmingham-Southern College to Reduce Tuition Price by 50 percent," *Alabama.com,* September 12, 2017, http://www.al.com/news/birmingham/index.ssf/2017/09/birmingham-southern_college_to.html
6. Rick Seltzer, "Sweet Briar Will Reset Tuition," *Inside Higher Education,* September 7, 2017, https://www.insidehighered.com/quicktakes/2017/09/07/sweet-briar-will-reset-tuition
7. Jon Marcus, "Universities and Colleges Struggle to Stem Big Drops in Enrollment," *Hechinger Report,* June 29, 2017, http://hechingerreport.org/universities-colleges-struggle-stem-big-drops-enrollment
8. Kelly Heyboer, "One of NJ's Costliest Colleges Slashes Tuition 20 Percent," *NJ.com,* September 11, 2017, http://www.nj.com/education/2017/09/one_of_njs_costliest_universities_slashes_tuition.html
9. Brandon Busteed, "It's Time for Elite Universities to Lead in Non-Elite Ways," *Gallup News,* August 9, 2017, http://www.gallup.com/opinion/gallup/215615/time-elite-universities-lead-non-elite-ways.aspx
10. Diana Hembree, "Western Governors University: The Best-Kept Secret in Online Colleges," *Forbes,* August 10, 2017, https://www.forbes.com/sites/dianahembree/2017/08/10/western-governors-university-the-best-kept-secret-in-online-colleges/#3106daf16b48
11. University of Utah Degree Plus Certificate Series home page, September 12, 2017, http://degreeplus.utah.edu
12. Jake Schwartz, Twitter post, August 2, 2017, 7:54 A.M., https://twitter.com/jakeschwartz/status/892715293537128448
13. "Community College FAQs," Columbia University Teacher's College, September 12, 2017, http://ccrc.tc.columbia.edu/Community-College-FAQs.html
14. "Fall 2010 Cohort Outcomes: Decline in College Completion Rates Reverse and Lead to Upward Trajectory for Great Recession Cohorts," *National Student Clearinghouse,* December 5, 2016, https://nscnews.org/fall-2010-cohort-outcomes
15. Susan Scrivener, Michael J. Weiss, Alyssa Ratledge, Timothy Rudd, Colleen Sommo, and Hannah Fresques, "Doubling Graduation Rates: Three-Year Effects of CUNY's Accelerated Study in Associate Programs (ASAP) for Developmental Education Students," *MDRC,* February 2015, http://www.mdrc.org/sites/default/files/doubling_graduation_rates_fr.pdf
16. "Students Need More Information to Help Reduce Challenges in Transferring College Credits," *GAO,* August 2017, http://www.gao.gov/assets/690/686530.pdf.
17. Scrivener et al., "Doubling Graduation Rates: Three-Year Effects of CUNY's Accelerated Study in Associate Programs (ASAP) for Developmental Education Students."
18. Natalie Bruzda, "Nevada Schools May Soon Go to Employer-Specific Training Programs," *Las Vegas Review-Journal,* February 24, 2017, https://

www.reviewjournal.com/news/politics-and-government/nevada/nevada
-schools-may-soon-go-to-employer-specific-training-programs

19. Paul Fain, "Helping Career Education Become a First Choice," *Inside Higher Education,* July 5, 2017, https://www.insidehighered.com/news/2017/07/05
/california-community-colleges-seek-rebrand-cte-state-kicks-new-money

20. Jessica Wang and Brian Yu, "Meet the Class of 2021," *Harvard Crimson,* http://
features.thecrimson.com/2017/freshman-survey/makeup

21. Roger Schank, "College Is Over," *LinkedIn,* January 3, 2017, https://www
.linkedin.com/pulse/college-over-roger-schank.

22. Shriya Sekhsaria, "Legacy status remains a factor in admissions," *Daily Princetonian,* May 7, 2017, http://www.dailyprincetonian.com/article/2015/05
/legacy-status-remains-a-factor-in-admissions

23. Susan Dynarski, "Simple Way to Help Low-Income Students: Make Every-one Take SAT or ACT," *New York Times,* July 14, 2017, https://www.nytimes
.com/2017/07/14/upshot/how-universal-college-admission-tests-help-low
-income-students.html

ACKNOWLEDGMENTS

In my work at University Ventures (UV) I'm extremely fortunate to have a great view of a wide range of precursors, as well as the first true faster + cheaper alternatives to college. Some of these programs found their way to us not only because UV is a potential source of capital but also because our views on the urgent need for faster + cheaper pathways to good first jobs are well known in the sector. So I'm most thankful to UV cofounder Daniel Pianko. UV wouldn't exist without Daniel. He is my perfect complement, a terrific partner, and a great friend.

Aanand Radia, Chris Mohr, Prateek Aneja, and Cassidy Leventhal also contributed a tremendous amount to our work and to this book specifically. Cassidy is solely responsible for the appendix—the first directory of faster + cheaper alternatives to college. I'm deeply appreciative for her contribution, one that I hope will be useful for many thousands of students.

Aanand, Chris, and Prateek have been terrific thought partners as we've navigated this exciting landscape over the past several years. I'm particularly grateful to Aanand for his work and leadership in the education-to-employment arena. It's great to be doing important work, but it's even greater to be doing it alongside someone you hold in such high regard. That's how I feel about Aanand.

Troy Williams joined UV two years ago and has helped lead the firm in exciting new directions. I've learned so much from Troy and am proud to be his partner.

Annie Zhang makes our firm run like clockwork. She's an essential team member and I'm grateful for her precision and work ethic. And Tara Jones has helped schedule most of the phone calls and meetings that produced the stories in this book. Thanks to Tara for her infinite patience. Thanks to John Minner and Larry Kane at Orrick, who continue to provide invaluable assistance to UV. Special thanks to Jasna for getting the UV Letters out like clockwork.

We wouldn't be able to do any of this without our limited partners. So my sincere thanks to: Thomas Rabe, Kay Krafft, Jarek Gabor, Kai Roemmelt, and Lee Noriega at Bertelsmann; Trace Harris, George Bushnell, Audrey Janin, and Debra Ford at Vivendi; Jamie Merisotis, Brad Kelsheimer, Dave Maas, Eileen Scott, John Duong, Cody Coppotelli, Holly McKiernan, Courtney Brown, Debra Humphreys, and Holly Zanville at Lumina Foundation; Jeremy Wheaton, Josh Susser, Chris Duncan, and Greg Van Guilder at ECMC, as well as Pete Taylor at the ECMC Foundation; Susan Chen and Jon Ellison at UTIMCO, along with their former colleagues Lindel Eakman and Lara Jeremko; Jon Sackler, Brian Olson, Brian Piacentino, and Don Hawks at Poco Bay; Yoji Nimura, Matt Greenfield, Loy Teik Ngan, David Pottruck, Lee Rierson, Elliot Sainer, Deborah Quazzo, Daniel Jinich, and Bob Hartman.

And special thanks to our friends and partners in innovation at Strada Education: Bill Hansen, Mark Pelesh, Dave Boodt, Carol D'Amico, Steve Ham, Matt Murphy, Scott Fleming, Andre Bennin, Michele Weise, Tom Dawson, Cebra Graves, Carlo Salerno, Leonard Gurin, Larry Lutz, Rick Buckingham, and Jinee Majors.

I'm grateful to my colleagues at Bridgepoint Education: Andrew Clark, Diane Thompson, Vickie Schray, Anurag Malik, Tom McCarty, and Abigail Flakes.

I treasure the excellent advice and wisdom I've received over the years from my godfather, Don Loeb.

Dalia Das provided inspiration when she was at Bertelsmann, and now I'd like to think she's taken some inspiration in launching her own faster + cheaper program in Hamburg, Germany: Neuefische (new fish). Congratulations, Dalia. I hope you're able to make some new fish, even if I won't be able to understand what they say.

My good friends at Whiteboard Advisors, led by Ben Wallerstein and Jenna Talbot, and including Sarah Herring, Ben Watsky, Noah Sudow, and Alison Griffin, continue to do a great job keeping me from doing too many outrageous things. There's no better communications team in education. And, hard to believe though it may be, they're also a lot of fun.

Other important sources of inspiration are Jeff Selingo, Paul Freedman, Trace Urdan, Michael Crow, Ann Kirschner, David Wolff, Robert Kelchen, Mimi Strouse, Ted Dintersmith, George Pernsteiner, Bryan Newman, Sean

Gallagher, Van Ton-Quinlivan, Sabrina Kay, Ben Walton, Laura Pinnie, Melissa Cheong, Andrew Kelly, Heather Terenzio, Al Rosabal, Bridget Burns, Yuanxia Ding, Michael Horn, Dvora Inwood, Nicole Weitz, Jon Barnett, Yael Lustmann, Peter Price, Matt Greenfield, Arrun Kapoor, Mike Bishop, Yelena Shapiro, Marian Craig, Sheldon Levy, Adam Newman, Chip Paucek, Nick Hammerschlag, Alan Harrison, Amy Laitenen, Dina Said, Jan Bucher, Srikanth Ramachandran, Ashwin Bharath, Justin Vianello, Joe Mitchell, Joe Vacca, Bryan Howlin, John Dow, Paul LeBlanc, Norm Allgood, Colin Malchow, Lowell VandeKamp, Jamie Kravcak, Rachel Magana, Josh Becker, Sara Martinez Tucker, Raj Kaji, Bill Song, Bob Hartman, Kevin Carey, Mitch Kapor, Freada Klein, David Coleman, Robert Gordon, Sae-young Kim, Joerg Draeger, Rich DiTieri, Lisa Baird, Beth Akers, Jonathan Finkelstein, Daniel Doktori, John Walber, Sheldon Kawarsky, Diana Kawarsky, Karen Kawarsky, Doug Belkin, Adam Markowitz, Troy Markowitz, Sylvain Kalache, Nasir Qadree, Brian Jones, Don Kilburn, Arthur Levine, Paxton Riter, Mac Hofeditz, Abigail Seldin, Tonio DeSorrento, Andrew Platt, Dave Lenihan, Carlos Rojas, Neil Waterman, Will Houghteling, Susan Cates, Jacqueline Loeb, Robin Levine, Jay Waterman, Phyllis Disenhouse, Pat Hackett, Adarsh Sarma, Ian Chiu, Michael London, Chris Nyren, Tony Miller, P. J. Pronger, Brian Weed, Kara Westrich, Mike Shannon, Preston Cooper, Alex Usher, Allison Williams, Michael Goldstein, Mary Alice McCarthy, Sam Hainer, Josh Macht, Athena Karp, Jason Palmer, Mark Grovic, Ryan Burke, Michael Sorrell, Ananth Krishnamurthy, Matthew Muench, Michael Meotti, Frank Britt, Jake Schwartz, Betsy Ziegler, Howard Weitz, Gwen Weitz, Phil Hill, Peter Smith, Wally Boston, Daniel Hamburger, Jonathan Kaplan, Daniel Greenstein, Iris Palmer, Louis Soares, Matt Chingos, Erdin Beshimov, Kip Wright, Bob Shireman, Josh Jarrett, Yahyin Shen, Elisabeth Klee, Ben Wildavsky, Dale Stephens, Goldie Blumenstyk, Brent Parton, Burck Smith, Kim Taylor, Paul Fain, Paul Bacsich, Jody Miller, Justin Ling, Gordon Jones, Nitzan Pelman, Nicos Nicolaou, Mike Willis, Rob Kingyens, Ankit Dhir, Gabe Moncayo, Danial Jameel, Bob Mattioli, Brent Grinna, Christos Vlachos, Elizabeth Gonzalez, Jessica Hinkle, Victor Nichols, Paul Breloff, Gary Beach, David Giampaolo, Howard Newman, Gene Holtzman, Lucas Swineford, Dale Crandall, Vivian Wu, Monica Simo, David Soo, Amit Avnet, Shannon Zoller, Kate Scott, Rooney Columbus, Gary Brahm, Susan Wolford, Jeff Silber, Joe May, Melissa Pianko, Gerry Heeger, Karan Khemka, Mark Leuba, Anne Enna, Jackie Weiss, Michael Brickman, Andy Chan, Matthew Bidwell, Liz Eggleston, Kash Shaikh, Jim

Rogers, Chris Keaveney, Lauren Pizer, Diane Auer Jones, Isabelle Hau, Nicole Craig, Jennifer Wisner, Bad Wendy, Good Wendy, Scott Turner, Euan Blair, Charlie Taibi, Brad Neese, Scott Pulsipher, Matt Sanders, Joy Chen, Tom Boasberg, Donna Henry, Gordon Freedman, Carl Lu, Tom Bewick, Dominic Gill, Kim Nichols, Brian Delle Donne, Jim Runcie, Brad Weeks, Bob LaBombard, David Weyerhaeuser, Dana Sokoll, Jackie Wolfson, Jaclyn Schlaikjer, Bryan Power, Steve Middleton, John Manning, Yahphen Chang, Monica Herk, John Bailey, Andy Smarick, James Leo, Dror Ben Naim, Leah Belsky, Alex Sarlin, Harish Venkatesan, Clint Schmidt, Jim Milton, Ethan Pollack, Eric Kelderman, Tigran Sloyan, Brian Subirana, Marvin Rosen, Michael Moe, Deborah Quazzo, John Moussach, and *Rumpus* magazine.

Thanks to everyone behind the Close It conference and to Byron Auguste and Karan Chopra of Opportunity@Work. Without you, there would be no competency-based hiring movement.

The entire team at Burning Glass has been very helpful, led by Matt Sigelman, whom I admire greatly.

Thank you to Caroline Howard at *Forbes* for publishing my rambling thoughts on higher education, and to Susan Adams, who's taken over this burden. I've also appreciated the opportunity to work with Doug Lederman at *Inside Higher Education* and Jon Shieber at *TechCrunch*. And thanks to Antonis Polemitis for his friendship, for his great work, and for helping me overcome my allergy to social media and join the vibrant higher education and workforce communities on Twitter.

Thanks to the faster + cheaper pioneers who were willing to share their stories: Trinae Adebayo, David Anderton, Tosin Awofeso, Skylar Bantley, Shannon Brennan, Quinton Bolt, Morgan Combs, Christina DiMartino, Haisam Elkewidy, Tommy Gaessler, Kenyatta Hardy, John Hersey, Simon Kim, Jeffrey King, Chrish Kumar, Juno Lee, Justin Marsh, Patrick Mateer, Sami Mustafa, Anthony Pegues, Wendy Pei, Mark Anthony Robles, Monica Robles, Maria Rodriguez, Yasmine Sadid, Nancy Tang, Matthew Theisen, Tessa Watson, Santiago Villaseñor, and Samantha Wolverton.

Major thanks to Carol Mann and Glenn Yeffeth for believing in this book. It wouldn't have been possible without you, and to Vy Tran, a terrific editor who significantly improved the manuscript with her care and commitment to telling this story.

When I started work on this book, I began interviewing several of these students and quickly realized I'm actually an awful interviewer. Fortunately, I have a sister who is not only a brilliant researcher, writer, and thinker, but an empathetic interlocutor. Laurel Waterman, Assistant Professor of Professional Writing and Communications at the University of Toronto, scheduled and conducted all the interviews for this book. Without Laurel, my ideas would be divorced from reality, and probably wrong. I'm extraordinarily grateful to Laurel for her hard work, in addition to being a very proud older brother. The students must be equally grateful that they had the opportunity to speak with Laurel and not with me. And don't worry, Laurel. The University of Toronto—our hometown school—is going to be just fine.

My college roommates are already well-represented in the stories I've included. Dave, Chris, Alex, Chris, and my brother, Aaron: I miss living with you guys. But I don't miss all the terrible things you did to me. You should be ashamed.

Leo, Hal, and Zev. Thanks for giving me the inspiration, and also the space by not barging into my office at all hours. Go to college or don't. As you can tell from this book, I don't have many thoughts on the question. You're all amazing. I love you.

I remain forever indebted to the generosity of my grandparents and parents who made it possible for me to attend college in a slightly warmer climate. I'm particularly grateful to my 103-year-old grandmother, Estelle Craig. Long may she reign, and she does with the amazing dedication of my aunt Robin. And every day I recognize I'm the freakishly predictable genetic byproduct of Collin Craig, my entrepreneur father, and Brenda Bennett, my mother the community college professor. Dad, you're also the source of my courage. Mom, you're also the source of my optimism. I love you both very much. I'm really glad neither of you opted for a faster + cheaper alternative to your first marriage.

Finally, I owe everything to a girl I met the first day of freshman English. We started with *The Iliad* and it's been an *Odyssey*. To my Penelope, my Molly Bloom. Yahlin: I'm not at home unless I'm home with you.

INDEX

ABOUT THE AUTHOR

Ryan is the Co-Founder and Managing Director of UV Capital Partners. Ryan's commentary on where the puck is going in higher education regularly appears in the *UV Letter, Forbes, TechCrunch, Inside Higher Education,* and *VentureBeat,* among others. He is also the author of *College Disrupted: The Great Unbundling of Higher Education.*

Prior to UV, Ryan led the Education & Training sector at Warburg Pincus where he was the founding Director of Bridgepoint Education (NYSE: BPI), one of the largest online universities in the United States. His prior experience in online education was at Columbia University. From 2004 to 2010, Ryan founded and built Wellspring, a national network of boarding schools and summer camps for overweight and obese children, adolescents, and young adults. He began his career at McKinsey & Co.

Ryan received bachelor's degrees summa cum laude and Phi Beta Kappa from Yale University and his law degree from the Yale Law School. He lives in Los Angeles with his wife Yahlin and sons Leo, Hal, and Zev.

While Ryan knows where the puck is going in higher education, he actually knows what to do with a puck because he hails from Toronto, Canada.